T0345617

DLR BOOK

How DAVID LEE ROTH Changed the World

DARREN PALTROWITZ

Backbeat
Books

ESSEX, CONNECTICUT

Backbeat Books

An imprint of Globe Pequot, the trade division of
The Rowman & Littlefield Publishing Group, Inc.
4501 Forbes Blvd., Ste. 200
Lanham, MD 20706
www.rowman.com

Distributed by NATIONAL BOOK NETWORK

British Library Cataloguing in Publication Information available

Library of Congress Cataloging-in-Publication Data

Names: Paltrowitz, Darren, author.
Title: DLR book : how David Lee Roth changed the world / Darren Paltrowitz.
Description: Essex, Connecticut : Backbeat Books, 2024. | Includes index. | Summary:
  "An intimate look at the epic career of David Lee Roth, from
  his start with Van Halen to today" —Provided by publisher.
Identifiers: LCCN 2023010080 (print) | LCCN 2023010081 (ebook) | ISBN
  9781493072521 (paperback) | ISBN 9781493072538 (epub)
Subjects: LCSH: Roth, David Lee, 1955- | Singers—United States—Biography. | Rock
  Musicians—United States—Biography. | Van Halen (Musical group)
Classification: LCC ML420.R882 P35 2024 (print) | LCC ML420.R882 (ebook) | DDC
  782.42166092 [B]—dc23/eng/20230301
LC record available at https://lccn.loc.gov/2023010080
LC ebook record available at https://lccn.loc.gov/2023010081

♾™ The paper used in this publication meets the minimum requirements of
American National Standard for Information Sciences—Permanence of Paper
for Printed Library Materials, ANSI/NISO Z39.48-1992.

Look at all the people here tonight . . .
—David Lee Roth

For Melissa and everyone else who encourages me to talk about David Lee Roth and Van Halen very frequently

Contents

Foreword

I didn't start wrestling until I was thirty-five years old. Fast forward thirty-something years and I'm a WWE Hall of Famer, an entrepreneur (DDPY has hundreds of thousands of subscribers), a best-selling author (for example, *Positively Unstoppable: The Art of Owning It*), an actor, and plenty of other things—yes, much like David Lee Roth, I love being a self-promoter—and it was a long, long road to get here.

Back in the late 1970s and early 1980s, I managed bars around the Jersey Shore before becoming a rock and dance club owner in Fort Myers, Florida. This all tied in with me managing Mark "Smittee" Smith, who was kind of a visual comedian, like John Belushi on steroids. In the early days of MTV, Smittee was a big deal. He was #4 on that MTV show *Puttin' on the Hits*, doing this Michael Jackson routine. He was *over huge* with college kids. I started to say, "I'm gonna get you out there." I brought him to MTV Spring Break and everyone went fucking crazy for him.

The next year I got Smittee on a bunch of stuff on MTV, and they brought him in to cohost with Alan Hunter. One night we were at The China Club in New York and we were getting ready to leave. As we are walking out, David Lee Roth is walking in. We are both ridiculous marks for Roth. We just went, "Holy shit, there's David Lee Roth." He looks, he walks over, and he goes, "Hey! The guy from MTV!" Smittee lost his mind that Dave knew who he was. We ended up talking to him, he loved Smit, all the stuff that he did. We got pictures with him, super-cool dude. Of course we lost the pictures.

Remember, back then, I was nobody at the time. I'm just running night-clubs and am Smittee's manager. I would go on to become a pretty top guy in the world, sure, but I never forgot that night. You have to treat people the way you want to be treated.

The author of this book, Darren Paltrowitz, is someone I first met in 2016. He interviewed me in the cafeteria of Viacom, where he used to work, and we have taped a bunch more interviews since then. He always does his research and always tries to sneak David Lee Roth–related questions into interviews. But as I have told him a few times, "Diamond Dave" . . . "Diamond Dallas Page" . . . sure, I love the guy's music, but it's just a coincidence.

Bottom line is this book makes for a great read, and David Lee Roth is one of the greatest entertainers to have ever hit a stage.

—Diamond Dallas Page, 2022

Meet Dave

"Hello, this is Diamond Dave," said the man on the other end of the phone line during an early morning phone call in the spring of 2003.

Surprised he had called himself "Diamond Dave" and that it was not a handler or third-party directly calling, I asked David Lee Roth how he was feeling that morning. He responded: "First thing in the morning, thunderbolt in your Cheerios, homeboy." That question was followed with my asking why a "rock god" like Roth would prefer to do interviews so early, especially given that he was dialing in from the West Coast. With a laugh he responded, "Well, I haven't slept since the late '80s." And that would be the first of many laughs Roth would get out there.

Van Halen has been a staple of my life for decades. You have your favorite sports team, and I have a timeless band that—at times simultaneously—accommodates my love for sing-along choruses, inventive guitar solos, amped-up tempos, Borscht Belt comedy, and acrobatics. Hence the launch of the podcast known as *The DLR Cast* in June 2020 alongside Steve Roth; as a fun fact, while not related to David Lee Roth, Steve Roth's father was also an ophthalmologist like Diamond Dave's.

I am proud to say that David Lee Roth lives in my earliest memories. As extra entertainment for my brother's bar mitzvah party at Temple Judea on Long Island, New York, my parents hired a local company called "Mock Rock." That excellent company—which would also serve as auxiliary entertainment at my bar mitzvah celebration at the Merrick Jewish Center—let bar mitzvah attendees lip-synch a live music video to an already-recorded hit song in front of a curtain while holding unplugged instruments. Within minutes of the song's ending, its employees would burn a VHS tape for you of that "performance." Really cutting-edge stuff for the 1980s. Which, in retrospect, probably violated some copyright laws.

"So what does any of that have to do with Van Halen?" At least one of the people who attended the bar mitzvah of Adam Paltrowitz—now a renowned choral teacher, composer, and podcaster—performed Van Halen's "Jump" via "Mock Rock." Back then, MTV and VH1 still played music videos more of the day than not, so I would ultimately be exposed to the big Van Halen hits and become a big fan of the band in the years to follow. No way of proving it, but I think I was aware of "Just a Gigolo" before I was aware of anything Van Halen put out from its first Sammy Hagar era.

Fast forward to the late 1990s, I wanted to get free albums and concert tickets but did not have the money saved to accomplish just that. My one-year-older friend Howard Davis had accepted an internship with a newspaper in my hometown called *Long Island Entertainment* but turned out to be too busy with college prep to fulfill the internship's responsibilities. He somehow passed along that internship to me, and I—as a high school junior—worked as hard as possible to deliver as much (teenage-minded) quality-oriented content as I could. "You need five albums reviewed this month? I'll give you ten. And need any live reviews or interviews done?" In turn, the second half of my teenage years were largely focused on networking, listening to advance copies of albums, and trying to act older than I was. Kind of like *Almost Famous*, without the bylines, money, backstage passes, women and . . . okay, it was nothing like *Almost Famous*.

When John Blenn—the founder of *Long Island Entertainment*—sold the newspaper to take on a gig as general manager of a huge Long Island concert venue, he recommended to the new owners that I be the newspaper's new editor. Probably it was right before my nineteenth birthday, but I definitely remember that I accepted that role for an "exorbitant" $400 per month. As part of that job promotion, it was up to me to provide a lot of coverage related to our advertisers. In other words, I would often have to interview artists associated with our advertisers, or coordinate others—writing for free, unless they also sold advertising beyond writing responsibilities—to interview those same artists.

In 2003, David Lee Roth was booked to play the very same concert venue managed by the aforementioned John Blenn in support of the *Diamond Dave* album. Roth's publicist at the time was a legendary publicist named Mitch Schneider, who ultimately spent over a decade working with Roth. The opportunity came for me to interview DLR by phone prior to his gig on Long Island's Westbury Music Fair—now known as the Theater at Westbury—and I happily accepted it.

Knowing what we know now, this interview was taped about one year after DLR coheadlined a tour with Sammy Hagar, and about one year before Van Halen did an ill-fated reunion tour with Hagar sans Roth. Just four years later Roth would rejoin Van Halen for an eight-year, on-again, off-again tenure, but before that started in 2007, Roth would contribute to a bluegrass-themed Van Halen tribute album and do syndicated morning radio in 2006. So it is unclear what Roth's long-term game plan was in 2003, but I do know that he was very patient with a very green reporter. Who actually asked his interview subject to record an outgoing voicemail message for him after completing the interview.

Going back to Roth's crack about not sleeping since the 1980s, early into our conversation I genuinely wanted to know more about his routine. Based on our phone call being scheduled for before 8:00 a.m. EST—even earlier than 5:00 a.m. his time—was he truly a morning person? Or had he simply not gone to sleep the night prior? "Routinely I do what I call 'boxer's hours,'" he began. "I started off in martial arts before I was even a teenager, and what you know by looking at and watching the *Rocky* movies, but naturally you wake up at about 4:35 in the morning, and I'll go until the middle of the afternoon and then I take a siesta. I do the whole thing over again until about midnight, so I get twice the light in half the time, and then I can reverse that to accommodate the road."

What exactly does Diamond Dave mean about reversing his body clock for the road? "Most people are just starting to hit cruise speed at nine o'clock at night and I'm supposed to combust, so you kind of learn your schedule. Whatever is most comfortable. People say, 'What's an average day like?' I don't have an average day, that's why I keep reenlisting."

As I later learned from our conversation, Roth believed his creativity to come from a natural place, much like his energy. "There's no lack of writer's block because I'm a genuine fan and even more importantly, like most of you reading this right now, I'm an elitist weenie." That one, of course, earned a laugh from the interviewee before the interviewer. "I think I know what's best. In fact, I know I know what's best and it's usually different than the rest of the crap, isn't that the way we all think? As long as you don't lose that, that ambitious fury, and I think there's a very thin line between fury and great art, and great art can be anything from graffiti on a brick wall to who designed the brick wall. Both require fury, preferably rage. I'd like to think that I have black rage in the most potent form." And yes, that was all in one linked thought.

Prying a bit further beyond that rage, Roth claims to have also found creative greatness in his more relaxed moments. He would go on to explain more about the Pasadena, California, home he often referred to as "the Mojo Dojo," where he was dialing in from. "I have a tennis court that several years ago I filled up with California beach sand from San Onofre Surf Beach. You may know it from the famous song 'Surf City USA.' . . . It's about a foot and a half deep here and I use it first thing in the morning. I call it 'the Zen pen,' because this is where all the ideas come from, or the best interviews in fact, and I can kind of actually go and walk along the beach."

Yet in the same conversation, he declared another constant source of creativity with what can best be described as a humblebrag. "Here's one of my favorite poems, and I saw it inscribed on a rock at the base of the Khumbu Icefall which leads to Everest. It doesn't rhyme but it's still poetry," he said before pausing. "'Go climb the treasure mountain and do not return empty handed. Where are you now?' Now in terms of poetry, that's an inspiration. Poetry is a lament or a simple reflection. That sounds like Coach Kelly from Pop Warner Football to me."

So if you are keeping score, we are just a few minutes into our interview in 2003, and Diamond Dave has already referenced *Rocky*, Jan & Dean, Pop Warner Football, and poetry written at the base of Mount Everest. To me, the immediate conclusion to draw is that David Lee Roth is a highly intellectual, cultured human being with a multitude of interests. Far from the buffoonish character singing the lyrics in "Goin' Crazy" or first-person Van Halen narratives heard in "Atomic Punk" or "Mean Street." Simply stated, Roth does both high brow and low brow.

But as he later told me during the conversation, reading has been even more of an inspiration for him than television. "I like to read. Most of what I know about showbiz I found off the printed page and still do. I just read an essay on Lenny Bruce, the Elvis of comedy. Was I a real fan of his humor? No. Has his life certainly lent color to mine and millions of others? You bet, yeah." After laughing hard, Roth continued: "Everything that I brought to the stage, and particularly my enthusiasms, come from having seen pictures of it and having read about it either as a kid or currently. I subscribe to thirty different magazines, I read them all every month. I read a book a week. I took the television out of my bedroom right after my birthday last October. I determined I wasn't reading enough."

Roth's love for reading was punctuated by an anecdote, which I could not confirm with an exact date: "A friend of mine, Kid Rock, was on the tour bus last season. He looked at me and said, 'Dave, I want to tell you and I'm proud of it. I don't think I've read a single book since high school.' I thought to myself, 'You don't have to tell me.'" Yes, a laugh from DLR followed.

That same narrative of Roth being a true connoisseur of entertainment's greats continued when I asked Roth about his then-new album *Diamond Dave*, which mostly consisted of cover songs from the 1960s and 1970s. "These are the songs that I grew up and learned at 'the college of musical knowledge.' There's the famous scene in *Stand By Me* where the twelve-year-olds are walking down the railroad track and they're singing 'Purple People Eater' or 'Polka Dot Bikini,'" he started. "Well, the conceptual leap from that to Wayne and Garth [from *Wayne's World*] doing 'Bohemian Rhapsody' and at the punchline you turn and point to each other, that is forever. Every generation has that." He would eventually break into song, proving his singing voice was still in top form.

During our conversation, Roth would boldly declare that his voice was "more famous than the Nike Swoosh," that you "hear Van Halen music more frequently than the National Anthem if you listen to rock radio with any regularity," and that he had "more hits than the Gottis." Seeking other great self-descriptors? "I'm a miracle dropper, Holmes. I'm that energy in your Alpha Bits first thing in the morning. I am your inner child and it turns out your inner child just wants to get away, so here's the soundtrack." Yet in the same talk, Roth modestly referred to his work with Van Halen as "why you're still bothering to talk to me today."

Also impressive about my lone conversation with David Lee Roth was that he appeared to remember *everything*. Seemingly out of nowhere he recalled a childhood play he was part of. "I just found my first pair of glasses that I ever wore as a star. I was seven years old as Mr. Bookworm, I can even sing you the song." After singing said song, he noted that his mother made him "these glasses that look like bookworm glasses" and he had found them in a cupboard recently. Which led to questionably applicable self-comparisons to Groucho Marx—not the only Groucho Marx reference you will see in this book—and Akira Kurosawa, and the following statement that yielded a laugh from him: "Think of me as the Wizard of Oz but with a little bit of echo."

As a long-time fan of Roth's full catalog, I had asked him if the upcoming Long Island concert I would be attending would feature "Slam Dunk," a single from the previous album, in its setlist. "The music we'll be playing is not necessarily in this order, it's 'California Girls,' 'Just a Gigolo,' all the classic Van Halen material, you name it, and a variety of what's coming from the new album as well." In other words, nope, the expected hits and some new album promotion. That intrigued me because you had someone who clearly aims to push all boundaries in life, yet the same person appeared content to primarily play the same songs he had been performing for decades. Even though he would later declare: "It's ambition to become better and better at what you do. . . . Do you ever completely master kendo? Or is it simply the process of a lifetime of having tried to master something that registers in your character?"

Prying more into the creative habits of Diamond Dave, making the earlier reference about the *Wizard of Oz* more applicable, he would make it clear that he was doing a lot more than singing. "I've managed to learn the vocabularies of what we do over the given summers. If you want to learn how to shoot film and edit and work in the edit bays, then that's a whole other vocabulary. If you want to do stage design and album covers and the computer graphic world, that's a whole other language again, all of which can be learned, but you're gonna have to not be 'the man' for a while."

Continued Roth about his ongoing pursuit of learning everything he can: "That's what usually stops most musicians from pursuing beyond what they simply do on the stage. 'Hey, I'm a guitar player and that's it.' You hire out to have somebody do your album cover, your stage design, your video, help you with the production and everything." He finished with the following statement, of course with a hearty laugh before I could start laughing: "At the end of the day you're going to wonder, 'What happened to the sound? What happened to the money?'"

Inexperienced journalists are likely to ask an artist who their influences were. As a still-green interviewer, I opted to ask Roth a variation upon that question, as to whether he ever thought about recording an album with artists he had influenced. "It's really, really easy to imitate a pair of pants, or pick up a bottle of Jack. It's really easy to imitate playing too fast on the guitar, which is usually how it winds up," he began. "My inspirations, the people that I would collaborate with would certainly be closer to the folks, the new faces in Linkin Park. I would collaborate with The Chemical Brothers. I would collaborate with Trevor Rabin, who I just heard a whole bunch of background music on that *Profiles from the Front Line* series that was just on about the military in Afghanistan, there's like eight episodes of that. The background, it sounds like *Cirque du Soleil*. I would go and find the individual who's responsible for the original music for Blue Man Group. That's inspired. In terms of serious vision, wrap-around smile and black rage, hey, take me along for speed, dash, and insecurity." That one ended with a laugh from DLR, as you would imagine. Interestingly enough, I spoke with a former Blue Man Group executive Todd Perlmutter, who turned out to have put out a Van Halen tribute album called *Everybody Wants Some! (Of Van Halen—A Loose Interpretation of the Musical Genius)* in 1997—he had said that Roth never reached out to collaborate—while later in the book you will read what Linkin Park's bassist Dave Farrell told me about Roth in 2020.

Toward the end of our interview, I asked David Lee Roth what used to be my "signature" closing question in interviews: "Any last words for the kids?" In reading other interviews done by Roth that same year, I saw that he gave a variation of the following response to questions asked by other journalists. He first mentioned recently losing his father, which I offered condolences for. "Ah, it was an antagonistic, love/hate relationship. You hear it in my voice, you hear it in my music, it was great. He wanted to be cremated and have his ashes thrown out around Aspen mountains, the great big beyond. I thought, 'Let me take my ashes and throw them around the [Greenwich] Village.'"

DLR added to these thoughts: "I've always spent my childhood, didn't know it at the time, trying to get downtown in New York. Whether it was *Mad Magazine*, which is quintessential downtown New York humor, to the books I ultimately read. All the [Jack] Kerouacs and the [Allen] Ginsburgs, and it turns out even Henry Miller was from New York. Jesus, you guys have a meeting without me or something?" Yes, a big laugh followed that one. "All my favorite poets, all my favorite pornography, it all comes from downtown. Throw my ashes in Washington Square Park." That park is indeed the same spot where Roth was strangely arrested in 1993 for purchasing a $5 bag—or $10, depending on the interview—of marijuana; the charge was later reduced to a citation and subsequently dismissed.

Yet there is far more to the upbringing of David Lee Roth than books, martial arts, Pop Warner Football, mother-made Dr. Bookworm glasses, and a love/hate relationship with his father. As it turns out, Diamond Dave is not the only Roth to have had footing in the entertainment business. Father Nathan, as you will later read, not only was a highly successful ophthalmologist, he also had some on-screen credits. Sisters Lisa and Allison have also found successful paths in and around entertainment. Uncle Manny, he is practically a book unto himself.

Allison Roth's IMDb page lists appearances in *Say Anything, Mask*—not the Jim Carrey–starring vehicle—and a few television programs. She is the founder of Allison Roth Creative. Her website for Allison Roth Voiceover currently shows work done on a series of Tinker Bell–related projects for Disney.

Lisa Roth is a well-regarded nutritionist, who helmed the *Rockabye Baby!* series of children-oriented music albums. When I interviewed her for the *Jewish Journal* in January 2019, the series had already released more than eighty albums, with close to two million CDs sold and plenty more than five hundred million tracks streamed to date. Her credits also included production work for the Discovery Channel and National Geographic.

Per my interview with Lisa Roth, I chose to take the high road and not to ask about her brother, believing that she had created her own success in entertainment. But he accidentally came up when I asked a question about whether the Roths kept kosher during her upbringing. "I was raised in a household where no pork was allowed, although I had an older brother that on the weekends walked up to the corner market and would buy bacon and come home and make it in our kitchen. My father would get furious and it was an ongoing struggle between the two of them. But I was raised to not eat pork." Slightly to the contrary, in David Lee Roth's memoir titled *Crazy from the Heat*, the Van Halen frontman mentioned that "Grandma Roth kept a kosher house."

As it turns out, her success in and around music turned out to be somewhat accidental. "I never aspired to be in the music industry . . . I can't carry a tune to save my life, but here I am thirteen years later and all is good."

Uncle Manny Roth, whose full name is reportedly "Manuel Lee Roth," was the owner of Café Wha?, a New York venue still in business. Aside from Van Halen famously playing Café Wha? in 2012, the venue was instrumental in the early careers of Bob Dylan, Joan Rivers, Woody Allen, Jimi Hendrix, Kool & The Gang—more on them coming later in the book—and Richard Pryor; Uncle Manny was also Pryor's first manager. Before that, Uncle Manny opened the Cock & Bull, a Broadway-themed club in Greenwich Village, which eventually became the still-open Bitter End. Uncle Manny would also be the first long-form guest on Roth's aforementioned syndicated morning radio show, sitting panel in 2006.

Yet in speaking with Dave's first cousin, Dr. Jack A. Roth, it turns out that there were plenty of other success stories in the Roth family. In a 2022 conversation, Jack—who will appear again later in this book—broke down the Roth family tree for me. "So the family, on the Roth side, which is my dad's side, Dora and Joe Roth were the parents. My dad was the oldest brother, Manny was the next oldest, and then there were four others. . . There were two sisters," he began. "Nate, who is David's father, and then the youngest brother is David, who was a neurosurgeon. He is currently alive and living in California, he's not on the greatest terms with David Lee. . . . But there is some contact with Lisa and Allison, his two sisters." Those two sisters were Toby, who Jack remembers being a competitive dancer, and Ruth, who he recalled being an attorney.

The "Grandma Roth" referenced in *Crazy from the Heat* was Dora Roth. "She came from Latvia, and my grandfather Joe came from Kiev in the Ukraine, so we have Ukrainian ancestry, believe it or not." Added Jack: "Joe Roth worked on a farm in Kiev, he managed the farm, and it's not clear exactly how he got to the U.S. There was some talk that he got to the U.S. to escape the Russo-Japanese War and get out of the military, but he managed to get over here. He and Dora met and were married in Indiana and of course they lived there in New Castle, Indiana. That's where their home was, that's where I would go down with my parents to meet all the rest of the family." Jack himself was born in LaPorte, Indiana, and when I mentioned my wife having family in Michigan City, Indiana, turns out so does he.

But to Jack, so many of the Roths finding success as professionals was a sign of the times. "In the early twentieth century, particularly first-generation immigrants, my grandparents were absolutely dedicated to having every one of their children go to college, no question. I went to college, then the question became, 'Well, how about professional school?'" Added Jack: "My dad actually loaned money and helped pay tuition for Nate and for [Uncle] David and made sure that they could cover their expenses. He was kind of like a surrogate father to them in many ways, helping them financially, making sure that they could meet their obligations, get through graduate school. One member of the family helping another. I think that played a role in everyone's eventual success."

According to Jack, things almost shaped up very differently for David's father, had there not been some family interference: "Nate actually started off as an optometrist, and my father persuaded him, 'Nate, you're a smart guy, you should go to medical school and become an ophthalmologist.' So he did, he specialized in retinal surgery and moved to Pasadena."

When David Lee Roth reemerged from a brief career hiatus in 2019 to promote his newly launched tattoo-oriented skincare line called INK the Original via a series of interviews, I decided it was time to try and interview him again. All requests went unanswered. Later that year, Roth announced a series of concerts in Las Vegas, and more interview requests followed, only to be unanswered. The same results followed in 2020, 2021—after he announced another Vegas residency, as quickly followed by a declaration of retirement via the *Las Vegas Review Journal*—and 2022. Rather than giving up on learning all there was to learn about DLR, I decided the correct course of action would be to speak with as many people as possible who have known, worked with, and/or appreciated Diamond Dave.

The byproduct of over one hundred interviews and a few trips to Las Vegas with my wife Melissa, you are now reading *DLR Book*, which covers the past forty-plus years of Roth's life from a multitude of perspectives. While not everyone holds the same opinions as far as his past, present, and future—one cannot confirm whether he "has more hits than the Gottis," for example—a few concepts remain indisputable:

- David Lee Roth is very intelligent,
- Diamond Dave is one of rock's all-time most memorable frontmen,

- most musicians could only dream of having long-term success like DLR, and
- somewhere, as you read this, a song featuring the vocals of Roth is probably playing on a radio station.

So no matter which era of David Lee Roth is your favorite, be prepared to learn about a man who has traveled the world many times over, never stops learning, and—according to some—never stops laughing.

Van Halen

Between 1978 and 1984, David Lee Roth released six full-length studio albums with Van Halen. All six of these Warner Bros. Records–released titles were produced by Ted Templeman, and all six of them would go on to be multi-platinum sellers; 1984's album titled *1984* would sell more than ten million copies in the United States alone. And prior to the release of *1984*, Van Halen would find its way into the *Guinness Book of World Records* as the highest-paid band for a single show, earning an estimated $1.5 million to headline 1983's US Festival.

But Van Halen was far from an overnight success. Years before 1978's self-titled album, the quartet regularly played five sets a night, mostly of cover songs. In the midst of all that came a production deal issued by KISS bassist Gene Simmons, and yet the band's Simmons-produced demo was turned down by every record label that heard it. Per Gene Simmons during our 2017 interview: "Do I own the twenty-four tracks? Yeah, I do, but you have to understand that above and beyond all that stuff, you've got to be able to go to sleep at night and just kind of say, 'I did the right thing.' When I couldn't get Van Halen a contract—they were signed to my production company—I tore up our contract right away . . . I did what lawyers and everybody around me said was the stupidest idea, but I sleep well at night." Simmons would later find success with producing, managing, and signing other artists, but he later added: "Van Halen was the only one I thought had the legs to go all the way, and that sure happened."

When the aforementioned Ted Templeman eventually heard Van Halen and decided he wanted to sign them to Warner Bros., as the story goes, he nearly had Eddie Van Halen, Alex Van Halen, and Michael Anthony axe Roth from the lineup due to his presumed limited vocal abilities. So once Van Halen took off in a big way, there was a determination rooted in "I told you so." Although as Roth would point out in his autobiography *Crazy from the Heat*, Van Halen's original deal with Warner Bros. Records gave them "the worst royalty rate in show business."

From early on it was evident that the carefree, flamboyant Diamond Dave character was not a separate being from David Lee Roth. "He is to being a frontman as Steve Martin is to being a stand-up comic," began Bowling for Soup frontman Jaret Reddick. "Steve Martin created this character and he crafted it and crafted it and crafted it, and it bore no resemblance to who he actually is as a person. He's actually a serious guy, but he's funny." Continued Reddick: "David Lee Roth, to me, is the ultimate frontman. . . . Think about it, he would just do karate. That's insane, but it worked."

Aron Stevens, a man also known to millions of WWE fans as Damien Sandow, slightly disagreed with Reddick's assessment of DLR. "I believe that the best characters are extensions of the individual playing them." Added Stevens: "Although on the surface the individual in real life may seem nothing like the persona they adhere to in public, the persona itself has to come from somewhere inside the individual. The greatest characters, showmen, performers, in public personalities are all at the very least an extension of some desire the individual wants to express for whatever reason."

As one of rock's all-time great managers, David Krebs was instrumental in the early careers of Aerosmith, AC/DC, Ted Nugent, The Scorpions, and Michael Bolton, to name just a few artists. He and concert promoter Louis Messina put together the long-running annual summer rock concert called the Texxas World Music Festival, as also known as Texxas Jam. Its inaugural 1978 edition featured Van Halen. Krebs met Roth backstage, and while the two engaged in only some brief conversation, Krebs told me that from those few minutes, "I concluded this was a brilliant guy." Interestingly, that same gig would be where legendary rock photographer Neil Zlozower first encouraged Van Halen, ultimately becoming the band's preferred photographer; some of Zlozower's work can be seen in the *Van Halen II* album artwork.

In speaking further with Krebs about the classic rock scene of the late 1970s, he asked me more about this book and what I had planned for it. He ultimately explained to me how rock band histories are often comparable to the Japanese film *Rashômon*. For the uninitiated—spoiler alert—the Akira Kurosawa–helmed *Rashômon* is the story of four people recounting different versions of the story of a murder and a rape. Grim stuff there, but what we are getting at is that people with shared histories tend to remember things very differently, especially when decades have passed.

So immediately putting that *Rashômon* comparison in play, in Neil Zlozower's book *Van Halen: A Visual History: 1978–1984*, KISS cofounder Paul Stanley described seeing Van Halen at The Starwood and then bringing Gene Simmons the following night to see them. In the same book, original Van Halen manager Marshall Berle mentions being tipped off to Van Halen by famed songwriter and producer Kim Fowley; Fowley would ultimately discover songwriter/producer Mike Viola, whose two cents on David Lee Roth are printed later in this book. Berle also referred to Roth, the first time he saw him, as being "the most amazing frontman/singer" he'd ever seen. So not only is who exactly discovered Van Halen debatable, but so is how great Roth was onstage before the band recorded its debut album.

However, one thing universally agreed upon is that it was evident from the early days of Van Halen that David Lee Roth was the most ambitious band member when it came to transitioning the group from playing covers in backyards to becoming a true headlining act. "In his book, he talked about checking the songs for dance-ability," began author Greg Renoff, who many regard as being *the* source when it comes to the early days of Van Halen history. "When you talked to people, Pasadena locals, they would talk about how much they hated it when Dave joined, because it changed the sound of the group. They didn't like Dave because in part they were doing less Black Sabbath covers and they were doing more pop stuff. Roth was like, 'Look guys, congratulations. We can play backyard parties 'til whenever,' but Roth was driven."

Renoff's research related to early Van Halen, as compiled for *Van Halen Rising: How a Southern California Backyard Party Band Saved Heavy Metal*, included a lot of exploration into Roth's pre–Van Halen band known as the Red Ball Jets: "A lot of the stuff Dave tested out in Red Ball Jets was a preview for later, like going down to the Sunset Strip with basically his high school group that was not ready to perform on the Sunset Strip, but getting his dad to pay for a Motown choreographer." That same father, as referenced in the previous chapter, has a proper IMDb page of his own. The Pasadena mansion he owned and raised his son David in, beyond being seen in a 1984 episode of *Lifestyles of the Rich & Famous* that spotlighted Dr. Roth, has appeared in multiple films. In his book about Van Halen, the aforementioned Neil Zlozower noted the mansion as being the site of many early Van Halen photo shoots because of "all the different locations and scenery" it had.

But back to Greg Renoff and DLR's early days: "The guys in Red Ball Jets told me this, this was Dave's idea to get this choreographer, to get them to have moves. . . . He understood that was the way to get a record deal. You're not going to get a record deal playing in some subdivision in Arcadia." This, however, was not entirely in tune with brothers Ed and Alex Van Halen. "They really wanted to be imagined like Black Sabbath. They thought, 'We're just going to stand there. Our hair hanging down, bashing away.' And Dave was kind of like, 'There already is a Black Sabbath, right?'" Continued Renoff: "[Dave] had his own, 'Let's make this into a different sort of sound and thing.' He brought his musicality to the table and changed it." However, Roth in his 1997 memoir *Crazy from the Heat* declared that when he was a part of the Red Ball Jets, "I was already Diamond Dave." Although just a few years later in that Zlozower book, said Roth, "I have often found that by the time my dreams come true, I've turned into someone else."

The previously mentioned John Blenn, an early mentor of mine as a writer, was drawn into Van Halen because of his Black Sabbath fandom: "I saw them four times on that tour, same results every night. Van Halen obliterated Black Sabbath and it turned out to be Ozzy's swan song." Added Blenn: "*Not* a coincidence that Ozzy formed a solo band *exactly* like Van Halen—cutting-edge guitarist, pounding rhythm section, Ozzy even wound up dying his hair blonde."

Black Sabbath was not the only hard rock band that Van Halen aimed to tackle in its early days. Per Renoff: "Roth talks about how he tried to sing the stuff that the brothers like, like the heavy metal, Grand Funk stuff. . . . He's like, 'We were terrible, it was so bad.' He liked Led Zeppelin and stuff, but it wasn't his thing to do that sort of stuff. He added much more of a pop Motown approach to songs. That's what he sang, but he was going to sing anything. . . . He wasn't going to be able to pull off 'Speed King' by Deep Purple effectively. It wasn't his thing."

Speaking of Deep Purple, when interviewing Deep Purple drummer Ian Paice in late 2021, I asked him whether he had ever encountered Roth. "I don't think I ever met the guy, he's not the sort of guy you'd forget." After pausing, he added: "I forgot meeting Phil Collins once. I said, 'Nice to meet you, man.' He said, 'We met last year in LA.' I just forgot." Before laughing, Paice noted, "Alcohol is a terrible thing."

Robin Trower was another artist covered by early Van Halen, specifically the song "The Fool in Me." An early recording of this can be found on bootlegs, and I brought this up to Trower when interviewing him in 2022. So when did he first hear about the cover? In the early 1980s? "Just then when you told me." Added Trower: "I don't think I've heard any Van Halen, apart from maybe the odd single or not. . . . That's quite a thing to have people cover your songs, I must say."

When seeing Michael Anthony—as part of Sammy Hagar & The Circle—live in Las Vegas in early 2022, the band covered Stevie Wonder's "Superstition" alongside Trombone Shorty. As it turns out, that was a song he had a lot of experience with performing live, as he explained in our interview just weeks after that Vegas gig. "There's a band called Beck Bogert & Appice, and that was a song that they played on their first album. So bands that I was playing in, and Van Halen, we were playing that song." Further making this a small world, the aforementioned "Appice"—legendary drummer Carmine Appice—had at least one rehearsal with Roth in the 1990s, nearly joining his solo band, as discussed in Zlozower's book.

Per Roth's *Crazy from the Heat* memoir, he specifically mentions songs by the Ohio Players, James Brown, KC & The Sunshine Band, Aerosmith, Elton John, and ZZ Top that Van Halen covered live in its early days. The criteria of these songs not only being "dance-ability" but also, as he learned from an old music teacher of his, "if it sounds good, it is good."

Vocal harmonies were an early staple of the Van Halen live show, per Anthony. After being complimented for his in-concert harmonies holding up for close to fifty years, he joked, "I tell people that I grew up in a family with like five kids. And so we were always yelling and screaming at each other, growing up. I take care of my voice. I don't smoke." He noted: "I don't drink as much as I used to in the early days, obviously. There are a few little things you can do that will take care of your voice and, luckily, it's lasted this long. I'm kind of surprised, actually."

Weirdly, while Roth's *Crazy from the Heat* book does mention Van Halen's bassist before Anthony, it wrongly identifies him as "Mike Stone" and not the correct name of "Mark Stone." Roth credits Stone as having created Van Halen's first proper stage banner.

Back to the singing of Diamond Dave, though. Per my brother Adam Paltrowitz—a master educator, composer, conductor, and clinician—I asked for his honest opinion about the long-standing argument of whether or not Roth was a strong vocalist. His answer? "As a starting point, I believe everyone can sing. In my opinion, we each have a voice, and with developed technique, we have better facility to communicate. Compare this to a young child who can express their emotions with 'happy' and 'sad.' As they develop more of a vocabulary, they are able to pinpoint more refined emotions such as disappointment, frustration, anger, worry, contentment, excitement, etc. David Lee Roth clearly has developed his technique to communicate at a level that has impacted millions of people around the world."

In a follow-up question, I referenced the joke that many had made about Roth being "the third best singer in Van Halen." Responded brother Adam: "To me, the best singers are the ones who can touch others with their ability to communicate. Let's see if 'the other two best singers in the group' could lead a concert for two hours straight, keep their voices going, and entertain the crowd. If they actually could, that's awesome. But, the facts are that in the role of singer, or frontman, David Lee Roth is a legend." Accolades of Adam aside, his wife Blair is a Broadway star, and he applied his experience with the Broadway world to DLR: "Some amazing singers would not fare well jumping around. I wouldn't classify them as less amazing singers because they can't jump around the stage. On the contrary, there are many Broadway performers who are known primarily as dancers who sing, as opposed to being primarily singers who also dance."

Ted Nugent was brought up earlier as not only being managed by David Krebs and then-partner Steve Leber but also as being an artist who played alongside Van Halen at the first Texxas Jam. During one of our interviews, he had a lot of kind words to say about Roth. "I admire and praise his entertainment gifts; he's a monster. Tell me that all that David Lee Roth music with Van Halen isn't a smile eruption in our life. I mean, what a fun, cocky, soulful guy. He really does evoke, emulate, and deliver touches of James Brown and Wilson Pickett and some Motown melodious grunt, and certainly the blues and the gospel and the rhythm and blues masters—you can hear that in David Lee Roth." Added Nugent: "I don't think he's ever been given credit for those talents and those musical capabilities that I just mentioned. So I'm glad I just mentioned them, because they should be attributed to him, 'cause he did deliver them with aplomb."

While Van Halen is often viewed as a "hard rock" band, its influence reached musicians in plenty of other genres. Said Kira Roessler, bassist of Black Flag, in our 2021 interview, "I had a cassette of a very early [Van Halen] gig at The Whiskey and it was pretty punk rock. I mean, aside from maybe the vocals, you could have seen that at The Whiskey any other night of the week." As a bit of a teaser, another Black Flag member is going to pop up a few times later on in this book.

While known to millions these days as the star of the series *Bar Rescue*, in the 1980s, Jon Taffer was managing The Troubadour in Los Angeles. So he was around David Lee Roth plenty, per a conversation we had in 2022. "At the same time the new wave thing was hitting, The Knack would be playing the day after Black Flag. . . . It was a very, very exciting time in music in those days."

Jack Irons, the founding drummer in the Red Hot Chili Peppers who would also play in Pearl Jam and The Wallflowers, also appreciated early Van Halen. When he was in high school, a friend told him he must see Van Halen in concert way before they were a household name. "You've got to check out this band Van Halen, they're the next big thing. I never saw them." Why not? "They were in Pasadena, we were in LA, and I was pretty young. I wasn't quite doing clubs or anything yet. Those guys are probably five to seven years older than me. But I've gotta say that first album, an unbelievable debut."

Warrant guitarist Joey Allen was in a similar boat as Jack Irons: "I tried to get to see Van Halen when I played in a band with Lars Ulrich from Metallica for a while, way before Metallica was ever formed." Continued Allen: "Both Lars and I went up The Starwood one time because we heard Van Halen was gonna play and it was actually a band called Snow, which was with Carlos Cavazo and his brother." While Van Halen did not play that evening, Allen finally saw them live in 1979. "Nobody could touch those guys when he was the frontman. Period. Hands down. There are a lot of guys in the LA scene that copied Dave because he was that good."

Author Lisa S. Johnson seems to have discovered Van Halen around the same time as Jack Irons and Joey Allen, despite the geographical differences:

"I grew up in Canada. . . . When I was fourteen, my boyfriend, who was two years older than me, introduced me to Van Halen. We would party around huge bonfires in wooded cutouts surrounded by our parked vehicles blasting Van Halen from a friend's van who had double doors that opened up and on each side of the doors were speakers covered with red velvet mushrooms. The sound was unlike anything we had heard, so electric, sexy, and invigorating!"

While Lisa S. Johnson was getting into Van Halen, so was Stacy Jones. The drumming of Van Halen continues to thrill Jones all these years later: "One of the things I just discovered they do every pre-chorus, not every but lots of their pre-choruses, leading into the chorus, Alex does this weird beat displacement shit and it stays in 4/4. But if you listen to 'Panama' or 'Unchained,' they do it even in 'Jump.' . . . He always does these little things in the pre-chorus where you kind of like, 'Wait, what's going on?' Then the chorus lands and he just lays it in there and it's incredible." On the small world end of things, Jones—not only the frontman of American Hi-Fi and an in-demand songwriter/producer but also Miley Cyrus' long-time drummer and music director—would take drum lessons in the mid-2000s from future Roth drummer Gregg Bissonette, just a few years after he had an album produced by future Roth producer Bob Rock.

Eric Dover, a Jellyfish and Imperial Drag member who also played with Slash's Snakepit and Alice Cooper, is another Van Halen devotee of note. Although he was into Led Zeppelin first, it was seeing Eddie Van Halen play that changed the course of his life. "Of course being fifteen years old, I was like, 'That's what I want to do, I want to play guitar.' I asked my dad to buy a guitar for me and he goes, 'Well, get a job.' So I got a job and bought my first guitar that way."

Overseas in Norway, TNT cofounder Ronni Le Tekrø was also early into the Van Halen craze. "I think the whole world loved Van Halen, my generation. I remember when the album came out, it didn't come out in Scandinavia until maybe half a year after America," he began to explain during a 2022 conversation we had. "But a friend of mine brought a copy to Norway because he was on a vacation in Los Angeles or something, and then that copy got copied. My entire town had it in forty-eight hours." Per Le Tekrø, though, "They didn't tour Norway much, but they should have because they were huge and are huge still in Scandinavia. Maybe bad management?" Later in our chat, he noted that beyond the hooks and the guitar work, he loved that "Van Halen brought humor back into rock."

Whynot Jansveld, a bassist/vocalist whose touring and/or recording credits include Butch Walker, The Wallflowers, Richard Marx, *and* Sara Bareilles, was a fan of Van Halen when growing up in the Netherlands. "I had the 45 of 'Runnin' with the Devil' . . . I still kind of remember how the treble sounded off of the actual vinyl, the high hat and stuff like that. I love that track so much. Then I got the *1984* album. It really blew my mind, it was sort of like the next evolution for me."

But was Jansveld aware of Van Halen's Dutch roots as a kid? "Amongst my peers, Van Halen was big and everyone knew who they were. But I didn't know they were Dutch at all. I knew that the name sounded Dutch and as cool as it sounds in English, it sounds super boring in Dutch." By the way, Whynot, how fluent were Alex and Eddie Van Halen in the Dutch language? "They're totally fluent. Eddie has more of an accent than Alex does, because he was just a couple years younger than Alex was."

Although a peer of the Van Halen band, Ratt's Stephen Pearcy is also a big fan from the early days. He told me about an early encounter he had with Roth in the 1970s in one of our 2021 interviews. "If it wasn't for him smoking a joint with me, I wouldn't have ever met Ed." Explained Pearcy: "I just wanted to meet Ed because I was mostly a guitar guy, even though I sang in Mickey Ratt. . . . I'd watch him at The Whiskey and sit on the stage cross-legged, fucking blew my mind, you know? I'd always say, 'Let my band open up.' It wasn't even up to him. Then one day we did open up some festival with them and it was fucking amazing."

Pearcy holds DLR in high regard all these years later. "Dave influenced everybody that was coming out of the '80s. How could you not? I'd introduced Robbin [Crosby] and Tommy [Asakawa] and Chris [Hager], all my friends, to the band. We'd literally go trade gear, go to Ed's house. It was fucking brilliant, they weren't really quite huge, they were just getting there." That brilliance inspired Pearcy to move Ratt up from San Diego to LA: "I'd go back and tell my guys in San Diego. . . . 'Nothing's gonna happen down here, guys. We gotta get the fuck up to LA. That's where it's all happening.'" The previously mentioned Marshall Berle was also the original manager of Ratt, and the previously discussed Neil Zlozower was also instrumental in the career of Ratt. And those are not the only commonalities between Van Halen and Ratt.

Enter David Jellison, who spoke with me a few times in 2022. "I joined Ratt in August 1980, and there was an influx of people from San Diego [moving to Los Angeles]. . . . The guys from Rough Cutt, Tawny Kitaen. . . . It was a group of about twenty of us. . . . Stephen Pearcy was first with his band, which was called Mickey Ratt at that point, and when he was up there, his bass player wanted to quit, he didn't like Los Angeles, and I moved there."

Continued Jellison: "I got a job at Charvel Guitars. So that's when I made a deal with Grover [Jackson] where I would work for $2.25 an hour in the shop, which was the going rate. In exchange, I would work for him eight hours, then I would get to build my own guitars for three hours using their materials. . . . I started building guitars for me, and people saw them. . . . They started hitting me up to make stuff for Carlos Cavazo [from Quiet Riot] and Donnie Dokken. . . . It was such a small, crazy community and everybody knew each other." Mötley Crüe included. "I remember Tommy Lee came out, he was painting houses with his uncle and the shed his uncle had was right next to across the street from the Jackson Chevelle [factory]. . . . We wanted to get him in the band, and he was already down the road with Mötley Crüe. . . . Everybody was just trying to find the combination to make it work. Jake E. Lee was also part of our collection. He was in Ratt for a while."

Jellison did not stick with Ratt long enough to experience its "Round and Round" heyday, but things worked out just fine for the guy. "I was with them for two years, basically, and I met the Van Halen guys through Tawny Kitaen, because my girlfriend at the time was one of Tawny's best friends." Little sidebar here, but that is indeed the same Tawny Kitaen who helped changed the state of the hard rock music video via her appearances in multiple Whitesnake music videos. And also the same person Roth criticizes in his *Crazy from the Heat* book for selling an O. J. Simpson–related story to a tabloid in the 1990s.

Anyway, David Jellison met Pete Angelus, Van Halen's lighting director at the time, via Kitaen and that crew. "He saw the guitars and he's like, 'Maybe you could make some stuff for Van Halen.' I just started doing freelance design work for them. . . . Over time, I started becoming more and more in their circle of trust and so forth."

Famed rock photographer Marc Weiss, a New Jersey native, was also pretty early on the scene for Van Halen. "One of my first assignments was in '79 at Convention Hall in Asbury Park for Van Halen, when they came up when the second album was released. It just snowballed, you know?"

Weiss notably was one of the few photographers who shot Van Halen and David Lee Roth solo. I asked during our 2021 interview whether he had been privy to Roth's plans to leave Van Halen in the mid-1980s. He answered: "Until you spend time shooting multiple dates with a band, you don't really get the inside scoop on what's going on."

Ralph Saenz briefly sang for L.A. Guns, but under different names, he has fronted Steel Panther and world-famous Van Halen tribute band The Atomic Punks. Early into the COVID-19 pandemic, we spoke via Zoom and I peppered him with a variety of Van Halen questions. With that, we briefly discussed Van Halen's 1981 show in Oakland, at which the band's "Unchained" and "So This Is Love" music videos were filmed. He had clued me in on Roth's savvy even back then when it came to videos: "Dave still made them rent out a soundstage, set up everything the same as it was behind him at the Oakland show and he did a bunch of cutaway B-roll shots for that. . . . They set up the whole stage and he filmed himself doing some screams. You could tell because his hair is different."

Stray Cats drummer Slim Jim Phantom was in similar circles as Van Halen at various points as a fellow early MTV staple artist, including performing alongside Eddie Van Halen on a 1988 Les Paul tribute show. In 2022 he told me about their paths crossing on a lot of occasions. "I met Dave quite a few times at nightclubs, hanging out in dressing rooms." But the most memorable interaction was in Italy. "We all did this Sanremo Festival in Italy, which was a funny one because there were international acts from all over the world, who were there to basically do one song. . . . I think Van Halen might have been doing something like 'Dancing in the Street.' . . . One of those things where you're stuck with someone for like seventeen hours in a dressing room. . . . I thought the guy was great, I still think he's great. I'd like to see him again someday, but we definitely know each other and he's a larger than life character."

Okay, back to David Jellison, who had a lot going on when he and Pete Angelus first connected. "In '82, I was still going to [Sassoon Academy] school, but also working, building guitars on the side, part time with Grover. Did the NAMM show, met Eddie Van Halen. . . . Pete Angelus said, 'Why don't you come on tour with us?' 'Alright, what do you want me to do?' 'I don't know, what do you want to do?' 'I can do anything.' . . . I sort of under-stood lighting and also had an S.A.S. sound system, because as the bass player, you're also obligated to become a responsible person." When I pointed out how surprisingly reliable he was in such a party-oriented era, Jellison was fast with a response. "I was the nondrug guy who just loved to play music. I was totally an outlier in that and also always had a girlfriend. . . . I viewed this as a career." And with that came being "in charge of the entire lighting system, which is massive and also working the board with Pete Angelus."

While folklore about life on the road with Van Halen makes it seem like it was a nonstop party for all involved, that was not the case for its road crew, per Jellison. "That's the mistake a lot of these kids made, that they thought that being on the road, that you were going to live a similar life to the band. When the exact opposite is true. You get up at 6:30. . . . You work nonstop. . . . I did the entire show and then you do the load out and then you go in your bunk at two in the morning. . . . You wake up five hours later. It's anti-glamorous." He added with a pause, "I mean, sure, once in a while, there'll be parties and events."

The Van Halen performance was generally the highlight for him, how-ever. "The shows, they're amazing, don't get me wrong. Watching Eddie Van Halen play every night was just spectacular. There was nothing better than that job. . . . Regardless of how coked up the band was and how angry they were at one another and whatever drama, their level of performance every night was at 95 percent. About every fifth show, Eddie would go beyond that to a stratospheric level, I would ask him about that riffing on 'Unchained.' He goes, 'I don't know, man. That shit just comes to me.' And that's really what it was, he was such a savant. . . . He was doing things nobody else could, honest to God. I would just sit there and enjoy."

As great as Van Halen was, *opening* for Van Halen was generally not easy for any band. Enter Joe Whiting, frontman of Joe Whiting & The Bandit Band, who chatted with me in late 2021. "I think it was '82 or early '83 and Van Halen played the Dome here in Syracuse. At the time it was their biggest show that they headlined themselves and it was promoted by my friend, the late Jack Belle. Jack worked closely with my agent David Rezak. So when After the Fire, who was opening for them at the time, they had that single that was taking off. They had to go and try to push themselves. Van Halen's manage-ment had approached Jack and said, 'Hey, we're going to need an opening act for the last couple of months of the tour. You got anybody in mind you could submit?' I had done a local single, probably within the last year, and so they submitted that and they liked it enough to say, 'Okay, we've got seven dates coming up and see how that works.'"

I asked Whiting if the old story about Van Halen wanting "t-shirt bands"—bands that did not interest the audience, so they would instead go to buy t-shirts—was true. "You're exactly right," he answered. So where did the tour kick off? "The first date was the Spectrum in Philadelphia. I'd played the Spectrum back when I was with Bobby Comstock. That's a tough audience. . . . I want to say thirty-one, thirty-seven, something like that. It was the last seven weeks of their *Diver Down* tour. The first seven dates went well, so they gave us a pay bump and committed to the end of the tour. So yeah, we were off to the races."

Sure, this all happened about forty years ago, but word is that Roth was not often seen hanging out backstage at the venue, while the rest of the band was known to be around and accessible. Does Whiting remember it that way? "Exactly what it was. And I think it's because Eddie was the guitar guy, but Dave was the star of the show as far as, I mean, he was a frontman. He was the face of it. And I think it was not that he was being a prima donna, it's just it was easier for him to keep a lower profile offstage because he had such a high profile onstage."

Whiting has fond memories of his time around the Van Halen band and crew. "They were very, very nice to us. Their rationale was, 'Hey, we were an opening act once and we were treated like shit. So, when we get a chance, we're not going to treat our opening acts like shit.' And they didn't. They left that to the audience." After pausing for a laugh, he continued: "It was an eye opener because I mean, when you get there for load in at two in the afternoon and already people are doing the tailgate and stuff. . . . You're in trouble."

One of the mysteries surrounding Van Halen is what is in "the vault." In Roth's *Crazy from the Heat* book, he refers to bringing tons of audio and video equipment on the road. In Roth's words: "We would film everything. We would document everything." Does Whiting remember these shows being recorded? "I've got plenty of audio tapes from the board. Like I said, their crew, for the most part, particularly the audio guys, the monitor guys, and the guys out front there, they were very professional. Very nice."

And Whiting also remembers the band's performances on the *Diver Down* tour very favorably: "I wasn't that familiar with him before [the tour]. . . . I'd been always a little bit more on the rhythm and blues side of town than that. So yeah, we would go out at least part of it of every night and catch some of the show." Expanded Whiting: "David Lee Roth was a great frontman. His lungs must've been made of leather because he gave it up every night. And what I liked most was that he would take no shit. I mean, people would throw stuff at them too, and he would stop the show. He'd say, 'I'm going to come down there and beat the shit out of you. And then I'm going to take your girlfriend and fuck her after the show.' And then of course, you've got the crowd on your side, you know? So I became a big David Lee Roth fan, just watching how he performed."

One more thing: Joe, in Sammy Hagar's autobiography *Red*, alludes to how Van Halen did not peak commercially until he was in the band, and how a lot of Van Halen's touring before *1984* was to unfilled arenas. Not exactly how Whiting remembers it. "Some sites were smaller than others, but honestly, I think every site that we played in was sold out or close to it. I mean, they were hot. They were hitting, you could see why. I mean, Eddie was a guitar guy, David Lee Roth was doing something as a frontman. Nobody was doing it at that time, you know?"

One of the bands ascending to global stardom around the same time as Van Halen was Hall & Oates. While few people would naturally think of Van Halen and Hall & Oates as peers, in 2022, John Oates painted a very different picture for me. "Our paths crossed with them all the time. We actually shared a lot of the same production people. We shared the same security guy, the same lighting designer, sound man, some of our roadies and technicians. So Van Halen would come off the road and the [crew] guys would go on the road with us, and vice versa, then they'd go back to Van Halen. We hung out with those guys, not a lot, because in those days you were moving so fast that the various solar systems would only kind of come in proximity, very seldom intersected. I mean, those guys are one of the great, great rock bands of all time, without a doubt." Oates' bandmate Daryl Hall made headlines when he declared that he had been considered by Eddie Van Halen as a replacement for David Lee Roth in the mid-1980s.

The previously mentioned *1984* album by Van Halen—Roth's last full-length album with the group for close to thirty years—was not only iconic for its music but also for its album cover. In the *Crazy from the Heat* book, Roth notes on page 215 that "I found that." Which is not exactly how the album's cover artist remembers it.

Per Margo Z. Nahas: "I think I got the job because the band wanted four dancing, chrome women, nude. I had done so many metal illustrations that people just automatically called me in the advertising and the record business. They knew it was going to be good, whatever I did." Rick Seireeni at Warner Bros. had asked her if she would do the album cover for the upcoming Van Halen album, per our 2021 conversation. "I was really nice about it, but I said, 'no, thank you.' I thought that was it, never thinking anything else about it."

Was it that Nahas was not a fan of the band? "I wasn't even that familiar with Van Halen. I had done something before, I think a billboard, but that was it, of their logo and metal, it was a big V." She continued: "So about two hours later, Rick Seireeni . . . called my husband [Jay Vigon] and asked me if he would go and take my portfolio over to the band the next day. . . . And he didn't listen to me. Jay took my portfolio over to the band and they were thumbing through. What they stopped on was this illustration, the only illustration in my portfolio that had never been used. Commercially, it had been used, I did it for this reference book called *The L.A. Workbook*. It was a huge two-volume, huge thick book, but it just gave references for photographers, designers, illustrators, makeup people, everybody. So at that time, the designer asked me if I would do a divider page. I said sure, because they always got artists to do those. Not always, but this particular year they did and I picked out photorealism and you had to pick out a style of art. So I'd always wanted to do something that looked real but could never be real."

It did not occur to me until I was speaking with Nahas that the kid shown on the *1984* album cover was a real human being and not just a realistic illustration. "I got my girlfriend at that time to let me photograph her son Carter Helm. He was probably about three years old. I went out with Dippity Do and with candy cigarettes. I put the Dippity Do on his hair to make him look like he had, well, a really cool haircut. Then he had a tantrum for about forty-five minutes." That memory made her laugh. "My girlfriend said, 'Just wait, just wait.' I brought out the candy and we went outside and the rest of that was history. I did Carter, sitting, I changed the coif, the picnic table, the sky, and I added a wing and that's really all I did. . . . That was the picture in the book of this little angel smoking a cigarette, kind of looking up to see if

God is watching over this little rebel angel and you know what? I really didn't think much about it. It got to be a divider page, which is just what they asked for. But other than that, I never went any further with it. It was just part of my portfolio."

Flashing back to the Van Halen part of the story, she continued: "So they stopped on that picture and I think thoughts of four Chrome women, scantily clothed, just flew out the window. They said, 'Oh, is this available?' My husband said, 'Yeah, I think so.' That was it. I must say, I didn't know much about it." And what does Carter Helm think of the album all these years later? Is he like the kid from Nirvana's *Nevermind* album cover? The answer is no. "He loves it." And things worked out well for Nahas? Does she own the art still? "I sold them only the rights to use it on their album and t-shirts, and that's it. I have owned the rights to this image for thirty-eight years? Something like that, thirty-seven, thirty-eight years, so no pushback in any way. They didn't ask me to change a thing, they liked it the way it was." (Coincidentally, her husband Jay wound up overseeing artwork for Roth's next few albums.)

The tour before *1984* was created was the *Diver Down*, which Joe Whiting had been part of and David Jellison was on the crew for. And apparently this tour was where the cracks really started to show for Roth and Van Halen. Per Jellison, the narrative presented about the tour's South American leg in Van Halen road manager Noel Monk's book is far from what actually happened. "Noel Monk's recollection of it, 'That was the best tour we ever did.' That's a fucking lie. The wheels came so close to flying off that thing every goddamn day, it was utterly surreal."

Rewinding a bit, why exactly was that? "You go to South America and in 1983, cocaine is, like, a dollar. Fucking ridiculous. As Roth said, 'I used to have a drug problem, but now I make enough money.' . . . So they are doing drugs on such a fucking high level that they flew out their doctor from Miami who somehow had a briefcase full of Valium, because they couldn't get Valium there. . . . Just every day, drama with chicks. . . . I could write a book on just the shows in South America alone." And yes, I told David Jellison that he should be writing that book. Fingers crossed.

Back to Roth's early influences as a performer, one name that came up plenty in the journey to write *DLR Book* was James Mangrum, the Black Oak Arkansas singer also known as "Jim Dandy." When interviewing Megadeth's Dave Mustaine in 2020—as the story goes, the roots of Megadeth go back to Mustaine being awoken by his then-neighbor Dave Ellefson playing the bass line of "Runnin' with the Devil"—I asked whether Van Halen was a key influence on him as a career performer. Mustaine's response? "I thought that David Lee Roth had a lot of difficulty singing, but he was an amazing front-man and I think that kind of came from him copying Jim Dandy from Black Oak Arkansas. I can't say that's for sure, but whenever I see any pictures of Jim Dandy or anything like that, a friend of mine was a huge fan of Black Oak Arkansas. . . . Whenever he would come over and play Black Oak Arkansas I would look at the picture on the album and I would think, 'Fuck, that looks like the dude from Van Halen.'"

Nashville Pussy's Ruyter Suys is another person I asked about whether Roth was influenced by Mangrum, whom she has performed alongside. "Yes, of course he did. I think almost anybody who ever put on a pair of white pants should be paying some kind of royalty to Jim Dandy and his fabulous ass. I know when I put on a pair of white pants I think of Jim Dandy." So did he ever ask Mangrum about Roth? "No way, I was just busy basking in his enthusiasm. He's a very enthusiastic person, to say the least, especially when he's had a couple shots of whiskey. . . . Jim Dandy seems to be smiling 24/7 and very relaxed, even with half his teeth. He's a pretty genuine man."

John Blenn, who I consider to be an expert on southern-style rock *and* Van Halen alike, is also someone I asked about this. "I see where someone might make a comparison between Jim Mangrum and Diamond Dave, blonde, shirtless, wisecrackin', etc. But you're really comparing pecan pie with a limited-edition French pastry. The big difference shows up when you start dissecting the lyrics both of them churned out."

Joe Whiting, who mentioned having more rhythm and blues roots than rock roots, also weighed in: "I saw Jim, I saw Black Oak. There was a physical resemblance, but to me, David Lee Roth was like a kingpin in that style. Black Oak, come on, I'm not putting them down, but they weren't in the same league. . . . I'd never thought about it until you mentioned that Black Oak thing. Like I say, physically, there certainly was a resemblance." Concluded Whiting: "But it's like comparing, I love Aerosmith, but are they The Rolling Stones? No."

For the record, Roth's *Crazy from the Heat* book does not specifically cite Mangrum's influence on him. However, page 84 does call out Walter Mitty's Rock & Grill in Pomona, California—a venue Roth had performed at before fame—as having only two songs on its jukebox that he remembers, one of which was "Jim Dandy to the Rescue." Meanwhile, Ted Nugent compared Roth to Mangrum in Neil Zlozower's book about Van Halen.

Whether or not Diamond Dave directly descends from Jim Dandy, the key is that there is no shortage of worshippers of Roth and Van Halen to this day. Per Ralph Saenz, while in character as Steel Panther's Michael Starr, "When Satchel and I were in The Atomic Punks, Dave [Grohl] and Taylor [Hawkins] asked if they could open for us at this small little club in North Hollywood or Van Nuys or Reseda, so the Foo Fighters opened up for The Atomic Punks. I'm sitting on the side of the stage with Jack Black, watching the Foo Fighters opening up for us."

Tracii Guns, the cofounder of L.A. Guns who is half of the namesake of Guns N' Roses, also never stopped being a fan of Roth or Van Halen, per our 2022 interview. "I'll always be a die-hard Roth fan. I love David Lee Roth. That was the first concert I ever went to and did cocaine at, the *Women & Children First* tour." Continuing the stories, Guns noted: "My cousin Willie. . . . We did some rails in the car and went and saw Van Halen and David Lee Roth, obviously something going through his veins, that was 1980, 1981, those were good times."

World-renowned professional wrestler Frankie Kazarian, who is also the bassist in the band Gutter Candy, is also a long-time die-hard fan. "My very first memory of David Lee Roth was from the 'Jump' video. I was a very young kid, and that song and video just mesmerized me. I know that is a very polarizing song in the Van Halen lore, but that is what hooked me on the band. Seeing David's stage presence and energy was incredibly impressionable. I was instantly hooked!"

Kazarian's Gutter Candy bandmate, frontman Jersey Dagger, then chimed in: "I guess the 'Jump' song was kinda my first introduction as well. Funny, because I got it confused with the Pointer Sisters song that came out the same year by the same name." He let out a laugh before continuing: "I bought the Pointer Sisters' cassette tape by mistake at the swap meet. Actually, I ended up loving both songs!"

Television host and producer Adam Richman also became a Van Halen loyalist via the *1984* album. "I'm the kid who went to yeshiva, learning how to write the Iron Maiden and Van Halen 'flying VH' logo on my looseleaf." Because he mentioned yeshiva, I asked Richman if Roth's background in

Judaism had anything to do with his fandom. "It was the music, man. It wasn't anyone in particular." For him it was "specifically the album *1984* and further cemented by that Claymation sequence in the movie *Better Off Dead.*"

But as one would hope, the former *Man vs. Food* host did have an anecdote to tack onto that: "I do laugh that one of the most wonderful chefs from Gramercy Tavern in New York is named Michael Anthony."

Lit bassist Kevin Baldes, whose photography can be seen in this book, has a tie to Van Halen that few may realize. And if you love the movie *The Decline of Western Civilization Part II: The Metal Years*, this one may widen your eyes. "We were doing very well on the Sunset Strip [as Razzle]. Bill Gazzarri's last prediction—he predicted The Doors, Ratt, Van Halen—to 'make it.' We were his last prediction. He died like a week later after he predicted us."

When speaking with Lit guitarist Jeremy Popoff a few months after speaking with Baldes, Van Halen came up naturally in our conversation. "Kevin and I met in junior high and the reason that we met was because we all loved heavy metal and rock and roll," he began. "Kevin was walking through the halls wearing a Van Halen shirt and I was wearing an Iron Maiden shirt. We're like, 'Hey, we should be friends because we like cool music,' you know? We actually used to go to concerts together just as fans before we ever talked about playing music together."

While the album referenced numerous times in this chapter is titled *1984*, it was actually recorded in 1983. The album helmed four hit singles—"Jump," "I'll Wait," "Panama" and "Hot for Teacher"—although only three music videos were released for the album. Close to one hundred concerts were played in support of the album, wrapping with Monsters of Rock shows in August and September 1984. So weirdly, one of David Lee Roth's last appearances in a music video while in Van Halen was as part of a cameo—alongside Eddie Van Halen in a limousine—in a video filmed to promote Frank Sinatra's "L.A. Is My Lady"; ironically, Roth would be recording "That's Life" within the next two years, but more on that later.

The aforementioned hit single "I'll Wait" is notable not only for not having an accompanying music video but also because it was the only original song from Van Halen's first six studio albums to feature a cowriter. That cowriter, Michael McDonald of The Doobie Brothers, had been recruited by Ted Templeman to help work on the song's chorus. When interviewing Kenny Loggins in 2022, I asked if he—as a frequent McDonald collaborator who was on the radar of Templeman, and a Pasadena City College attendee like Roth—had ever nearly collaborated with Van Halen. The short answer was no, but Loggins explained that he thought Van Halen at the time was "trying really hard to be Led Zeppelin," and that was not the direction that he "was going," even if he "loved some of the stuff" they put out.

As the often-repeated story goes, when touring wrapped in support of *1984*, David Lee Roth was itching to tour more *and* get back into the studio, while the majority of his bandmates were looking for some time off. So what did Diamond Dave, as an unmarried and infinitely creative individual, opt to do? He wrote a screenplay, got into the studio for a solo project, made some music videos, and accidentally got himself kicked out of Van Halen.

Crazy from the Heat EP

In the summer of 1985, a *Rolling Stone* article led to millions of people learning that David Lee Roth was no longer the lead singer of Van Halen. Depending on who you asked, this was either very shocking or very expected. And depending on who you asked, Roth had either quit or been fired by one of the biggest bands in the world. However, per Roth's autobiography titled *Crazy from the Heat*, "I left on good faith and asked for no quarter. I asked for no settlement, nothing. And I guess that's precisely what I got." He claimed to have also departed Van Halen with a screenplay but "no movie deal," no band, and no equipment to rehearse with.

Going back a few months prior to Dave's announced departure, David Lee Roth released his first solo recordings, titled *Crazy from the Heat*, on January 28, 1985. Composed of four cover songs—two of which ultimately had MTV Video Music Award–nominated accompanying music videos, totaling more VMA nominations than any other artist had ever earned in a single year—*Crazy from the Heat* featured a "who's who" of backing musicians. It also included the production talents of Ted Templeman, the long-time producer of Van Halen who was also responsible for getting the band signed to Warner Bros. Records. Artwork and other production duties on the EP had also been handled by people who had worked for Van Halen.

Crazy from the Heat was also set to be the title of a film cowritten and directed by Roth. Starring Roth with a budget of over $10 million, the movie was supposed to be released in 1986 via CBS Pictures. Kind of like George Costanza's "summer of George" on *Seinfeld*, 1986 was slated to be "the year of Dave." And then came 1985's one-two-three punch of Roth being dismissed by Van Halen in a less-than-flattering way, Diamond Dave not winning any of his MTV VMA nominations, and CBS Pictures going belly up before filming on *Crazy from the Heat* began.

While it may be easy to blame Diamond Dave for leaving Van Halen to be a "movie star"—as Eddie Van Halen said in a mid-1980s interview with *Rolling Stone*—and to selfishly pursue non–Van Halen projects, this narrative has proven to be entirely one sided. For starters, contributing a guitar solo to Michael Jackson's "Beat It" was not the only time Eddie Van Halen had worked on a nonband project while sharing a band with Roth. As a few examples of this, he composed music for the films *The Seduction of Gina* (starring wife Valerie Bertinelli) and *The Wild Life* (an unofficial sequel to *Fast Times at Ridgemont High*), he played guitar on a Ted Templeman–produced album by Nicolette Larson, he produced and played guitar on Dweezil Zappa's debut single "My Mother Is a Space Cadet," he contributed an instrumental track to *Back to the Future*, and he was part of Brian May's Star Fleet Project album in 1983.

The making of the *Crazy from the Heat* EP was apparently not being kept a secret from the music industry, per engineer Garry Rindfuss. "It was never a secret. I guess a week or two before it happened, the studio manager called me up, 'Do you want to work on this new David Lee Roth project?' I didn't know what to think." Per the secrecy I referenced, Rindfuss clarified that some projects he worked on were kept very quiet: "'Under Pressure,' Queen and David Bowie, and that was a couple years earlier. That was a secret project. If you look at the tape box, the actual multitrack and the mixdown tapes, there is no mention of any names. It's just a management company."

On the small world end, one of Ted Templeman's last projects before working on *Crazy from the Heat* was *V.O.A.*, Sammy Hagar's last studio album before replacing Roth in Van Halen. Rindfuss worked on that also as well. "I think they were, like, a year apart and *Crazy from the Heat* was the first one. Because that was the first time I worked with Ted Templeman. I was second engineer, all those projects. The main guy was a guy named Jeff Hendrickson, and he did an awful lot of work with Ted, who is an absolute sweetheart. He's one of the nicest people you'd ever want to meet."

Continued Rindfuss about Team Templeman: "So Jeff was back and forth from LA to New York and all that, and he would bring projects in, including David Lee Roth. . . . I guess after that record came out, it was at that point it had become obvious that David Lee Roth was no longer a member of Van Halen. And I thought, 'Well, it's kind of a funny way to launch your solo career with an EP of covers.'"

In retrospect, Rindfuss still looks back on his time with Roth fondly: "There's nothing really scandalous about the David Lee Roth record. Nothing salacious to report. I can only say I feel very fortunate." About Roth himself, Rindfuss remembers kindness. "Quite frankly, he could not have been nicer. His was one of the most enjoyable projects I can recall from that time period. He was bright, he was funny, not obnoxious." He also recalled the team behind the solid musicianship: "It was unbelievable. John Robinson on drums, Edgar Winter, a personal hero of mine, on the keyboards, Willie Weeks on bass, and . . . Eddie Martinez on guitar, and Brian Mann on synthesizers, and we had Sid McGinnis on guitar too."

Rindfuss ultimately tied that in with an explanation of how close the team at The Power Station studio in New York at the time was: "Besides myself, it was James Farber and Scott Litt, Jeff Hendrickson and Neil Dorfman and Bob Clearmountain, that's who got the place on the map. We talk about it sometimes because I'm in touch with all of them, James, especially. . . . We talk about how lucky we were. I mean, we could have ended up at any number of major studios in New York—Hit Factory, Record Plant, Electric Lady, you name it."

While not immediately named by Rindfuss, also along for the ride that was the *Crazy from the Heat* EP was percussionist Sammy Figueroa, who spoke with me in 2020. "I was one of those fortunate guys that I was at the right place at the right time, you know?" Continued Figueroa: "I'm from New York City, everybody and their mother lived there, from Herbie Hancock to Chaka Khan to Diana Ross . . . I was right there in the middle of all that, so I'm very grateful that that happened."

So how did Figueroa wind up in the *Crazy from the Heat* sessions? "I was very close to Ted. . . . He would call me for everything. I'd go 'Ted, are you sure?' 'Yeah, man, I want you on this gig.' But he said something to me very interesting. . . . He said to me, 'Look, it's not just about the playing, the playing is great, but it's your vibe and the character that you bring into the studio

and your jokes and your personality, because you know we can get anybody
we want.' . . . To get somebody that has character and who's funny and that's
on time all the time and that can cover this kind of rock and roll, he said very
few people can do that."

Figueroa remains fond not only of Templeman but also of Roth himself.
"David and I hit it off immediately. We were pals and I was talking to David
Lee Roth like almost every day on the phone. 'Hey man, what are you doing,
bro? . . . Come on over to my house, man, let's go hang out.' Then he lived in
Central Park at that time . . . at his brownstone, talking about music, playing,
jamming. He even bought a set of percussion so I can come and play."

One of the recurring themes you will see in this book is that DLR projects
tend to be overrehearsed or improvisation oriented. Which one was *Crazy
from the Heat*? Was everything prepared long in advance? Per Figueroa:
"They called me and I went in the studio, there were no charts, there was
nothing. They had a lead sheet and then the ending and we sort of went in
there and we rehearsed. We were jamming, really that's what we're doing. . . .
Then by the third hour we said. . . . ' Let's just record now,' and the engineer
was Bob Clearmountain."

Rindfuss remembers the sessions going very smoothly, like Figueroa does:
"We did all the basic tracks and some overdubbing, and then they moved the
session to LA." Wait, what? "That's when they did Carl Wilson and Chris-
topher Cross and that sort of thing. Then they came back to New York and
we mixed the record in Power Station Studio B." He added with a laugh, "So
I didn't get to work with Carl Wilson, dammit." Was he part of the full EP
then? "I was on the project for the duration. . . . You just stayed with it."

Did Rindfuss know that *Crazy from the Heat* was going to be an EP and
not an album? Or how many songs were being recorded? "I don't know if
I knew before the record started that it was going to be an EP. I don't have
any recollection of that. But at a certain point, obviously, we tracked the four
songs and that's it." Any recollection about Dave tracking the vocals live with
the band, or later on? "He would have done guide vocals, certainly. And I
don't remember doing a lot of lead vocal overdubs and, like, a vocal day. . . .
I seem to remember that no, the overdubbing was mostly in LA. That we just
did the basic tracks and recorded mix. He might have kept his guide vocals in,
in some instances, because a good singer will quite often just nail it with the
band in the studio, and won't have to replace it."

As mentioned by Rindfuss, Edgar Winter was part of the *Crazy from the Heat* sessions and is someone I had the pleasure of speaking with in 2022. Per Winter, Roth just called him up and asked him to get involved. "He wanted to do 'Easy Street' and he wanted it to be the real deal, the authentic thing, and asked if I would be on that." The answer was yes. Further discussion ensued. "He said, 'I've got this weird song you've never heard.' . . . I said, 'Oh you mean Sam Butera that played one of my favorite sax players.' . . . I knew the song." That song was indeed "Just a Gigolo/I Ain't Got Nobody." More on that one later.

I asked Winter, who's generally known to be reserved while offstage, what Roth was like during these sessions. Responded Winter: "Some comedians are always on all the time, that's the way Dave is, his stage persona. I'm not that way. Like, when I get on and say, 'Hello everybody, are you ready to rock and roll?' That's not really me. People meet me and then they say, 'Oh, you're so mild mannered and soft spoken and articulate.' . . . Diamond Dave, that's who he is."

Roth has steadily praised Winter over the years. In a 1988 interview with Dan Neer, Diamond Dave said the following of Winter, who at that point he had worked with only on *Crazy from the Heat*. "Working with Edgar Winter was really a gift experience to me. Edgar was always one of my big heroes. He had a lot of stage pizazz and at the same time was super accelerated musically. . . . He was in there with the original version of 'Easy Street' with Dan Hartman. So when he came in, it was sort of like watching a master at work."

Prolific session player and Toto cofounder Steve Lukather nearly wound up playing on that album, per an interview we taped in 2021. "There was talk when his first solo album came out, James Newton Howard was going to be involved as a producer and he asked me to play on it. So I went to Eddie [Van Halen] and I said, 'Is this going to be weird? Because I won't do it.' This is when they had fallen apart the first time and he looked at me, he goes, 'Yeah, do it but don't play so good,'" he laughed. "It just never happened and I really wasn't the right guy for the job." More on Luke to follow.

The first of the four songs released from *Crazy from the Heat* was a take on The Beach Boys' "California Girls." Per Roth's *Crazy from the Heat* memoir, the music video for "California Girls" required five weeks of pre-production and won Roth a Kodak Cinematographer Award; it did not win any of its three MTV VMA nominations. His inspiration for recording that song, per the same 1988 interview with Dan Neer, came from his security guard (and later his manager) Eddie Anderson while vacationing in Puerto Vallarta.

The second single and subsequent music video was for "Just a Gigolo/I Ain't Got Nobody"; it did not win any of its five MTV VMA nominations. Per Roth's *Crazy from the Heat* memoir, this music video was made after he had started to write the follow up to *1984* with Van Halen. Which begs the question as to whether any of Van Halen's *5150* album, its first studio effort with Sammy Hagar as lead vocalist, was actually cowritten by Roth; ASCAP and BMI song registrations say no, although Van Halen song registrations have been revised over the years to exclude Michael Anthony from *1984* songwriter credits. There would be no live concerts in support of these single releases, unless you count Diamond Dave lip synching "Just a Gigolo/I Ain't Got Nobody" at a well-attended Mexican beauty pageant in 1985.

In a 1994 interview with *MTV News*, David Lee Roth referred to the music video of "Just a Gigolo/I Ain't Got Nobody" as "satire." He referred to it as featuring "familiar characters and types and putting them in scenarios that would never ever happen." One of the actors seen in both the music videos from the *Crazy from the Heat* EP is Durga McBroom, who talked DLR with me in 2022. "I actually started as an actress. I was a theater art major at UCLA . . . and within six months was cast in *Flashdance*," began McBroom.

So how exactly did she wind up on Diamond Dave's radar? "It was just one of those kismet things. . . . I was watching MTV and 'Hot for Teacher' was on and I was watching it. I was thinking to myself, 'I really like Van Halen.' No, you know, I really liked David Lee Roth. . . . So as the video was fading on my television, I kid you not, my phone rang. It was my agent saying I had an audition for 'California Girls.' So I went in and I auditioned." But it was not as simple as that, unfortunately. "They wanted to cast me, but it was a nonunion shoot. So my agent was like, 'Oh well, that's too bad.' Then they called me back five minutes later saying, 'You know what? They don't care that you're union, they're going to pay you union rates.'"

Music videos were not the only work that McBroom did in relation to David Lee Roth. "When the album was coming out, Dave had a big listening party and he wanted to invite all the music execs from the different labels. So they hired me. I had these five-inch spike heels, just the nastiest, dirty girl shoes, and I had this dress, I still have it. It's made of black fishnet, basically." She paused before continuing: "They hired me to wear that, leading two little people on a chain with a whip, and they were covered with gauze and duct tape and crap all over their faces. They would let me into these music executives' offices, because the receptionist or whatever was in on it. These guys, one of them would have the invitation in his mouth, and I would, like, whip them over to the table. . . . I'm six-foot-three in these shoes. . . . These guys would be on the phone talking to somebody. . . . These little people were coming in, they'd just be growling and I'd drop the invitation on their desk. The guy would be, like, with his mouth wide open. And I'd say, 'David would really love it if you attended. Have a great day,' and lead them out. I went to, like, twenty offices. It was so funny."

The back cover of the *Crazy from the Heat* memoir shows Diamond Dave walking beside two little people. The *No Holds Bar-B-Que* video discussed later in this book has a little person in it. I asked David Jellison what gives on all of that—is it because Roth strives to be an equal-opportunity employer? Not exactly. "Dave always had a fascination with involving the little people with specific events—live shows, parties, videos, etc. His attitude was that it added to the circus-like atmosphere, and they were purely there for entertainment." If *Crazy from the Heat* is correct, the two gentlemen who had been paraded around by McBroom were Jimmy and Danny, former Barnum & Bailey employees.

Anyway, back to Durga McBroom. While asking her about her music video work with Dave, it led to discussion related to the previously referenced music video he had written. "So in that video, I'm wearing a dress, it was custom made. It's a dress covered with flowers that were basically sewn or glued onto a corset that was really tight. . . . Originally the outfit had a hat, a wide brimmed hat that was like three, four feet across, and it had a big purple wig ponytail coming out of the top. It weighed about eight million pounds. Now that dress was made for me for the *Crazy from the Heat* movie. . . . Unfortunately that project never came to fruition." More to follow on that film project, but that anecdote was tied up with the more compassionate side of DLR: "The whole outfit, it was so heavy that it was hurting my neck, and Dave came in and he said, 'She's beautiful. Why do we gotta put all that crap on her?' So that's why I wound up wearing my own hair in that scene."

As alluded to earlier, photographer Marc Weiss knew how to do things so that he had access to both Van Halen and DLR in this era. "I was kind of like the girlfriend that they didn't talk about. They use other photographers too, but I would go on the road," he began. "I would shoot Black Sabbath and then I would shoot Ozzy. I wouldn't tell the other one about the other one, you know? I don't know if they cared, but I'm sure they wouldn't want me to be talking about 'Oh, I just got off the road with Black Sabbath.'"

Continued Weiss: "When David went solo, he hired me to shoot some solo shots and actually when he was in Van Halen he wanted me to shoot solo photos before he even went solo. I kind of had a feeling things were kind of taking a shift. . . . When Sammy entered the picture, on the other side, they hired me to take their photos like for the *Monsters of Rock* tour book. I did several photo shoots with them and again, I didn't tell them."

Producer, songwriter, and solo artist Mike Viola, who also had ties in his early days to Kim Fowley like Van Halen did, saw Van Halen on its *Diver Down* tour. While we have had conversations about his appreciation for hotshot guitarists of the 1970s and 1980s, he is not someone who followed Roth after he went solo, per our 2022 discussion. "When David Lee Roth left the group I lost interest in Van Halen. It wasn't just his voice but possibly the rock aesthetic he brought to it. After he left everything felt 'too pop' for me." Viola expanded further: "I love pop music, but I didn't want that from Van Halen. I always thought David Lee Roth solo albums were a bit of a lark for him. Without Van Halen diffusing the showbiz, it all got turned up too much for me. The music videos always seemed a little porny." But is Roth one of the greatest frontmen of all time? Per Viola, "I don't think anybody can argue with that."

In the previously referenced 1988 interview Roth did with Dan Neer, he was asked about his time with Van Halen. Keeping it cordial yet honest, Roth opened up to Neer: "People are people, people change, people's personalities change. . . . You age seven years every year out on the road. I haven't seen the Van Halens in years." He further commented: "Now when the issue comes up, I choose to dwell only on the good things we contributed to music together. I think Van Halen was at one time a pretty influential band, maybe it still is."

But with regard to Van Halen's success following his departure from the band, Roth threw one of the best barbs I have ever heard when prompted by Neer: "If I build you a Cessna, it better fly without me."

Crazy from the Heat Movie

Making sure we are still on same page here:

- *Crazy from the Heat* was the name of David Lee Roth's solo EP, as released in 1985
- *Crazy from the Heat* was the name of David Lee Roth's memoir, as released in 1997
- *Crazy from the Heat*, as you are about to learn, was the name of the screenplay that was supposed to be filmed in 1986
- "Crazy from the Heat" is a lyric in the song "Goin' Crazy," which you will read about in another chapter

So yes, one-liners and self-deprecating jokes are not the only thing that Diamond Dave has repurposed over the years.

Crazy from the Heat, starring, cowritten, and directed by David Lee Roth, was contracted to be released by CBS Studios. Per the previously mentioned David Jellison, "I went to Japan on a tour. . . . And then Dave's team called. 'Hey, we're gonna do a movie. He wants you involved.' Pete Angelus was involved as well. And, John Dahl, who was their storyboard artist, is the guy that really sort of helped propel me into the film world." Jellison added that he enjoyed watching Dahl, who graduated from short films and music videos to writing and directing feature films, "do storyboards every day."

Primarily working on the *Crazy from the Heat* script with Diamond Dave was Jerry Perzigian. Perzigian, the "Jerry" who Roth refers to on page 103 of his memoir, would later win an Emmy and work as a showrunner, writer, and/or producer on some of the most successful half-hour sitcoms in television history. In the DLR universe, Perzigian would also appear in multiple Roth music videos; he ultimately declined multiple interview requests from yours truly, and a little Googling around into his family history may help to explain why that is the case.

However, Jellison—who worked under Roth as an assistant director on *Crazy from the Heat*—remembers what Roth's creative process was like in those days. "It's very 'anti rock and roll,' but he'd get up at seven in the morning and work out with Benny 'The Jet' Urquidez for, like, two hours a day. . . . Then come to the office, smoke pot, and then just sort of go over the day's events." Continued Jellison: "Then at night, starting at seven, they would write and they would bring in these [script] punch-up guys. . . . He had a legit office staff. Gail Liss was the accountant and he had secretaries and people to manage the business."

Sam Ingraffia was one of the actors who met with David Lee Roth about being part of *Crazy from the Heat*. "I had a very good manager at the time, and she and I had talked about David Lee Roth," he began in our 2022 interview. "I thought he was funny, and even though I wasn't born in LA, I grew up kind of my teen years in LA. I was a huge rock and roll fan, so I saw just about everybody who was anybody because there were so many great clubs in LA. Gazzarri', The Whiskey, The Roxy, all those places, a lot of bands played in those before they got to be stadium act bands. And I never saw Van Halen, but I knew of Van Halen because I lived in Sherman Oaks and they lived in Pasadena, so it wasn't very far away."

Continued Ingraffia: "Everybody kind of knew about Van Halen, they were this kind of really hip, kind of semi-local band that everybody thought was going to get really hot. So I had talked to my manager about Van Halen, because I remember saying to them, 'I'm surprised nobody's made a movie about the band.' Between the interrelations between David Lee Roth and Eddie Van Halen, and the fact that they had this kind of meteoric rise from being club guys to being superstars. . . . I was really surprised that nobody made a movie, and that was the conversation." Or so he thought. "Then she said, 'Well, he's doing a movie. You want to go in for it?' And I said, 'Yeah, sure.'"

That conversation led to a meeting with Roth for Ingraffia. "The thing that sticks out in my head is, I'm generally pretty healthy, but I had a cold. And I almost didn't go to the meeting, because I had a cold. But I thought, 'You know, I'm almost over the cold, and I'm probably not contagious or anything, so it'll be okay.' But my voice was kind of scratchy as a result of the cold." And he turned out to be not the only person in attendance with a shaky voice. "So I go in and meet with him, and I said, 'I apologize, sorry, my voice is kind of scratchy because I've got a cold.' He starts talking to me and his voice is really scratchy. And I say, 'Do you have a cold also?' He goes, 'No, it's a lifetime of rock and roll.' It was basically from being the frontman for Van Halen for all those years. He had, I think, probably burned some of his vocal cords."

Vocal difficulties aside, Ingraffia enjoyed his time around Roth. "He was very funny. . . . The videos were very clever and very funny, and he was kind of poking fun at himself. The rock star image, he was kind of making fun of himself. I remember we talked about that, that so many actors are unwilling to poke fun at themselves, and take themselves so seriously. That they're serious artists. He said, 'Well, rock stars are even worse than that.' We had a nice conversation."

I asked Ingraffia if he recalled reading the *Crazy from the Heat* script, and if so, what he had thought about it. "I don't know if they had a script. If they did, I never got a chance to read it." Instead, it was more of a summary, he recalled. "There was like a one-page kind of description of what they wanted to try and do and who they were looking for. And I have played, when I was younger, a lot of sleazy bad guys, a lot of sleazy lawyers. I think they were considering me to play a sleazy lawyer."

Around the time that Diamond Dave had met up with Sam Ingraffia, Roth had also been a guest on *The Tonight Show with Johnny Carson* in October 1985 when it was guest hosted by Joan Rivers. In that interview segment, Roth discussed auditioning talent for *Crazy from the Heat*, with classified ads helping to recruit everyday people for these auditions. He noted that the film was set to start shooting in January 1986. To Rivers—who would also have Roth on as her first guest in the first episode of *The Late Show Starring Joan Rivers* in October 1986—he also went into depth about himself and Angelus being "the Fabulous Picasso Brothers" and how their directing aliases were intended to sound like "high art meets pizza delivery."

But per Jellison, who was slated to work as assistant director on *Crazy from the Heat*, the cancellation of the film came very suddenly. "So we're here at CBS lot for six months, basically prepping this film. Then CBS had seven flops in a row. . . . They just canceled Dave's movie a week before we were to shoot it. We were a week away from principal photography." Roth's *Crazy from the Heat* memoir noted his film to be one of eight films axed by CBS at that time.

While 20/20 hindsight says that a film centered on David Lee Roth would never have worked, and that music was always supposed to be his focus, Jellison explained to me that *Crazy from the Heat* was supposed to be far more than a raunchy comedy. "The film was going to be a springboard, everybody thought, to Dave's next level, whatever that is." He continued, "There was no instant pressure, because it didn't appear like the Van Halen guys were getting out of the gate with a project very quickly either."

While the script of *Crazy from the Heat* references a band, Jellison noted that the DLR band featured in the film—whom he dubbed "The Yankee Rose Band" in his *Crazy from the Heat* memoir—was the result of Roth "building a band . . . because he wanted his music in the film." Roth remembers things directly in that memoir, insisting that the film was intended to be a "sidebar" and not a career, but both Roth and Jellison agree that the songs that would become 1986's *Eat 'Em and Smile* were all slated to be part of the *Crazy from the Heat* film. Then again, Steven Tyler went on the record in a 1980s television interview about Roth asking Aerosmith to write music for his film.

Aerosmith aside, Jellison expanded further on that soundtrack's planned music: "Dave wasn't doing a lot [of music] while we were working on the film. He was doing some writing and they were laying down some tracks with [Steve] Vai, with Billy [Sheehan], but then once the film collapsed, then everything went into that. It's like, 'Okay, you've got to get out there.'" And it as it turned out, rumblings had emerged about Van Halen moving ahead with a new singer with planned touring. As Jellison noted, "Dave's a supercompetitive person," thus plans were properly adapted for a proper album cycle via Team Roth.

The first member of Roth's band recruited appears to have been bassist Billy Sheehan. The Buffalo, New York, native had first encountered Roth years earlier when his band Talas had toured with Van Halen. However, touring with Van Halen was not the career-defining big break for Talas, nor did it lead to a proper record deal.

When speaking with Sheehan in 2021, I inquired about Buffalo's entertainment scene in the late 1970s and early 1980s, which included a young Harvey Weinstein. "Stage One was the club that Harvey had. It was used to showcase national acts but we'd play every Monday and one Monday he'd bring a national act as the opening act because they were just on their way up," he began. "I said, 'Who's playing with us tonight?' I remember him saying something about a submarine. 'What are you talking about, a submarine?' So the band got up and it was U2, which is a German submarine. . . . At least that's what I thought it was. They got up and played and left a little note in the dressing room, 'Thanks a lot,' signed The Edge."

U2 was not the only future superstar band that Sheehan and Talas would cross paths with in Buffalo. "The Police came through [Buffalo] on their station wagon tour and they used our P.A. and lights. We didn't perform with them on that, but I was at that show right up front watching them. So Harvey's club was a significant thing." Added Sheehan with a laugh, "I'm somewhat proud to say that Harvey and I ended on very bad terms."

After leaving Talas in 1985, Sheehan joined up with Roth and the *Crazy from the Heat* film he recalls as being the first order of business. "They worked on that script. . . . Dave flew me out, it was before Steve [Vai] or Gregg [Bissonette] or anybody. We hung out and they were working. I would go to the movie office to go see everybody during the day, I think it was on the CBS lot. They were working all the time and their scriptwriters and stuff were there, so they kind of already had it mapped out as I was there."

For those who read the *Crazy from the Heat* script closely, they will notice a stage direction referencing the song "Shy Boy," a song written by Sheehan that he had performed with Talas. I asked whether Dave had always wanted the song in there or if it was added to the script later to the process. "Once I was there and Dave decided to do that song, it was concurrent in the timeframe there that it would be in there. I still have my copy of the script too." Noted Sheehan about the quality of the film's script: "It's pretty good, I stayed up and read the whole thing one night when I first got it. It was pretty exciting, I thought. I think it might have been a riot to do."

So how far along does he remember the film being production-wise? Far enough for the wardrobe to have been worked on. "A lot of the clothes we had onstage . . . I got this big, long leopard coat that was 'the pimp coat' from whoever played that character."

Overall, in retrospect, Sheehan looks at *Crazy from the Heat* with a balanced viewpoint. "I remember it was a drag when CBS pulled the plug. If you think the record business is cutthroat, you've got a couple steps up to the movie business. It's unbelievable. . . . I felt bad for Dave because he worked his ass off on that movie and he put his heart and soul in it. But that's Hollywood, the movie business—put your heart and soul into something they will yank it out of your chest."

Continued Sheehan after a pause: "I was at the office with Dave the day it came down, and I think he had just moved his office to Sunset Boulevard, to right on the Strip. I went there and I remember saying, 'Hey, we've got a great record. Let's just go out and tour and do what we do,' and we did."

Ultimately, David Lee Roth took legal action against CBS for its cancellation of the *Crazy from the Heat* film. He came away with a multi-million-dollar settlement believed to match his intended director's fee. In a July 10, 1986, interview with Larry King, Roth said that he "absolutely" plans to make another movie, planning to make a "rock and roll sex comedy." While Roth would ultimately direct a film, this is not something that would happen within the next decade.

Eat 'Em and Smile

When speaking with Larry King on July 10, 1986, David Lee Roth told the legendary interviewer, "I make records as an excuse to go on the road." While the sort of thing Roth has said in countless interviews, the reality was that the full-length album that became *Eat 'Em and Smile* was initially recorded to be the soundtrack to the film *Crazy from the Heat*.

In the previous chapter, it was discussed how bassist Billy Sheehan was the first of Roth's solo band members to join what the *Crazy from the Heat* memoir referred to as "The Yankee Rose Band." However, keeping *Rashô-mon* fresh in your mind, a grain of salt may be needed for this time. For starters, Roth's book fails to mention any of the musicians he had considered (for example, guitarist Steve Stevens) or the chosen musicians he had recruited (for example, drummer Chris Frazier) before that lineup came into place.

When speaking with guitarist Steve Vai in 2021 about his then-new album *Inviolate*, I tossed in a few Roth-related questions, like how he wound up playing with DLR. "Billy had brought me in and this was after that, from what I understand. Billy would be a good person to ask." After pausing, Vai continued: "I think they had tried out, or they were working with, three other guitar players." This narrative varies a bit from Roth's memoir, in which he talks about meeting Vai outside the Zero One Gallery—an after-hours spot Roth coowned—during a police raid.

Prior to landing the gig with Diamond Dave, after studying at the prestigious Berklee College of Music, Steve Vai had been in Frank Zappa's band. While playing with Zappa, Vai met Eddie Van Halen for the first time. While conversing, Vai told Van Halen about Zappa's home studio, which is believed to be what inspired Eddie Van Halen to build his home-based 5150 studio. Per Vai during our conversation, "If you saw Frank's studio, you, anybody would want one." On the small world end of things, one can argue that Eddie being able to make music on his own terms at home would contribute to Roth's frustration with Van Halen and subsequent departure from the band.

When speaking with Vai, I asked him about the previously mentioned Chris Frazier and the rumors about him originally having the gig with Roth. "Now, Chris is a great drummer. I've used him on many records. . . . It just takes a certain kind of sound and just rock and roll sensibility for something like that, and Dave needed to feel comfortable." Continued Vai: "Chris was great, it doesn't diminish him as an artist at all. . . . Dave wanted us to try out some other drummers and we, Billy and I, held auditions." Those auditions indeed led to the drummer that Vai, Sheehan, and Roth would all instantly agree upon. "When Gregg Bissonette entered the room, there was no question anymore. There was just an instant recognition of, 'Okay, he's the right guy.'" And Frazier would later play with the Eddie Van Halen–produced band Private Life.

Hailing from a music-centric family in Detroit, Gregg Bissonette is the son of a drummer (father Bud) and a piano/vibraphonist (mother Phyllis). He and brother Matt—lots more on Matt to come in later chapters—got to see The Beatles live in 1966, but it wasn't all rock and roll for the Bissonettes. "We grew up playing a lot of weddings, a lot of parties," Bissonette told me in a joint interview with his brother Matt. "Matt, I've got a picture of you playing with Chris Nordman and you're about fifteen years old and you're just staring at his left hand." Added Matt about Gregg: "Gregg started doing gigs with my dad, playing drums, and my dad would want to take a break and not play the disco songs or the rock songs, so Gregg would jump on the drums and play."

Detroit proved to be an ideal musical hub for the Bissonettes as both performers and fans, per Gregg. "When [John] Coltrane played with Elvin Jones and Jimmy Garrison and McCoy Tyner, they only played in two cities ever, I think. They did live in Paris, but in America they jockeyed between Manhattan and Detroit. Elvin Jones, of course, was from Detroit. But a great music town, we had this station that we grew up listening to, it was from Windsor, Canada, it's called CKLW, a Canadian station, but it was kind of the Motown station." He continued: "We left when we were young, like seventeen, eighteen years old. We'd come back for the summers and to do gigs, to make money to pay for college. We didn't really experience the playing at Harpo's and all the stuff that our friends did. . . . But we knew enough about it to know that Grand Funk, and Iggy Pop, and all that was there."

Back to the Zappas, musician, author, director, and all-around Van Halen historian Frank Meyer—frontman of The Streetwalkin' Cheetahs—was around the formation of the aforementioned Yankee Rose Band. "I grew up with Dweezil Zappa and all the Zappas. So I met Eddie a few times in the eighties around the time of when Sammy first joined the band; he and Dweezil were good friends, Dweezil had made a single called 'My Mother's a Space Cadet' when he was twelve years old. Eddie not only produced it with Frank but plays guitar on that intro riff. I met Dweezil about a year after that, but I had known his brother Ahmet and his sister Moon for years, we all went to grade school together and summer camp together, so I'd grown up with them."

Sidebar here, but was Dweezil a good guitarist as a kid? He was indeed, per Meyer. "Dweezil played at the talent show and Eddie Van Halen showed up at the soundcheck rehearsal of the talent show and brought Dweezil a guitar in front of all of his friends and. . . . I think that he even jammed with them at the rehearsal, but I don't think he did at the talent show."

But back to the DLR show here. "One day Dweezil calls me up because we lived down the street from each other and he says, 'Hey, are you home? I'm coming to pick you up.' And I said okay. He came down my driveway to pick me up, I was living at my parents' house and Steve Vai is in the passenger seat." Meyer paused. "At this point, Steve had played in Frank's band and I had met Steve because he hung around the house a lot. But also, he had played in Alcatrazz. . . . He goes, 'Hey Frank, you remember Steve. Steve's playing me his new record with David Lee Roth.' We knew that the rumor was they were playing together. This is six months probably before *Eat 'Em and Smile* came out. So these were rough mixes and he pops in 'Tobacco Road' as the first song. . . . Blew my brains out. Then by the time we got home, we sat there and listened to the song 'Yankee Rose,' and again, this is way before it came out. The only thing he'd done outside of Van Halen was the 'California Girls' thing, which did not sound like this."

The previously discussed Edgar Winter, known to be a big influence on Dave, had a hit decades earlier with "Tobacco Road." When speaking with Winter in 2022, I asked whether Roth covered "Tobacco Road" because of him. "I would assume so . . . I never really asked him that question directly, but I always made that assumption."

Of the ten songs featured on *Eat 'Em and Smile*, only six of them were originals written for the album, and all six of those were cowritten by Vai. During our late 2021 Zoom call, I asked Vai about his overall creative process as a songwriter. "What I do is find snippets . . . I'll find a snippet of something that I recorded that has some kind of energy in it. . . . Then I start fleshing it out. . . . For me, sometimes if there's a foundation of a groove that inspires you to play something on it, that works." He later added: "I think music comes to me, not unlike it comes to other musicians. There are various methods." A bit of a different mindset from Roth, who told TV2000's Lisa Robinson in 1985 that he writes lyrics when television commercials come on; joking or not, that interview included an alternate version of the "Mr. Bookworm" anecdote Roth told me in 2003.

While not named with the *Crazy from the Heat* memoir, another musician present for the *Eat 'Em and Smile* album was Jesse Harms. Although the album's liner notes only have him contributing keyboards to a few songs on the album, he told me during our 2020 interview that "I was there the whole time."

Harms, who ironically played with Sammy Hagar for decades and was part of the *I Never Said Goodbye* album by Hagar that featured Eddie Van Halen on bass, was recruited to *Eat 'Em and Smile* by Ted Templeman. "Ted was a really good producer, but he wasn't the kind of producer that would tell you what to play. In other words, his strategy—and actually he wrote a book about it—he wasn't the kind of guy that would tell you what to play, he would get the best players and try to get them to be creative. But if something wasn't right for him, it just didn't end up on the record." Further explained Harms, "I played on more tracks, but some of the stuff just didn't get on the record. There's nothing wrong with that, but I'm not sure exactly how the whole process went down."

Yet Roth was clearly happy with Harms' performances and studio demeanor, per a conversation that happened toward the end of the album's tracking. "We were kind of wrapping up everything, we're all hanging out, and Dave said to me, 'Jesse, look you're one of us, and do you want to be in the band?' Well you knew this is a trio and they didn't have a keyboardist in Van Halen, so I said, 'Well Dave, am I going to be on the stage or off the stage?' He said, 'We'll start out, you're going to probably be off the stage.' I'd just been with Sammy and I was trying to learn how to write songs on my own and everything. So I said, 'Well, I don't know, Dave, let me think about it.' And he never talked to me again." Harms ended that one with a laugh before continuing.

"He was obviously insulted, but I wasn't trying to be insulting. I was just trying to figure out what's best for me. It was really good for Brett Tuggle, who I've already said is a great guy and really good player and everything. So Brett really made something out of it." Harms, who also found success cowriting songs for REO Speedwagon, Heart, Eddie Money, and Guitar Shorty, has no regrets but still seemed a bit unsure of what happened: "I have to say it wasn't because I wasn't accepted by those guys [in his band], because I definitely was. So I don't really know what happened in the whole process of recording, but I could say after that day I never talked to Dave again, except for when we did the *Sam & Dave* tour. Then we did speak and he was nice."

Also around for the making of *Eat 'Em and Smile* while not referenced in the *Crazy from the Heat* book was Sammy Figueroa, who had played on the *Crazy from the Heat* EP. "I was there for the whole thing. We spent about a week or two living in the studio, eating there, from 10:00 in the morning until 1:00 in the morning," he told me via Zoom. "I never got tired, I wanted more because we were having so much fun laughing and reading great books and comparing knowledge. Steve and I were really good friends because Steve didn't drink or smoke. . . . We got to exchange a lot of wisdom and knowledge and we were both into the same things, metaphysics, science, biology, quantum physics . . . I was a big book collector and I had thousands of books. Like some people collect records, I collected books."

Further notable about *Eat 'Em and Smile*—which Roth claimed in *Crazy from the Heat* was a reference to an old fruit crate label he saw, and not a dig at Van Halen, although their *OU812* album title was a dig at Roth—is that

David Lee Roth recorded the full album in Spanish under the name *Sonrisa Salvaje*. The story behind that is bassist Billy Sheehan telling Roth about an article he had read that mentioned how approximately 20 percent of all hard rock music purchased within the Los Angeles metro area was purchased by Spanish speakers. Well, Diamond Dave is a Spanish speaker, but not everyone in his band was.

"I cut them with him," began Sheehan in our interview, when asked if he sang on *Sonrisa Salvaje*. "The harmonies are just me on that record. So we went into a studio in LA in the evening, but during the day Missing Persons were there. Terry Bozzio's crazy electronic kit was set up and the microphone was the one Dale Bozzio sang on. It had her lipstick and makeup all over the windscreen, so I could smell her perfume. I got a kick out of that because she was a beautiful girl." Continued Sheehan: "I sang it phonetically but Dave is pretty good at español, he can speak it pretty well, so he just coached me."

While *Sonrisa Salvaje* is regularly in rotation in the Paltrowitz household, it did not exactly set any sales records. "I don't know how successful it was, because it wasn't my record deal, that was Warner and Dave," responded Sheehan about its commercial success. "But every time I go to South America, man, people got them [albums] all over the place. I've signed thousands of them down there, but what a riot. That was a cool idea. A couple other people have tried to do something in another language, but unless you actually speak it, you can kind of make a fool of yourself pretty easily. Fortunately Dave knew what he was doing."

Per Sheehan, the Spanish sung by Roth on *Sonrisa Salvaje* was not universally approved. "We had to change some lyrics though because, especially with Mexico being a Catholic country, they don't like a lot of lewd stuff. . . . They were a little concerned about the atmosphere at the time because that was '86. Things were different back then than they are now."

Steve Vai confirmed in our conversation that he missed those sessions and that it was indeed Sheehan and Roth on vocal duties. "I didn't go to the studio. Dave did knock that off in like a day or two. They just took the masters and just overdubbed Dave singing in Spanish on them."

Surprisingly, Sammy Figueroa was not there either, although he did enjoy conversing in Spanish with Dave. "He came up to me one day in the studio while I was in my booth and he sat there and he started speaking Spanish. I said, 'Holy shit, you speak Spanish.' He said, 'Claro que sí.' . . . We spoke

Spanish for about twenty minutes but then we had to go back to work, so we waited 'til the session was over late in the night and then we started speaking more Spanish."

Figueroa added more to that story: "All the rest of the guys in the band were cracking up because they didn't know what the hell we were talking about. . . . He made it his business to learn Spanish. . . . At the time he had a Puerto Rican girlfriend and then he had another girlfriend that was Spanish a year later. He was all into the whole culture, the food. He'd love to go to Cuban, Puerto Rican, all kinds of Latin restaurants and have food after the sessions."

Weirdly enough, Roth's performance at a 1985 Mexican beauty pageant— reportedly televised to over seventy million homes, per his *Crazy from the Heat* book—had nothing to do with *Sonrisa Salvaje*. But *Sonrisa Salvaje*, per conversations I have had in recent years, does have fans in The Mavericks' Raul Malo and Fozzy's Chris Jericho.

As noted earlier, Jesse Harms' passing on the offer to hit the road with DLR ultimately led to Brett Tuggle joining the band. Steve Vai remembers this all happening after recording on *Eat 'Em and Smile* had wrapped. "We had written the music and recorded it and the keyboards were something that were very gently massaged into a couple of songs. . . . We didn't know anything about Brett. . . . He wasn't there beforehand." The decision to go with Tuggle was a mix between his strong musicianship and his easygoing demeanor. "When you hire a musician to go on tour. . . . They've got to be a happy camper. They've got to enjoy being away from home, or at least be able to tolerate it."

The *Eat 'Em and Smile* album was released via Warner Bros. Records on July 7, 1986. Its North American tour kicked off a little over two months later in Hampton, Virginia, on August 16, 1986. Van Halen's *5150* tour had kicked off nearly a half-year earlier on March 27, 1986, just days after the release of the *5150* studio album. Supporting acts for Roth's tour included Tesla and Cinderella; Duran Duran's Andy Taylor was initially announced as an opener for tour dates but does not appear to have been part of the tour, which did not hit Europe, Asia, Australia, or South America.

The average Van Halen setlist on the *5150* tour included only three DLR-era Van Halen songs (including "You Really Got Me," which was a Kinks cover), instead focusing more on Van Hagar tracks. Meanwhile, Roth's

Eat 'Em and Smile tour setlist included eight DLR-era Van Halen (covers included), showing him to have one foot in the past and one foot in the future. As with Van Halen tours of the past, Roth would perform a song on a mini-stage in the middle of the venue at each performance. However, Dave's tour did include a signature segment each night when Sheehan and Vai would have a dueling solo spot where they would physically chase one another. Per The Stray Cats' Slim Jim Phantom, that version of Roth's band "was one of the greatest rock bands ever."

While the *Eat 'Em and Smile* tour included plenty of tracks from the album in its setlist and a backdrop that showed the album cover, the live show had little to do with Roth's solo music videos, which had all done well on MTV. "I was fascinated by the videos because MTV was such a phenomenon at that time," began Less Than Jake's Chris Demakes. "'Yankee Rose,' that video was of course a classic." Roth told interviewer Dan Neer in early 1988, when it came to writing the stylistically unique "Yankee Rose," it was rooted in drawing "water from many wells," because "that's how rock and roll improves."

Gutter Candy singer Jersey Dagger agrees with Demakes' assessment of "Yankee Rose": "It transitions from like a Madonna video to the beginning liquor store sequence of 'Yankee Rose.' I was glued to this, my adolescent brain was about to explode by the time Roth rolls up to the cash register in tribal paint and says the classic line, 'Give me a bottle of anything and a glazed donut to go!' Then the guitar rips in, and Roth jumps off the drum riser with a split kick. Fuckin' forget-about-it! Butt shakin' spandex. I could not stop thinking about it the rest of the day. . . . It's still one of my favorite songs ever." Gutter Candy bassist and IMPACT Wrestling star Frankie Kazarian echoed his bandmate's praise and also noted that it shows that "Billy Sheehan was a monster bass player."

Jeff Cardoni, a film and television composer whose credits include *Young Sheldon, Silicon Valley, Undercover Boss, Wilfred,* and *Heels,* still views *Eat 'Em and Smile* as an important album in his musical development. "I could play *Eat 'Em and Smile* front to back. I had the book and I was a freak for that stuff," he explained to me in 2020. "I liked a lot of the songs that weren't hits on it. I liked 'Ladies Night in Buffalo,' the solo on that was a good one . . . 'Shy Boy,' 'Tobacco Road' . . . I guess over time your tastes change and your perspective changes, but at that point in time it was like guitar gymnastics. . . . It had humor, it had really catchy songs, and ridiculous musicianship."

Ultimately, three music videos were released from the *Eat 'Em and Smile* album: "Yankee Rose," "Goin' Crazy" and "That's Life." "Goin' Crazy," which Roth enthusiastically showed a clip from during his 1986 appearance on Joan Rivers' talk show, featured Roth in heavy prosthetics—a "fat suit," if you will—for some of its scenes, as he played more than character in the video. The lesser scene "That's Life" was a compilation of clips from other videos from Roth, almost like a "greatest hits" clip.

"Of course when Dave's *Eat 'Em and Smile* album came out, it didn't leave my car's tape deck for months. And his videos for 'Just a Gigolo/I Ain't Got Nobody' and 'Goin' Crazy' were everything back then," I was told by Amanda Cagan, a top-tier music industry publicist who will pop up again later in this book. "His manager at the time, who's also in those videos, Pete Angelus, wound up managing The Black Crowes too, who Mitch Schneider worked with starting with their first album when I was Mitch's assistant."

Warner Bros. would further promote the launch of David Lee Roth's solo career with a 1986 VHS release. Featuring music videos from *Crazy from the Heat* and *Eat 'Em and Smile*—although weirdly not "That's Life"—along with "never-before-seen interview footage," the video runs about thirty minutes in length. In recent years, Roth has uploaded a version of it to his YouTube channel that features some overdubbed commentary from the man himself.

But unlike what many major label artists did at the time, a live home video was not released by Warner Bros. for this tour, nor was there an MTV concert. At the time of this book's writing, Wikipedia referenced the Lakeland, Florida, show of the *Eat 'Em and Smile* tour having been filmed, and I asked Billy Sheehan about that. "It's so incredulous to me that I often question my own memory. But as far as I know, on that hard drive right over there, there's a full show video and audio of *Eat 'Em and Smile*." Continued Sheehan: "Now I don't own that, it's Dave's show, so I wouldn't violate his trust of course or do anything with it. I don't think I've ever even shown anybody the thing, but I have a full video of the *Eat 'Em and Smile Tour* pro-shot and pro-recorded. . . . I would hand it to Dave instantly. It's his property and I'm the caretaker for it. . . . Someday that would be nice to put out."

Another byproduct of the success of *Eat 'Em and Smile* was comedian Joe Piscopo doing a "Yankee Rose"–style parody titled "I Wish I Was You So I Could Make Love to Me" as part of his 1987 HBO comedy special *The Joe*

Piscopo Halloween Party. As Piscopo declined multiple requests for an inter-view, I asked his previously referenced collaborator Sam Ingraffia—the same gentleman who nearly appeared in the *Crazy from the Heat* film—whether Jersey Joe was a friend of Diamond Dave.

"That seems unlikely," started Ingraffia. "Knowing Piscopo pretty well, I doubt it. . . . Joe was doing all these characters and he did a lot of research, so he did like an impersonation. It wasn't like a parody, he actually did a pretty spot-on impersonation of the person. His Frank Sinatra was pretty remarkable." When I referenced a photo of Piscopo and Roth together from the mid-1980s circulating online, Ingraffia insisted that Piscopo "might have been hanging out with David Lee Roth to try and get his mannerisms down." However, it was likely "David Lee Roth thought it was funny that somebody was doing an impersonation of him."

Speaking of "Yankee Rose," that one also has lived on for decades in the life of Durga McBroom. She regularly attends to the NAMM trade show in Los Angeles, and a few years back she ran into Billy Sheehan, who was there to perform alongside Bissonette, Tuggle, and Vai. "I was there and I saw them and they're like, 'Oh my God, you're here. You've got to come up on stage and say it,'" referring to her lines from the intro of the music video.

While a very successful tour and era from a critical and commercial stand-point for David Lee Roth, this would prove to be David Jellison's last DLR tour, aside from doing design work on the next one. Jellison looks back on his Van Halen–related years fondly but is also glad he left the touring world behind. "It's exhausting being around those personalities. . . . You're work-ing around these guys six months nonstop. . . . You're with them every day, day in, day out," he started. "Because of the drugs and the sort of contentious nature of being in a band, it's like being married to four people you don't like, that's my analogy. Then you just throw in drugs and sex and money." He has since directed almost one thousand commercials, and his credits include work with the NFL, PGA, Mercedes, Jaguar, Washington Mutual, and EA Sports.

In 1982, 1983, and 1984, David Lee Roth recorded and toured the world alongside Van Halen. In 1985, 1986, and 1987, David Lee Roth nearly made a big studio movie and kicked off a successful solo career. Somehow in the midst of all that he ran the New York City Marathon in 1987, clocking in at 6:04:43. So he would slow down and take off 1988, right? Not a chance.

In his own words from the *Crazy from the Heat* book: "I 'spect I have not wound up with a significant other 'cause I'm not happy with me. Always something new to prove. Always a new treasure mountain to climb."

Enter *Skyscraper.*

Skyscraper

As released in January 1988, *Skyscraper* was the second full-length album—and third solo release overall, counting *Crazy from the Heat*—from David Lee Roth. Recorded in at least six studios over the course of 1987, per Roth's promotional *1988 Japan Interview* release, it was an ambitious effort on all ends. It was Roth's first studio album without Ted Templeman as producer and his first solo effort to not feature any covers.

As with *Eat 'Em and Smile*, *Skyscraper* was recorded around the greater Los Angeles area. "When the Red Hot Chili Peppers were recording at Capitol Studios, Roth and I had side by side urinals," famed drummer Jack Irons told me when pressed if he had any Roth-related anecdotes. "He looked at me and was like, 'You're one of those Chili Peppers, right?' 'Yeah.' And that was it."

Skyscraper would find the upgrading of Brett Tuggle from touring keyboardist to proper Roth band member, per Steve Vai, who produced the album with Roth. "I believe that coming from Van Halen and then the 'power rock' kind of foundation that bands had at the time, keyboards were not really something that was associated with Van Halen very much until "Jump" and all that stuff, and it still was Edward playing." He continued: "Brett started out off-stage sort of like, 'Hey, I think there's a keyboard player.' . . . He became an integral part."

One of Tuggle's contributions to *Skyscraper* was the foundation to the song "Just Like Paradise," as cowritten by Roth and Vai. In a February 1988 interview with tastemaker New York radio station Z100 and its *Z Morning Zoo*, Roth was asked plenty about the song, which eventually peaked at #6 on the *Billboard* 200. "There's always somebody special in the back of my mind when I'm writing these songs . . . it's the spirit more than anything . . . we know that paradise doesn't really exist."

Just a few weeks earlier in January 1988, Roth told Dan Neer of the same song: "Lyrically the song 'Paradise' has nothing literally to do with mountain climbing or rock climbing. Climbing is a visualization of how it sounded to me for that song. Not necessarily that long walk in the woods in paradise. Quite the contrary. I'd rather ride a Harley anytime. But for the feeling, the vibe that you'll get while you're there, is pure rock and roll. . . . A careening rush towards an unpredictable finish, that's what I get in the studio and what I get on the rock slab." Per Roth to Z100, the song's popular music video—which actually featured Roth mountain climbing—almost killed Vai. Although on a brighter note, per Roth's *Crazy from the Heat* book, the video did inspire scenes from the film *Cliffhanger*, per director Renny Harlin.

Another song of note from *Skyscraper* was "Damn Good." Roth told Neer in 1988 that "Damn Good" was a song that was "close to my heart" and that he was "singing it to specific people and to specific times and places and people who inspired the lyrics. I had a cold when I sang the song, you can hear it at the end." In a 2022 interview Vai conducted with *eonmusic*, he clarified that "Damn Good" was developed from a piece called "Scandinavian Air Solo," which was originally slated to appear on his *Passion and Warfare* solo album. While the song charted and had a proper release to radio, a music video was not filmed for it.

In our 2021 conversation, Vai explained to me that it is generally a coincidence when he has written something commercial or radio accessible: "Part of my brain lives in a fantasy because I think all my stuff is radio-friendly. . . . People know an inspired song, you feel it." He continued: "But everybody is stimulated differently, so luckily there are people who are making music that stimulate[s] those people and every great artist expresses their true, creative desires most effectively when they follow those things that are most exciting to them on a creative level."

"Stand Up" from *Skyscraper*, however, did have a music video filmed for it. A keyboard-centric song cowritten by Roth and Tuggle, its music features a car driving through clouds, dancing scantily clad women, a leather-clad dancing DLR, road cases made to look like skyscrapers . . . it is very '80s indeed. As arguably '80s as *Skyscraper* featuring a backward message hidden in the album, as confirmed in different interviews with Roth and Vai over the years: "Obey your parents and use a condom."

Noticeable in "Just Like Paradise" and "Stand Up," both Tuggle-written songs, are low-end sounds coming from a keyboard and not a bass guitar. Perhaps not so coincidentally, while Billy Sheehan played on *Skyscraper*, he exited the DLR band before the touring cycle in support of it; Mr. Big formed in 1988 and released its self-titled debut album in 1989, which scored a hit with "Addicted to That Rush," a song Sheehan had performed with the band Talas.

During the previously mentioned Z100 radio interview in 1988, a caller asked Roth about Sheehan's status with Roth. "We're moving different people around, different musicians, there's a whole different thing moving along in the '80s and every time you get a group identity over a long period of time, which I've done, you have to compromise a little bit." Continued Roth: "And rock and roll is not about compromise. So we just changed bassists and we're looking to make this engine runs as hot as we can, so stick with us."

Sheehan's replacement? The previously mentioned Matt Bissonette, brother of drummer Gregg. A commonly used quip from Roth in this era, about his band having sibling musicians: "two brothers, that sounds familiar?" Roth did give a slightly different answer about Sheehan's departure in the promotional *1988 Japan Interview* release: "The split with Billy was very happy . . . it was my decision and we talked about it."

By the way, a slightly different perspective when you speak with Billy Sheehan in the 2020s, I found: "Dave was generally there but not always, and that's one of the reasons why the album didn't sit right with me, because we didn't play it like we did on *Eat 'Em and Smile*." Continued Sheehan, both honestly and diplomatically: "I give Dave credit for doing something different. Instead of playing to the formula, he had the courage to do something different. So as much as that record isn't a personal favorite of mine, I think it was a well-recorded record. I'm glad they took a chance."

Per coverage by the *Los Angeles Times* in January 1988, the launch of *Skyscraper* coincided with an unforgettable stunt on the Sunset Strip in which Roth scaled "an eight-foot Styrofoam mountain atop the Tower Records building" with several bikini-clad dancers and the USC marching band" on hand. As it turns out, Warner Bros. Records did not have a permit for the mountain, roof signs were not permitted per local city ordinances, and crowd control issues came about.

Touring in support of *Skyscraper* kicked off on March 4, 1988, in Lakeland, Florida. Running for nearly 150 shows, the *Skyscraper* tour would not only extensively cover North America like the *Eat 'Em and Smile* tour did but also go out to Europe, Japan, and Australia. Openers included Poison, Faster Pussycat (replacing Guns N' Roses), Great White, Zinatra, and Zero Nine. Ironically, when Poison was unable to perform during the tour's Vancouver stop in May 1988, infamous punk band D.O.A. served as a last-minute replacement. And perhaps even more humorously, Roth's *Crazy from the Heat* memoir specifically calls out Great White and Poison for having bad episodes of *MTV Unplugged*, which were both within two years of them being on the road with DLR.

As with the *Eat 'Em and Smile* tour, Roth's setlist was a mix of solo selections and Van Halen classics. Yet on the production end, this was a state-of-the-art tour unlike anything Roth or Van Halen had ever attempted before. There was a part of the show where everyone in the band (and members of the crew) played steel drums in a marching band–like exhibition. There was an acoustic performance. There was an elevated boxing ring where Dave performed "Panama" and a surfboard he rode over the crowd while singing "California Girls." Vai had a three-neck guitar for "Just Like Paradise." Tuggle had two keyboard rigs. Oh, and like the Tower Records stunt, Diamond Dave would come down from way above the stage on a rope for "Skyscraper." As Roth said in that promotional 1988 Japanese interview: "The new stage is as exactly as the music sounds."

As a complex stage show, the setlist on the *Skyscraper* tour did not vary from night to night, and the opening song each night was the *Skyscraper* track "The Bottom Line." It was a fast-paced track with a nearly impossible bass solo and soulful call-and-response singing. I asked Sheehan about what it was like recording that one. "I'd go in and record bass alone. They'd have the drum tracks recorded, the guitar, and I'd be in there by myself with the engineer." And what about the bass solo, was that fully him playing or was there some editing in there? "As far as the solo, I wish we could have done some shenanigans because I wanted more. But I basically come in, 'Okay, do the solo, one take.' 'Okay, this is it bro, you've gotta hit it or not.' So there's a little bit of pressure to play it right. . . . They just want to do the bass. 'Okay, here we go, I hope I get this right.'"

As the studio recording of "The Bottom Line" features vocals that sound like something the McBroom Sisters would have recorded, I asked Durga McBroom if that was her on the track. Oddly enough, the answer was no. "I'm really mad that David never hired me as a singer. I always told him he should have, especially when he did one of the Vegas residencies. . . . When he met me, I was still just mostly acting."

Back to Matt Bissonette and his joining Roth's band, I asked him about "The Bottom Line," which brother Gregg noted as having "the best bass solo live." Matt Bissonette stated that in opening the *Skyscraper* tour with that particular song, "you'd get warmed up." Gregg Bissonette compared that to how the band would open the *Eat 'Em and Smile* tour shows with "Shy Boy," another one of Roth's faster songs. In Gregg's words: "It's kind of a statement. Like, 'here we go.'"

While the average David Lee Roth fan may not have known about Matt Bissonette before he replaced Billy Sheehan, he had great recording and touring credits beforehand. "When I got the gig with Roth, I had a band called A440 and we came out on the same label that Bon Jovi's *Slippery When Wet* came out, the same weekend our records opened up. We weren't hanging much after that because Bon Jovi took over the world."

This setback ultimately led A440 to break up and Matt to head back to Detroit for Christmas. "My dad organized a Gregg Bissonnette autograph session at our house in the middle of winter, because my dad loved us so much. He was so proud of us and I remember this line of people that would never give us the time of the day growing up were in line getting bro's signature, and I remember my dad going, 'Hey Matt, get up there and you could sign it too.' My dad, he equated your success musically with who you're playing with."

In our 2020 conversation, Gregg Bissonette gave kudos to Matt as being a great songwriter, while he was more of a road-ready drummer. "I'm always networking, 'Go to Guitar Center and hang out and see who's looking for gigs.' I find out through the grapevines of grapevines on the phone while we're in Detroit that Rod Stewart's looking for a bass player. So I tell Matt and I tell my dad and my dad's going, 'Matt, Rod Stewart audition when you get back in January after New Year's.' Finally Matt just snapped. He goes, 'I don't want to play with Rod Stewart.'"

For those keeping score, by the way, there are other musical Bissonettes out there. Per Gregg, their sister Kathy "works in the entertainment industry, too. She works down at AEG Live in Hollywood and she is the biggest music fan. Her hero's Donny Osmond. She lives to go see Donny Osmond." Per Matt: "She can actually sing better than any of us." Later Gregg told me: "Matt's wife Chariya, they met when they were playing in the band that comes up on Space Mountain at Disneyland. All four of our kids played drums."

As with the *Eat 'Em and Smile* tour, a home video release of a *Skyscraper*-era concert never materialized. Yet weirdly, at least one full *Skyscraper* concert was filmed for a Japanese television special, as sponsored by Toshiba. Some YouTube digging will find you some television commercials Roth filmed for the Japanese market in that era, and as you will read later, those were not the only international commercials Roth would participate in.

Another head scratcher from this era is that in Roth's *Crazy from the Heat* memoir, he mentions that the then-new television series *Beverly Hills 90210* wanted to use "Just Like Paradise" as its theme, but his manager—believed to be Pete Angelus—never told him about this. While believable on the surface, this sort of usage would likely also need to have been vetted by Warner Bros. Records as the owner of the song's master recording, Brett as cocomposers, and the music publisher for Tuggle. In other words, this request would have had to go to multiple parties, per music clearance protocol.

When interviewing legendary concert promoter Danny Zelisko—a man who promoted shows for numerous eras of Van Halen, Montrose, Sammy Hagar, and Dave solo—with Steve Roth for the *DLR Cast*, it came up that he had promoted one of the dates on the *Skyscraper* tour. "It was in El Paso. Don't ask me how I ended up with El Paso, but I did. I went there, we had a good show, a lot of people showed up," Zelisko began. "Afterwards, the crew guys and a couple of band guys said, 'Let's go across to Juarez.' I go, 'I've never been there before.' So I figured they had a car, we'll go over. We had to park at the state line to the country, and we got out and walked."

Continued Zelisko: "They took me into this place called Cesar's Palace and left me there. About four in the morning, I woke up, no clothes, no wallet, nothing. Somebody there found them for me. They said they put them away to keep them safe. I had to walk back to El Paso. I don't know, I could never blame Dave for that one, but it was a fantastic show. I just thought, 'I can't ever book a show with these guys again, they're gonna think I'm a lightweight.'" After laughing, he added, "I did end up doing more Dave shows after that, but none quite like that."

Per Trixter guitarist Steve Brown—whose touring and/or recording credits also include Def Leppard, Styx's Dennis DeYoung, Danger Danger, Jim Breuer, and Broadway's *Rock of Ages*—was an attendee of both Roth's *Eat 'Em and Smile* and *Skyscraper* tours. "I had a handmade *Eat 'Em and Smile* sheet that was hand painted, that I still have hanging in my garage. It was in the *Dream Come True* Trixter documentary that I did." Declared Brown in our 2021 interview: "*Eat 'Em and Smile* and *Skyscraper* still rank for me up there as good as *5150* and *OU812*."

Going back to *Skyscraper* single "Damn Good," that track would ultimately play a big role in the career of then-unknown guitarist Andy Timmons. "The first time I met Steve was in 1988 and so he was in Roth's band at the time. I had just recorded my first instrumental track called 'It's Getting Better,' which even though it was recorded in '88, it came out on my first solo record called *Ear X-Tacy* in 1994. But it was the first instrumental I'd ever done in this particular recording studio called January Sound in Carrollton, Texas." Continued Timmons in our 2022 conversation: "Steve, I heard, was coming through Dallas on tour and he needed to rent out a recording studio to edit the song 'Damn Good Times' to make it shorter for radio, so he'd rented out one of the small editing suites at January Sound." The studio engineer at January Sound tipped Timmons off to this. "'He's going to be here this night, come down and meet him.'"

After Vai finished doing the work that he needed to do, per Timmons, the studio "had this whole thing planned" where they were going to show Vai the studio and Timmons' track, "So they had my song cued up on the multitrack tape. . . . He's listening to the track, he's looking at me going, 'This is you?' I'm getting a nod of approval from who at the moment is the biggest guitar star. He did say to me after the track played, as he's leaving the studio, he was very impressed. He was very kind to me. . . . There's such a magnetism and a spirituality. . . . There was, like, very much a halo around his being. He says, 'Man, I know who I'll recommend if I ever leave David Lee Roth's band.' Obviously nothing came of that." Added Timmons: "That was a nice compliment for me, because I hadn't really gotten out there on any kind of national or international level. It was right after that, that's when I got the Danger Danger gig and life went on the path that it went down."

The year 1989 would bring the long-rumored departure of Vai from Roth's band. At the time, Vai was still helming the previously referenced *Passion & Warfare* but opted to join Whitesnake for its *Slip of the Tongue* album. In Roth's *Crazy from the Heat* book, he says little about Vai, even though the Long Island native was Roth's main musical collaborator from 1985 through 1989. He does say in the memoir that Vai did not like "Just Like Paradise" and preferred more abstract music. However, Vai was willing to partake in the "Yankee Rose Band" reunion that nearly happened in 2015, did perform with that band (sans Roth) in 2019 at the NAMM show referenced by Durga McBroom, and has collaborated with Bissonette and/or Sheehan on numerous occasions throughout the years.

Almost thirty-five years after its original release, *Skyscraper* is a multi-platinum album that undeniably serves as the commercial peak of David Lee Roth's solo career. Yet for those who like controversy, comedy, and unexplainable risk-taking in their DLR lore, it gets a whole lot better after *Skyscraper* . . .

A Little Ain't Enough

"Are you still Diamond Dave?" That was an actual question David Letterman asked David Lee Roth in a 1991 *Late Night with David Letterman* talk show appearance, as Roth was there to promote his then-new album *A Little Ain't Enough*.

Roth's long-winded response to Letterman included the following: "Diamond Dave comes from going to schools on the other side of town. We were listening to all Motown, all rhythm and blues at the Friday night dance. When I stepped across the other side of town, it was integrational busing. I had my pants up to here, my suspenders, my two-tone shoes with the Cuban heels, they'd say 'sparkle like a diamond.'"

On January 10, 1991, David Lee Roth world premiered *A Little Ain't Enough* via a syndicated Album Network radio special with radio personality Doug "Redbeard" Hill. While Roth had released new music in 1984 (Van Halen's *1984*), 1985 (*Crazy from the Heat*), 1986 (*Eat 'Em and Smile*) and 1988 (*Skyscraper*)—beyond completing several world tours, countless interviews, and a screenplay in midst of all that—a lot of fuss was made about *A Little Ain't Enough* being Roth's first new music in three years.

In turn, it was played up as if Diamond Dave had been hidden away for a long time before releasing *A Little Ain't Enough*. As he told Redbeard, whose introduction noted that Roth had sold twenty-four million albums in the United States alone: "When I disappear . . . when I'm gone, I is truly gone

. . . I don't create well under a microscope . . . I remove myself completely from the public eye . . . I'm a big people watcher and I see what's happening around me. I can only do that if people aren't looking at me." And how did Roth make that happen? "The best way to literally do that is cut my hair. So I go off to these far-away countries for a little bit, and two-thirds of my time is spent in the studio, the proverbial basement, working up songs. I do a lot of going to the movies, listening to the radio, but none of it is in the public eye." That response was later tagged with a Van Halen reference via "heard you missed us, we're back."

A week later on January 17, 1991, David Lee Roth appeared on *The Howard Stern Show*. While the majority of interviewers tend to get steamrolled by Roth's charm and quick wit—this author included—Howard Stern's interviews with Roth were often a rarity not only in getting Roth to answer questions that went off script but also getting humility out of Roth at times. When Roth entered the studio, Stern complimented DLR as looking "the most fit I've ever seen."

Earlier in this interview, he got Roth to admit to the album cover of *A Little Ain't Enough* being a statement on censorship, that touring was a profit center, and that Vai quit his band due to a "difference in musical opinions." Then again, Roth mentioned not speaking to the Van Halens in five or six years, although in his *Crazy from the Heat* book, he references running into Eddie Van Halen and Valerie Bertinelli on the streets of New York City in the early 1990s, and that his father Nathan had reached out to Eddie about wanting him to be on better terms with Dave. In turn, the timeline of it all is a bit convoluted, and that is not the first time this happens with relation to Dave's Howard Stern interviews.

Throughout Roth's 1991 discussion with Stern, there were numerous instances in which Stern badmouths Eddie Van Halen, Alex Van Halen, Michael Anthony, Sammy Hagar, *and* Valerie Bertinelli, yet Dave never takes the bait. He mentions that rock stars trying to be actors is "ridiculous," seemingly forgetting to mention the *Crazy from the Heat* film aspirations he once held. Then again, Howard Stern mocks entertainers running for public office in that interview, yet he would wage a campaign for the New York State governorship within a few years of this. Roth also declared that Van Halen never made demos or shopped itself to record companies in its early days, which is not true, while Stern—who has reinvented himself as a major advocate for LGBTQIA+ rights and matters—threatens to take Roth to "the homo room."

Stern did manage to extract interesting Van Halen tidbits from Roth, who had then been out of the band for fewer than six years. One of them being this quote: "The Van Halens and I were never the best of pals . . . that's why the music was so fiery." But then this one: "I don't even remember why Van Halen broke up, it's been a while." And when Howard Stern mocks Don Henley's then-refusal to talk about the Eagles, who would interestingly reform about three years later via the same manager who would help Van Halen reunite with Roth in 2006, Roth agreed: "You don't just chop out years of your life and say that was no good, that was a mistake."

On air with David Lee Roth, Howard Stern played portions of most of the songs on *A Little Ain't Enough*, regularly interrupting the songs and offering unrelated commentary.

In an April 1994 interview with New York radio station WNEW, about three years after *A Little Ain't Enough*'s release, Roth opened up about what the album was intended to mean overall: "[It] was a good statement of me in the times we were bouncing around in." He later added: "Often when I look back on old videos or old work, if you take it in 1994, you get kind of a giggle because it's so much a reflection of its time . . . I'd like to think that my music is just like that."

As told to *Off the Record* host Mary Turner—whom Stern mocked in that 1991 interview—in May 1991, he and his band spent four and a half months in Vancouver to make *A Little Ain't Enough*. Rather than staying at a five-star hotel, he chose the much less posh Nelson Place Hotel in downtown Vancouver. This hotel was in a rougher part of town, which he said helped inspire the lyrics to "Dogtown Shuffle," which he told the WNEW host is about "how people really live."

The final album cover to *A Little Ain't Enough* did not end up as Roth had first conceptualized. Per an interview with WNEW in 1991, Roth explained that he had come up with the following album cover: "It was a picture of a gal sitting against an airplane and the airplane was in the background, it looked like a B-17 bomber, but it had a human face on the front of the cockpit. She was sitting in the front in a see-through negligee with a pair of scissors. The name of the album was *Cuttin' Out*. So I guess the question in the censor's mind was 'Exactly what was she cutting?' The censors are particularly riled, particularly sensitive these days. I don't know, for something like that, it's not like I'm making a political statement. It's not like my career is based on 'You didn't like this picture.' There's a million other pictures that you could pick."

Continued Roth, who clearly had disdain for censorship: "Getting serious here for a second here, censorship is an insidious, corrosive thing. Something that works from the inside out. You don't even know it's working. . . . You get a label on your record, it means one hundred thousand more sales."

The band backing Roth on *A Little Ain't Enough* also did not come out as Roth had first conceptualized. With Steve Vai's departure following the *Skyscraper* tour came Roth's quest for the next groundbreaking guitar hero. That would be Jason Becker, who played alongside future Megadeth guitarist (and future Japanese musical icon) Marty Friedman in the band Cacophony long before his twenty-first birthday.

In Roth's 1991 interview with WNEW, he referred to Becker as "Shreddy Krueger . . . the hot new guitar slinger." He also noted that he recorded with a rhythm guitarist for the first time ever on an album for the sake of simplifying overdubs. That led to some sort of anecdote about Becker sometimes messing up due to his young age, hence him using Steve Hunter—whose credits include B. B. King, Aerosmith, Eric Clapton, and Peter Gabriel—because "he never misses." Furthermore, Roth said that he likes "to keep it fresh" because "there are people who are imminently qualified to kick butt in the studio, but they just don't quite serve it up onstage. There are people who are great onstage, but you never want to put a microphone in front of them connected to a tape recorder."

Closer to the truth was that in the midst of recording *A Little Ain't Enough*, Jason Becker became ill and began to suffer the effects of what was later diagnosed as ALS. He was unable to tour with Roth in support of *A Little Ain't Enough*, and as DLR declared on air via WNEW, "it's a different gang than I recorded with." Per influential music journalist and author Brad Tolinski—coauthor of *Eruption: Conversations with Eddie Van Halen*—a conversation we had in 2022, Roth was asking trusted guitar experts about who should replace Becker, and he had directly recommended Eric Gales in their one and only conversation. Ultimately, in place of Becker and Hunter on the road would initially be Joe Holmes and Desi Rexx.

The previously mentioned Mitch Schneider has represented Ozzy Osbourne, Aerosmith, David Bowie, Tom Petty, Dolly Parton, and Slash as a publicist, to name just a few key artists. He started working with Roth in 1991 around the *A Little Ain't Enough* album campaign. In our 2020 interview alongside Steve Roth, Schneider described Roth as "a true visionary and not warm and fuzzy to be around," but quickly added, "that really goes for a lot of rock and roll greats that I've worked with . . . they want to get it right, they're really detailed."

Schneider came on board with DLR when it was time to put together the press kit for the album. "I had to interview him for his bio prior to the photo shoot, and I think that was the second time I met him. The first time was in the office in West Hollywood," he said before pausing. "So I sit down, take out my tape recorder, I still am in journalist mode. . . . So I take out my questions and he takes the questions from my hand he goes, 'Oh let me look at this.' He looks at it and then he gives it back to me, but he doesn't actually physically give it back to me. He just turns the piece of paper over and puts it on the table and says, 'Oh you won't need these.'" Schneider paused and briefly laughed. "Then he just talks for like ninety minutes, which admittedly was incredible. However, he still didn't answer some of the questions I had."

Musician, author, and wearer-of-many-hats Frank Meyer is a fan of Mitch Schneider, much like myself. "I like Mitch a lot and a lot of folks I know came under Mitch's tutelage, like Mitch groomed some of the greatest publicists ever, and he is one of the greatest publicists ever."

One of those publicists Meyer was undoubtedly referring to is Amanda Cagan, who answered questions for me in 2022. "Mitch was always just perfect with him. Mitch got everything Dave was about. He speaks the same colorful language as Dave, so they were always on the same page. Dave trusted his opinions about press that Mitch had secured for him."

Per Cagan, while Roth did get on the phone with Schneider, he did still have office staff in 1991. "He did have a personal associate that Mitch and I mainly dealt with when it came to arranging interviews, sending options and clips, etc., especially once Levine/Schneider turned into MSO in 1995 and I was doing more hands-on PR type of work, not just assistant stuff. There was always something cool, exciting, and interesting to take care of during all of those times! He always kept us on 'tour toes.'"

Those "tour toes" could include visits to the MSO office. "'Holding court' is an understatement when it comes to Dave," began Cagan. "He takes command of a room, and always did anytime I was with him. I've got a vivid memory of him being at MSO's office to do interviews, and when he was done, he stood at the front of the office space and just riffed for the entire staff about stuff for thirty minutes! It was mesmerizing. We all just couldn't move or speak until he had left, because we were all just in awe of him. Such an amazing moment."

Unique about *A Little Ain't Enough* as an album is that its songwriting credits are all over the place. Some of the songs were written with Roth's band members and other songs by outside writers. This was clarified in several interviews, including the WNEW interview in 1991. Per Roth: "I got a lot of tapes from publishing houses . . . I chose none of them, but I found some excellent songwriters to work with."

One of those songwriters is Robbie Nevil, whom Howard Stern referred to as a "cute guy" in that 1991 interview. Nevil, who has been a top-tier composer for film, television, and other artists' albums beyond having a solo career of his own, looks back on his time around Roth with warmth. He did not come to Roth via a "publishing house," as had been alluded to, however. And for the record, Nevil never took Stern's jokes about him seriously: "Howard started making fun of me, which I love, I don't care. I don't take myself too seriously."

"It started with a mutual friend of ours, Keith Olsen," began Nevil. "He was an amazing cat and had introduced me to David. . . . The first time we got together, I went to David's house and it was a blast because I grew up listening to Van Halen too. I remember being in club bands, cover bands when they were first starting to really take off, and it was a certain kind of rock star thing that's not the same today."

Nevil recalls that the first song Nevil and Roth had worked on was "Shoot It," which wound up being the second song on the album. "I didn't have anything to do with the music, he had the track and I think he had some melodic ideas. He sort of said, 'Why don't you take this, mess around with it, and come back and see what happens?' So I think we talked about it a little bit and he might have some other words. So I took it, wrote some lyrics to it, and then came back to his house."

There was some humorous back and forth before they got to the finished product, according to Nevil. "There's one thing he said to me when I came back with a lyric that I just never forget. I wrote what I thought would be right for him, I think I had a lot of the hook and maybe the verses too . . . I was telling him about it in a kind of like apologetic manner . . . I was sort of saying, 'Hey listen, you know this is this thing I have. If it's not cool I'll rewrite it again or I'll tweak it.' He just looked at me at one point and he's just like, he didn't understand my trying to be really diplomatic, overly diplomatic perhaps, it's just my personality type. He's got a large personality. He looked to me, he goes, 'Did your mother hit you as a child?'" Nevil laughed when telling me that. "I will never forget that. We just started laughing, I just started laughing, it was just such a classic line. He just has a line for everything and he's a great dude. So we finished that one up and I wasn't there when he sang it."

Yet that was not the end of the road for Nevil as a Roth collaborator. "He was a great guy and he's super super fun and so I just went back and I'm like, 'I want to come up with something that kind of reminds me of my favorite David Lee Roth and Van Halen stuff, just my take on it.' So I started 'A Lil' Ain't Enough' without him. I had access to a studio because I was signed to MCA Publishing, they had a studio, so I went down with a band and I cut 'A Lil' Ain't Enough.' It wasn't that at that time, I just called it 'Living in Luxury,' and I sang, I did the basic track, not the one that's on the record. He redid it with Bob Rock and did an amazing job."

Nevil expanded further upon the creative process behind the song: "I did the basic track and then I put a scratch vocal where I was singing the melodies. During that hook line I would say 'living in luxury,' which I think still ends up in the line, but that was my whole thing . . . I sent it to him. . . . He just goes, 'Oh this is great, man.' But you never know in those situations, like maybe he'll take it or maybe it won't make it."

While *A Little Ain't Enough* was produced by iconic rock producer Bob Rock—who also helmed key albums by Metallica and Mötley Crüe—Nevil remembers getting a call from Bob Ezrin, who was briefly attached to produce the album. "He's like, 'I'm working with David, we're thinking about cutting that song.' I was thrilled because I always loved the song, but you don't have control over that, you know? Then I didn't hear from them for quite a while."

How long was it before Robbie Nevil heard more about the status of the song "A Lil' Ain't Enough"? "I'm sure it was months, because the next thing I know I heard from David that they did the album with Bob Rock and that it could be the first single or something, which was just mind blowing. I mean, it was exciting you know for obvious reasons, I was still doing the artist thing at that point where I was recording my own albums. So I always enjoyed playing those two roles. . . . When that record came out, I was just like, 'God damn.'"

Did he and Roth ever hang out again? "I think we hung out a few times. I think he invited me to a karaoke thing one night or something. It was so much fun, he's a great cat, he's good people. . . . The thing that's so amazing about him, aside from the music, I just can't believe how rapid fire he is. He has some crazy amazing line to say about everything and I wonder sometimes, 'Is he improvising them or does he just have this endless supply of one-liners?' It never ends. His energy burns so bright. He's an amazing guy." But back to David Letterman's question that opened this chapter: Is he still Diamond Dave? According to Nevil, Roth "could turn it up to ten and it wasn't always like that, not that intense."

Mirroring something that Ted Nugent had told me, Nevil had similar conversations with Roth about him not being primarily influenced by rock. "We were just talking about vocal styles. . . . He goes, 'You know what, man? I always thought of myself as an R&B singer.' I just thought, 'What a trip,' but I get it in a weird way, I get it from his perspective. That's the fun part about music, and how we all take from everything and then we kind of redo it and comes out in our own way. When I did [the demo of] 'A Lil' Ain't Enough,' I did what I thought he would, but he probably heard it and was like, 'I don't know about that.' The original track was cool, but they definitely did a brilliant other thing."

So did Nevil's successes related to David Lee Roth lead to any other work coming in for him? "Well I don't remember someone saying they wanted that, because that was so in the 'David Lee Roth meets Van Halen' kind of genre. . . . But I remember bumping into Jon Bon Jovi at a recording studio and he's like, 'Man that's so cool. I heard that you did that thing.' I had met him in Sweden. . . . He said, 'Man, we've got to get together,' and we did a little cowrite with him and Southside Johnny. It came as a result of that. . . . It wasn't like Southside Johnny wanted that at all." He ended that one with a laugh.

Another collaborator who David Lee Roth worked with on *A Little Ain't Enough* was Rocket Ritchotte, who cowrote the song "Last Call." How exactly did that one happen? "We used to just get together at Gregg's house when he used to live off Topanga in Woodland Hills. He had a little studio in there and you'd just come up with ideas. I don't remember who came up with that." He added: "I haven't heard the song in so long. . . . We'd just do a demo, a bunch of demos, a bunch of different ideas."

Per Ritchotte, Roth was not in the room when it was written: "It had been given to David. . . . He was never there, so he was never involved. They just would give him a song, he'd fall in love with it." The guitar hero continued: "When he hears a demo, he falls in love with them. . . . The demo I did on that record. . . . I can't remember what it was called, but he [Jason Becker] played the same exact slides that I played because Dave fell in love with it, and he's a really good player. He can come up with something probably way better, but that's how David is. . . . The demo he gets, he gets so used to it."

Rocket Ritchotte corroborated what Robbie Nevil had said about Bob Ezrin being attached to *A Little Ain't Enough* at one point. "I remember [Bob] Rock coming in. Bob Ezrin, I don't know what had happened. . . . When they were doing that, those records, I think it was Ezrin who got Becker in the band. I think he said, 'You need a real hot flashy guitar player.' He is really a good guitar player. . . . Then Jason got kind of sick and he didn't take them on the road."

Singer Marc LaFrance was around for the making of *A Little Ain't Enough*, as recruited by producer Bob Rock. "I did a lot of stuff with Bob and I did stuff with Bruce Fairbairn as well. I did Poison and The Scorpions and a variety of work with him," he began. "I ended up at Little Mountain Sound, which was kind of the center of the universe when I moved here in 1980. . . . I moved to Vancouver and the first day I moved here I was at a meeting at GGRP, a jingle house, and everything exploded. The album sessions happened there. You'd be singing on a commercial and Bob Rock would walk by and say, 'Hey Marc, are you available to do a session? I'm just producing this band called Blue Murder.' Another time you'd be doing the album session and somebody would come by, one of the jingle people, and say, 'Hey, you want to do a McDonald's ad tomorrow?'"

Per LaFrance, who is also a reputable drummer, "you were in the studio almost every day, so you really got used to working in the studio." This is why major artists would often utilize local performers. "A lot of people just get nervous and especially as a singer if you get nervous, your vocal cords tighten up, it's hard to sing." Bob Rock often used LaFrance and vocalist Dave Steele together on sessions. "We did a lot of stuff combined because our voices complemented each other."

LaFrance remembers being around for a lot of the making of *A Little Ain't Enough*. "We did the whole album, because you go in one day and you'd be doing some stuff and then they'd work on some other stuff. Of course you get, 'Can you come on in again? We want to try some new stuff.'" About Roth himself, LaFrance has only positive things to say. "David was amazing to work with, because a lot of the other singers, they didn't necessarily participate in the background vocals. But he would come in and sing with us and do stuff. He was very colorful and a very super-fun guy to work with. He's one of the guys that really stands out. He was just super friendly and charismatic."

Roth ultimately made a big impression on the recording studio as a whole, per LaFrance. "Little Mountain was famous for their loading bay, which was a huge room that they used for natural reverb. It kind of gave Little Mountain a sound they're famous for, the drum sound there, because they use that." Continued LaFrance before laughing: "He had his wall-climbing setup in there in the loading bay." LaFrance also confirmed what Roth said about his lodging in Vancouver while rehearsing: "He had this mobile home that he had parked, I guess to travel around, but he's a character too. The hotel room, he could afford any hotel, but he chose this kind of weird hotel in downtown Vancouver. He blasted the wall out so he turned it into a big penthouse or something."

He did see Roth again after completing work on *A Little Ain't Enough*. "I actually did a live show where I [vocally] warmed up David Lee Roth. We were at the Commodore [Ballroom in Vancouver]. I remember when we were in the studio, he's telling me, 'Marc, you ain't been to a backstage like mine ever in your life.' It was something to see.'" Sounds like Club Dave. "That was Club Dave, yeah. There were a lot of females in the back. It had to be over one hundred or something. I'd never seen anything quite like that. He was a true ladies man, for sure."

As for some of the other recordings where you can hear Marc LaFrance sing, try The Cult's *Sonic Temple* album, Glass Tiger's "Don't Forget Me (When I'm Gone)," Poison's "Unskinny Bop," and Bon Jovi's *Keep the Faith* album. Although don't expect to see LaFrance credited as a vocalist on all of those: "A lot of stuff was like union sessions or whatever, but some bands didn't like to give credits. They'd give you an 'extra extra special thanks,' even though you're actually singing. Some bands didn't want to let their fans know that they had to bring in other people to do stuff on their records, I guess."

If you recall the *Skyscraper* chapter, bassist Billy Sheehan left Roth's band after recording the album, replaced by Matt Bissonette. Similar circumstances happened with this one as Matt Bissonette recorded *A Little Ain't Enough* and did not do the corresponding world tour, although brother Gregg did. Per Bissonette: "Dave runs the show and he's pretty adamant about who's in his band. At that time music was changing a lot and Dave always liked to stay a step ahead musically so I think he was just trying new combinations, etc." Added Bissonette: "Things were changing quickly, from what I heard."

When I pried a bit more, the always unbelievably nice Matt Bissonette opened up a bit more about his time with DLR: "I gotta say when I got the call to play with Dave it was shocking and fast. I was playing with my own band at the time, called A440, and just did a tour with Sheena Easton and a little time with Gino Vanelli. When Dave called it was 'hurry up and jump into this crazy circus.' It was awesome and fun to work with such a great band and to see Dave give 100 percent every night." Continued Bissonette, who has played with Elton John since 2012, about Diamond Dave: "He reinforced my belief that if you work hard and stay consistent you will reap the benefits. My mind was in million different directions at the time and I really wanted to write more, so I know everything worked out for everyone when we parted ways. I'm just incredibly grateful that I'm still playing music, and thankful to have played in Dave's band when I did."

While he was there to promote *A Little Ain't Enough* in his 1991 interview with WNEW, Roth emphasized the live element to be his favorite part of the process: "Touring is where it all starts. Everything else is a hobby. I love travel. I love playing live onstage. Everything I do on record is a representation of what I do live onstage." Continued Dave: "There isn't enough countries for me to go to. Last tour we did twenty-something countries, we're going to do the same thing, twenty-two countries, something like that. Living on the road is an art. When you are continually nowhere specific, that becomes your somewhere, and you have to learn to live out there. . . . I always perceived rock and roll as a passport. Let this take me everywhere and then I'll have more things to write about and then I'll go even further." When asked about possible props and tricks he had planned for the tour, he answered: "It's going to be of epic proportions. I think the Latin term is 'gimongous.'"

A Little Ain't Enough was released on January 15, 1991, and its corresponding world tour kicked off in Europe in the winter of 1991. Warrant was the slated support act for the European leg of the tour, then riding high off its *Cherry Pie* album. Per guitarist Joey Allen: "We started the European run. We were supposed to be the only opening band for that entire run and we only ended up doing four shows." I asked Allen during our 2021 conversation if that was due to the rumors of Warrant frontman Jani Lane getting hurt during a show. "There's two versions of that story. We can leave it 'PG' and say, 'Yeah, he got hurt and went home.' But in all reality, his wife of the week was driving around LA with some other guy in his car, and he left in the middle of the night without telling any of us."

Musician and podcaster Rob Lane—no relation to Jani—was one of the fans aiming to see Warrant open for David Lee Roth. "That album to this day is huge for me so I was buzzed to learn they were coming over as support to David Lee Roth in early 1991," he told about *Cherry Pie*. "My friend and I grabbed our tickets for the show and bus—this was when ticket operators ran bus trips to shows. Once we got on the bus we were told that 'the support band' had canceled. We couldn't believe it! Apparently Jani Lane had fell through the stage the previous night, but since I've heard other stories. Seriously we were crushed." But Lane added: "Luckily though the Dave show more than made up for it and I was all in from that point on!"

Dropping out of the *A Little Ain't Enough* tour would mean more to Roth than it would to Warrant, per Allen. "When we abruptly got back to the States, when Dave finished his tour, Dave reached out to us—I think he called Jani or Erik [Turner], he got somebody's number, it wasn't me—he said, 'The way I look at it, you owe me a tour and a bottle of Jack Daniel's.'"

Funny quip aside, Allen remembers those first shows with DLR fondly: "On the first night of the European tour with Dave, when we actually walked into the arena he was onstage soundchecking. He got offstage and came over and said hi to everybody. It was a very nice, cordial, 'welcome to the tour, make yourself at home, if you need anything.' Just very cool. We've never had an artist do that at that point."

So why did Warrant owe Dave a bottle of Jack Daniels? "I'd known Dave since way prior to that, but the first night we were in our dressing room and we didn't have any Jack Daniel's, and Dave always has Jack Daniel's. So we sent one of our guys over to his dressing room and said, 'You said if you need anything and we need some Jack Daniel's.' Our guy came back with a bottle, so that's why he said that when he called, 'You owe me a tour and a bottle of

Jack Daniel's.'" But about that tour, that did not pan out for good reason, per Allen. "The *Cherry Pie* record was doing huge in America and we got offers to go out on our own. That's the only reason we didn't go out with Dave."

Side note here, but in a 2022 interview with Jack Daniel's Brand Ambassador E. T. Tecosky, I established that the brand loves Roth back: "I mean, is there a list of the greatest rock frontmen that does not put Diamond Dave in the top ten? . . . The kicks alone put him high on the list." Continued Tecosky: "I do have a great story about the time I accidentally spilled a very large beer on a very large, angry man at a Van Halen concert. Luckily, I am here to tell the story and happy to do so next time we share a glass of Jack together."

When DLR was being interviewed by Mary Turner in 1991, he was asked who was in his backing band and he declined to name the previously referenced Desi Rexx. However, Allen remembers Rexx being there. "Yeah, Desi Rexx on rhythm guitar and then Joe Holmes was playing lead guitar, I do believe." Any idea why Rexx may not have made it through the whole tour? "Sometimes when you have a new record or you've got some new band members, you want to tighten it up, and that's maybe what he was doing." Holmes, who later played with Ozzy Osbourne but declined to be interviewed for this book, was viewed by Allen as "a nice guy . . . a super-easy, mellow dude." Per Rexx, who also declined to be interviewed and has since moved to Utah, Allen "didn't know he was in Roth's band" until he "saw him onstage shaking his ass, as he does so well or used to."

Going back to how Allen, who arguably did not become prominent until 1989, had known Roth, I asked about that as well. "We never toured with Van Halen, obviously. When he was in Van Halen, Warrant was a thing, barely, in '84." He continued: "I met him through a friend of mine that was good friends with his girlfriend that he was dating at the time, a girl named Kate Brooks who is the daughter of Jean Simmons, the actress. . . . My buddy was good friends with Kate, platonic friends, and they were going to The Rainbow one night and it was in '83, like right after the US Festival. . . . It was within months of that because I remember it was that era of Dave. They said, 'Hey, you want to go to dinner? Dave's going to be there.' I said, 'That'd be great, I'd love to meet Dave.' I went and had dinner with David Lee Roth at The Rainbow and he was great. He pulled into the booth, sat right next to me, and started talking. He's always been very very nice to me."

For the North American run of the *A Little Ain't Enough* tour, different openers were slotted after Warrant could not do those dates. "Trixter got offered to open up for Dave on that summer of '91 tour that he did that Extreme wound up going out on," began Trixter guitarist Steve Brown. "Thank god we didn't do it, because we would have lost the Warrant tour, which was hugely successful."

But it was not easy for Brown, a die-hard Van Halen fan who caught the *Eat 'Em and Smile* and *Skyscraper* tours as a fan, to decline the *A Little Ain't Enough Tour*. "Turning down the *A Little Ain't Enough* summer tour, that was a hard decision for me. But I was smart enough at that point to where I knew that the Warrant tour, first off we were getting paid a lot more money, and I just had a feeling it was going to be a better fit, you know? I also knew that the *A Little Ain't Enough* record wasn't selling that well. So my managers and the band, we were like, 'The Warrant thing's going to be a lot better for us.' It turned out to be more than a home run for us and for everybody, for Warrant and for Firehouse. By the time that tour ended they had almost a #1 single on the charts, so it was great."

Like Roth's prior two solo tours, the *A Little Ain't Enough* tour setlist was a mix of both solo and Van Halen classics. Possibly due to the poor advance ticket sales that led to some of its shows being canceled, the production on the tour was not "gimongous" as promised. It did have the wall of Marshall amplifiers seen in the "A Lil' Ain't Enough" video, a huge inflatable mic he rode on, and a large set of women's legs that wrapped around Gregg Bissonette's drum riser. Roth's *Crazy from the Heat* memoir referenced the tour having a boxing ring that sprayed Jack Daniel's, although that is not something this author has viewed in any available bootleg videos from the tour.

A bit of a conflicting story, but in Roth's previously mentioned 1991 appearance on *Late Night with David Letterman*—which featured him performing "Tell The Truth," another single from *A Little Ain't Enough*, with Paul Shaffer, the *Late Show* band, and a pair of background singers—he told Letterman that the *A Little Ain't Enough* tour had already "sold out" in fourteen European countries.

Another big change in the *A Little Ain't Enough* era for Diamond Dave was that he was no longer working with manager and frequent creative collaborator Pete Angelus. While Angelus declined comment for this book, I did ask Black Crowes guitarist Isaiah Mitchell if the story about The Black

Crowes—also managed by Angelus—having difficulty with Roth in the early 1990s was true. "Yeah, Chris [Robinson] told [me] a story. . . . The Crowes were going to LA for the first time and I think they were playing for some record people and whatever. David Lee Roth was there and I think he was all gacked out and he was just telling them they're all wrong . . . and just being David Lee Roth. . . . The way Chris tells it was pretty funny, but I think it's amazing. . . . You're in your early twenties and boom, you go to LA and you're starstruck as it is and you're, like, 'We're here, we're doing this.' And then David Lee Roth is directing you, like you've got to be like, 'Wow, this is amazing. And fuck this guy.'"

While Roth's music video for "California Girls" reportedly required five weeks of pre-production, his video for "A Lil' Ain't Enough" was arguably his most ambitious music video yet. Per DLR in a 1991 MTV News segment about the video, there were twenty-two sets and more than 150 characters involved. In his words, "What we do musically here, and as far as what goes on the screen, I take it seriously as a heart attack. It's what other people think of me that I don't take seriously at all." And, "It's a question of balancing fury with a little sense of humor." Yeah, I don't get it, either.

Going back to Roth's 1991 interview with Howard Stern, he was asked about the "A Lil' Ain't Enough" music video, which Stern cohost Robin Quivers was a big fan of. Roth sort of clarified to Stern that the video is not meant to mean a whole lot: "We sat around the table, a bunch of us, and said, 'what does "A Lil' Ain't Enough" mean to you?'" He later admitted the music video has very little to do with its lyrics, which Robbie Nevil played a part in writing.

The music video for "A Lil' Ain't Enough" was initially banned by MTV and later unbanned. But it made headlines in late 2021 when Roth announced his retirement to a Las Vegas newspaper on October 1, 2021, literally within two weeks of the date shown at the end of the "A Lil' Ain't Enough" music video as being his final show: October 10, 2021. Decades later, this led long-time DLR fans to try to guess whether this was a coincidence or whether Roth knew that he planned on retiring in thirty years; this author is guessing it was coincidence based on Diamond Dave's birthday being October 10.

The year 1991 yielded a few other gems in the DLR universe. Rockcards—hard rock's attempt at collectible trading cards—came out with a set, and Roth was the only artist to have four cards in the set. Roth also voiced Brian the Brain in a series of Nintendo Gameboy commercials that appear to have aired only in the United Kingdom and are not currently documented in the IMDb universe.

Possibly seeing that the writing was on the wall for him as a mainstream rock solo artist, David Lee Roth's interviews in 1991 often touched upon his legacy. As told to Canada's MuchMusic in 1991: "I know that when I'm gone, I ain't gonna get no monument. I'd rather have people walk past my gravestone and say, 'How come Dave didn't get no monument?' As opposed to 'How come Dave got a monument?'" When asked about his next intended steps as a musician in that interview, he mentions a "blues album." That sort of happened.

Your Filthy Little Mouth

With no world tour, new album, or mainstream projects to speak of, 1992 was a quiet year from David Lee Roth. The year 1993 was slated to be more of the same until April 16, 1993, happened. If media coverage is to be believed—as the related court and criminal records appear to be sealed and/or deleted—Roth was arrested for attempting to purchase marijuana from an undercover cop in New York City's Washington Square Park. Via good lawyering, this charge eventually pled down to what he has called a "traffic citation." But a key takeaway from the related coverage of Roth's pot bust was that he was living in New York in 1993.

March 8, 1994, brought the release of *Your Filthy Little Mouth*, the fourth full-length solo album by David Lee Roth. Produced by Chic's Nile Rodgers, this was yet another title recorded by Roth for Warner Music, although Reprise Records was its branded label. While not exactly the "blues album" Roth had promised in that 1991 interview with MuchMusic, it definitely did not sound much like *Eat 'Em and Smile, Skyscraper*, or *1984*. Yet in a 1994 interview taped for MTV News, Roth described *Your Filthy Little Mouth* as being "like a diary." A *Music Scope* recorded that same year found Roth describing himself being in his "artist in a loft phase."

In a 1994 interview taped for MTV's *Jon Stewart Show*—just a few years before Stewart was hosting Comedy Central's *The Daily Show*—Roth had a grittier version of Diamond Dave on display than prior album press cycles.

Responding to whether he was happy with *Your Filthy Little Mouth*, at one point Roth answered with the following: "What is happy, you know? People tell me 'Dave, was it fun making the record?' 'Dave, are you happy with the record?' 'Dave, is it still fun to go on the road?' It was never fun. I'm never happy. I'm only happy when I'm miserable . . . I'm never happy unless I'm miserable, I'm overworked, too many deadlines, gotta be here, gotta be there, gotta be both places, kid. Hey, c'mon, the world is run by people who never feel well."

In a 1994 interview with WNEW's Dan Neer, Roth seemed eager to emphasize that he had evolved as both a human being and an artist. One example of that: "I look different seven years from now than I did seven years ago. That is living life. That is the scenic route. That is how I want to drive. At any given time, I'm gonna reflect on what's around me." Another example: "I change, just like all of you listening to this." And another: "It is always a temptation to repeat prior successes. It is always a temptation to try and repaint the *Mona Lisa* a little bit better. I prefer to move on. There are so many things that excite me and inspire me musically and otherwise that I change, I look forward to it."

A frequent collaborator of Nile Rodgers since the late 1980s, Richard Hilton's credits as a performer, engineer, and/or composer include David Bowie, Eric Clapton, Bob Dylan, Elton John, Paul Simon, Steve Winwood, Stevie Ray Vaughan, Duran Duran, Freddie Mercury, Kid Rock, and Maroon 5. In 1993, with Rodgers in heavy demand as a producer, per Hilton, "there was always the next project."

"Dave showed up one day at The Hit Factory while we were working with David Bowie," Hilton told Steve Roth and myself during a Zoom interview. "I distinctly remember him by the ping pong table. We had a ping pong table we used to travel with, we were all fairly decent, serviceable ping pong players. . . . We would have good games." Back on topic here, Rich. "Anyway. I remember Dave kind of showing up around the time when we were playing ping pong and it was like, 'Oh cool, we're going to work with Dave.' I wasn't privy to the planning stages, so it was a pleasant surprise for me at the time because I'm a fan."

The sessions that became *Your Filthy Little Mouth* were recorded at The Hit Factory in New York City at 54th and Broadway, as also known as "the Broadway Hit Factory." For the basic track sessions, you had Tony Beard on drums, John Regan on bass, Terry Kilgore on guitar, and DLR doing most of the tracking, per Hilton. "I don't think I played any of the basics on that record. I think it was pretty much guitar trio and Dave singing the original vocals, the vocals that end up getting supplemented later. Then there was time in the production later where other things got added in."

Although not directly named earlier, Terry Kilgore—who originally agreed to be interviewed for this book and then later declined such without explanation—was friends with Roth back in high school. He was a member of the Red Ball Jets, Roth's last band of note before Van Halen. Some people dare to call him a "guitar rival" of Eddie Van Halen, and others dare say he was finger tapping before Eddie Van Halen was.

Because Kilgore opted not to participate, I asked a few likely experts about him. Ratt's Stephen Pearcy, in short, was not very familiar with him. "That's the guitar player that everybody's saying Eddie got the finger tapping from? I don't know if that's all that true. I'm not that big of a guitar nerd to know that kind of shit." I referenced that Kilgore cowrote the song "All or Nothing" on a Ratt album, per album credits I had read. He responded before laughing, "If we did that's good, but I don't recall. Put it this way, there's people out there that say they were in Ratt and Mickey Ratt, and I don't know who the fuck these people are."

Posing the same question to Warrant's Joey Allen, he answered: "If Stephen hasn't heard of him, he's got a writing credit, that's bizarre. Maybe he was one of Robbin's friends or Warren's friends or something, I don't know. If I'd heard of him I would tell you."

Early Ratt bassist Dave Jellison, who worked with Van Halen and DLR solo, was in a similar boat as Pearcy and Allen: "I did not remember hearing his name ever mentioned and had to look him up to place him in the '80s mix. I remember hearing briefly about his band Reddi Kilowatt, but they weren't part of the scene."

Whatever the story is, Hilton told me that he thinks "very highly of Terry's playing" and work on *Your Filthy Little Mouth*.

Surprising to Hilton in the making of *Your Filthy Little Mouth* was how open DLR was to collaboration with its recording sessions. "I was allowed to sing parts to him . . . I was allowed to make a suggestion and it wasn't taken in a way that I was invading his space or anything like that, because there came a point in the project where I became pretty deeply involved in helping him with the vocal arrangements, because a lot of these vocal arrangements were done electronically." Giving an example, Hilton discussed the remix version of "You're Breathin' It": "There's a lot of the electronic vocals exposed there . . . I started taking alternate lead vocal takes and producing background vocal parts by playing melodic material underneath it. He walked in one day and said, 'Whoa, what's that?' Pretty soon, it's a thing, and it's kind of a defining thing for that record, if I do say so."

I pointed out to Hilton that he has a cowriting credit on "You're Breathin' It," which he was very modest about. "I helped Dave write vocal parts in one section of the song, and he was very kind to include me as a cowriter, but the song substantially started with him and Terry. I came on it and was asked if I had an idea for a certain thing and sure enough I did . . . I consider it to be an act of true friendship and generosity on the part of Dave, because I have contributed more and gotten less in my life."

Hilton expanded further on the collaborative process between Roth and the session players: "As much as he had a vision for how it should be and what it should do, he was listening to what the people he had were doing. I'm not talking about me necessarily, I'm talking about all of these guys and going, 'That's cool.' He wasn't set in his ways at all. He's a really, really, creative and receptive person. . . . He's interested in a lot of different things. And when you talk to him, maybe I should say, when you listen to him. . . . He's very, very smart and well read and intellectually motivated, Dave. So you are not going to have a boring day with Dave Roth."

The compliments do not end there when Hilton is discussing Roth, of course. "The man is one of the most brilliant lyricists I've ever been around and I've been around some pretty brilliant lyricists. . . . You could just quote him, they just come flying out of him and then they start showing up in the songs. . . . Every song has some kind of very cool story basis to it." One example, per Hilton, is "Your Filthy Little Mouth": "A pretty amazing song. . . . The stylistic breadth of the thing was something that really made it so much fun, because you're not trying to make a Van Halen album, basically. Not that that wouldn't be fun, but just that that's not really what he was there to do."

Per an April 1994 interview with WNEW's Dan Neer, Travis Tritt's duet on *Your Filthy Little Mouth*—the only duet Roth has ever had on a solo album—was not as odd of a pairing to DLR as many thought. "Travis and I probably come from the same background as far as playing all the clubs and bars, putting in those kinds of hours. The voices sound almost identical. . . . That comes from some mileage and a little bit of experience. . . . Rock and roll and country western have a lot in common."

When I interviewed Travis Tritt in 2021, he explained that he got a call from Roth directly: "He said, 'Man, first of all I just want to tell you I love what you do and I love the Southern rock aspect of what you do for your music.' He said, 'I've got this song called "Cheating Heart I" that I want to do on this new album and you'd be the perfect guy to do it with.' I was honored and kind of intimidated by the whole idea until I heard the song. I thought, 'Man this is perfect.' Then of course we had a chance to work with Nile Rodgers, he produced that track, and it was just a great experience all the way around, man. I had a ton of fun on that."

The album's first single, "She's My Machine," definitely fit the "blues album" mold that DLR had hinted at in 1991. Yet in a 1994 interview taped for ABC, he described its influence as coming from "that global village" after name dropping Dr. Dre, Red Hot Chili Peppers, Elvis, and George Jetson. When asked about the sexualized lyrics of "She's My Machine" in that 1994 interview taped for *Music Scope* with a not-yet-famous Kelly Ripa, he asked back, "Since when has a car just been about a car?"

That very same song may have been the point at which Steel Panther's Michael Starr stopped following Roth's career. "He started losing me a little bit with 'She's My Machine.' I don't know if you know that song . . . I was like, 'What, dude? That is *not* Van Halen.' But *A Little Ain't Enough* came out and I liked that record."

Another single from *Your Filthy Little Mouth* that yielded a music video was "Nightlife," a Willie Nelson cover. As noted in Roth's 1994 interview with WNEW, the song is simultaneously happy and sad, and Willie Nelson is one of "relatively few artists" who has the credibility to sing sad lyrics.

While *Your Filthy Little Mouth* was a very collaborative and experimental album, Hilton did not remember the musicians recording much more than what made the final tracklisting. "There's only one song I remember that he decided not to include, and I don't even remember what it was called. If I thought really long and hard, maybe I'd come up with it, but I don't think you want to wait for that."

As our conversation with Hilton was video based, early into the talk I had complimented him on a piece of artwork seen behind him that resembled Donald Duck. As it turned out, Roth drew it, which led to discussion about the singer's overall artistic abilities. "When we did *Your Filthy Little Mouth*, I believe every song has a work of art. That is the lyric sheet, every song. I think the original booklet for the album contains some of these, if I'm not mistaken. I can tell you absolutely categorically that when I saw a video of the last Van Halen tour with those giant video screens behind them, there were times where the hand-drawn David Lee Roth lyric sheets went by, because I saw them . . . I had the sense when we made the record that this wasn't the first time he had done them. I think this is part of his sort of Zen preparation for how to approach and create this song when he's finished."

Speaking of artwork, early into researching this book, a catch-up conversation with a friend Louis Stenerson led to the realization that his old friend Jonathan Shlafer did the artwork for *Your Filthy Little Mouth*. Shlafer, as it turned out, was graciously open to a conversation about DLR.

So how exactly did Jonathan Shlafer—a sculptor and an in-demand fine artist—wind up doing the artwork for *Your Filthy Little Mouth*? "We had a mutual friend who was a dancer at Stringfellow's," he answered without hesitation. "I was rock climbing with her at the time and mountain biking and stuff like that and going over to Stringfellow's with my job and some friends back at that time. She and I just went over to his house one day to smoke some weed, and there you go."

Simply put, for Shlafer, it was one of those "if you don't ask, you don't get" scenarios. "He lived right around the corner from both of us, so we went over there, we hit it off, hanging out, talking, and I was an art director for an advertising agency at the time he was doing this album. I had a small little agency with some friends of mine. . . . I asked Dave, 'We can do stuff.' He's like, 'Yeah, sure. Let's do it.' We did it." Sort of joking, I asked Shlafer if this was the only gig he had gotten from frequenting a club like Stringfellow's, and the answer was a resounding yes.

Shlafer was a fan of classic Van Halen at the time of doing the artwork for *Your Filthy Little Mouth* and had a lot of respect for Diamond Dave's self-invention as an artist. "'Let's see if I can reinvent myself and have a Las Vegas thing,' like that sort of style. I mean, that fits his personality as being like a rock and roll clown. . . . He was always seeing what's out there, so I respect that. He cut his hair short and tried to make a go of it, doing that."

What sort of direction did Shlafer receive so he could start this project for Roth? "He told us the name of the album was *Your Filthy Little Mouth*. . . . It had so much subtext to what was going on, especially for him, like the whole industry feeding off guys like him. So, I mean, there was a lot you could read into it. . . . We showed him a bunch of different ideas.. He's an artist, so he likes to dig away. . . . He enjoyed the process, but once we picked that cover image, we're done."

But of course there were plenty more opportunities to hang with Roth. "We were hanging out with the guy, it was cool. We were going to Pete's Tavern, eating cheeseburgers upstairs." Was he always in Diamond Dave mode? "He would go in and out of character, it's funny. So he could be super down and then all of a sudden, got that shit-eating grin." Super down indeed. "When this thing was close to being over, I have the tape somewhere—I've moved so many times—I get this message on my answering machine, just chewing me out. And me and my friend, we thought it was the funniest thing, because he was pissed about something. I don't remember what it was, but he was flexing his muscles. We all laughed it off."

Did his work on *Your Filthy Little Mouth* lead to more work for DLR? "Not really. . . . It came out. It was fun. It wasn't very successful. . . . We might've done some posters for a show here or there or something like that, but we didn't blow it out into a whole merch line or anything." No holiday cards from Dave, no, but a few quick run-ins at social gatherings. "There was no bad blood. It was just. . . . He's a big rock star and everyone wants a piece of him. So I guess he's hard to get close to."

Your Filthy Little Mouth had the distinction of featuring three different credited drummers on the album. And interestingly, none of those three drummers hit the road for the world tour in support of the album. That distinction went to Ron Wikso.

The backstory of Ron Wikso is truly one of those "job A leads to job B," "job B leads to job C," "job C leads to job D" sorts of scenarios. A recurring Studio City, California, softball game in the 1980s alongside Ricky Phillips, Pat Torpey, Jesse Harms, Dave Amato, Chuck Wright, and other rockers led to a Giuffria audition, which led to playing The Storm, which led to being part of Cher's band.

In late 1993, Wikso was on the road with a blues artist named Mike Finnegan for a short tour between Christmas and New Year's Eve when he got the call to audition for David Lee Roth. In early 1994 the band The Storm still existed but was relatively inactive due to record label reshuffling. "So my audition with Dave was at his house in Pasadena, which is the same house where Van Halen rehearsed and did all that stuff," began Wikso in an interview he taped for *The DLR Cast.* "I was down there in the basement with the guitar player, which was Terry Kilgore at that time, and the bass player Jamie Hunting and we just went through these songs that they had asked me to learn. Unbeknownst to me, Dave was upstairs listening but he didn't show himself. Then he came down after whatever it was, a half-hour or an hour or whatever it was, and they go, 'You want the gig?'"

But getting the DLR gig actually led to what may have been the hardest three weeks of Wikso's life. "For the few weeks of that gig, I had gigs with The Storm, they were all up in the Bay Area. So the gigs are at night but I had Dave rehearsals during the day in Pasadena. So what I would do was I'd finish the Dave rehearsal, then I'd drive to Burbank Airport, catch a Southwest flight up to Oakland. Ross [Valory] or somebody would pick me up and we'd go do the gig with The Storm, then the next morning Gregg [Rolie] would drive me back to the airport, I'd fly back down for Dave's rehearsal, and I did that for like two weeks." Added Wikso: "It was brutal. My hands were killing me because that's a lot of playing, and then plus the traveling and everything, I was just dying. But you know you've got to get through it."

While Roth and band were out to push the *Your Filthy Little Mouth* album, Wikso learned quickly into the gig about a separate release they had unknowingly been part of. "One of the first things we did was this show at Capitol Studios in Hollywood.. It was for Westwood One or something like that, and there's actually an audience. It's a very small audience so you could only fit whatever it was, forty or fifty people on chairs in the studio there." Wikso continued: "They recorded that and it became a double album . . . like two limited-edition discs, only I think five songs on each CD or something like that. So it's out there, I think it's called *Night Life.*"

How exactly did he learn about it? "So we're in England, we had done a short tour, like a promo tour in the States and then we went to Japan and then we went to England. One of the first gigs in England was with Jason Bonham's band called Motherland, they were opening for us and I was really interested in meeting Jason because I was a huge fan of his father's and all that. The first gig at soundcheck when they were soundchecking I went out into the house to listen to him and when I went out there, there were all these flyers on the seats for this new David Lee Roth limited-edition CD and it said it had live versions of some of the songs from the *Your Filthy Little Mouth* record." Wikso took a pause. "I thought, 'How could there be live versions? We're the only band that's played it live.' There was 'Big Train' on it and then there was a couple of Van Halen cuts . . . I was like, 'Wow, I wonder what's the deal with this?'"

Rather than just wondering, Wikso asked management. "'Oh yeah, it's just this little promo thing. It's no big deal.' The big deal to us was that they hadn't paid us for it," he laughed. "His manager told me, 'Oh it's not even for sale in the stores or anything. It's just this little promo thing we're doing.' So the next day I went down to Tower Records in Piccadilly Circus and I bought it and I went, 'I thought it wasn't for sale?' You know, I still never got paid for it." That one was also followed with a laugh. "The record does exist, I even have a copy of it somewhere, although it's in a box."

Attending one of the British shows on the *Your Filthy Little Mouth* tour was podcaster and musician Rob Lane. "The *Your Filthy Little Mouth* tour was far from the arena show I'd seen in 1991 but it was still in a good-sized theater and pretty full. The UK tends to stay pretty loyal for a lot of, let's say, classic and legacy acts in the hard rock world. . . . I was so stoked to grab front-row seats; there was no standing pit as this was a theater."

Lane recalled Motherland opening the show, as Wikso had, and with good reason. "The band that opened was Motherland featuring Jason Bonham. They were pretty great and I was stoked to see John Smithson on bass. Smithson had been in the band Bonham previously but I knew him from seeing him play with Paul Rodgers earlier that year and thought he was really cool. Strangely, I'd gone to that Paul Rodgers show because his backing band should have been the guys from Hardline: Todd Jensen, Neal Schon, and Deen Castronovo." The same Todd Jensen who had replaced Matt Bissonette in Roth's band for the *A Little Ain't Enough* tour and would later work as a tour manager for Roth. "I'd become a *huge* Hardline fan after seeing Todd perform with Dave back in 1991. Everything is connected!"

Continued Lane: "Dave's show was a lot of fun but it did feel kinda strange. Everything had the vibe of the tracks from *Your Filthy Little Mouth*, and from what I recall the old Van Halen and Dave tunes had that too, which was a little weird. I believe they had a backdrop with the album art, but that was pretty much it. Seeing Dave that close was pretty fun though and as it was a fairly local show we hung around after and grabbed his autograph." Did Lane purchase that *Night Life* EP that Wikso had referenced? "I did have the *Night Life* EP and managed to swipe me one of the promo record store promotional standees, which I still have."

Another one of the people who went to see Roth on the *Your Filthy Little Mouth* tour was Thomas Lennon, an actor, screenwriter, and comedian I interviewed during a 2022 *Reno 911!* junket. After asking about a little-seen video that featured him and other cast members from MTV's *The State* lip synching to Van Halen's "Panama" at an MTV holiday party, he mentioned being a Roth fan. "We went to see David Lee Roth at Town Hall [in New York City] and he told the story, he had just been arrested in Washington Square Park, he'd been buying a dimebag of weed. . . . We went to the after party at The Tunnel."

Added *Reno 911!* costar Kerri Kenney-Silver: "Another fun fact about that [MTV holiday party] video is that the next morning I believe was my *SNL* audition, which you can guess by the state of me in that video did not go great."

Mitch Schneider, as Roth's publicist for the *Your Filthy Little Mouth* album, absolutely understood that Diamond Dave was in a rough position in 1994. "Look, he's no longer in Van Halen. . . . I think that people had a hard time wrapping their head around David Lee Roth solo, because for David it wasn't just merely about rock and roll, it was about pop culture. He saw himself not merely as a vocalist and songwriter, 'Where's my place in pop culture?'" Schneider explained that DLR had different goals than most artists when it came to securing press. "He was happy when I brought back a feature in that cool downtown New York publication called *Paper*. That meant more to him than me bringing back a big story in a music publication. It was always about, 'What is my cachet with the groovy people?' That meant a lot to him because he felt he had it sewn up with the rock fans."

Because a lot of people going to Roth's shows in the *Your Filthy Little Mouth* era were going for the sake of hearing Van Halen classics, I asked drummer Ron Wikso whether he had a lot of creative license when it came to performing live. "There are certain parts that you just have to play it like the record or as close to it as you can, depending on what it is. The rest of it, as long as it has the right feel and is recognizable, you can have a little bit of license with it."

This then led to a story about when, in the middle of the tour, Dave decided that he wanted to add "Dance the Night Away" to the setlist. Per Wikso: "We learned it that day. I charted it out in my hotel room and we're at soundcheck and I used to have a tom drum right to my left and I just taped it to that so that I could kind of glance at it and look at it. I left it there during the gig and Dave saw it. He was not happy about it. He's like, 'What are you doing with that chart?' I was like, 'I just didn't want to make a mistake, man. I didn't want to screw up your song.' But anyway, it was fine. I think he was just giving me a hard time. That's just how I go about it." Added Wikso: "I probably still have a lot of those charts in envelopes. I save them all in case I ever need to use them."

Ultimately he did not go into the Roth gig expecting it to be long term, and his assumption proved to be correct. "I was only in the band from January of that year 'til I think October of the same year, because then I joined Foreigner in January of '95. That was essentially basically the entire *Your Filthy Little Mouth* tour, if I remember correctly. I did the whole tour. . . . After that I think he did his Vegas thing." Correct. "I had an amazing experience playing all that music. The guys in the band were great and Dave could be great, too. But I think he was going through some stuff at the time. It wasn't the same as like, you know, the 'Yankee Rose' and all that stuff. We were playing smaller venues and I think there were some record company issues, so I think he was a little stressed out."

Wikso made that conclusion not just based on what he saw but conversations with keyboardist Brett Tuggle. "Brett Tuggle was on that tour, so he knew the difference between what we were doing then and what they had done on the 'Yankee Rose' and 'Just Like Paradise' tours, whatever those were called. I'm pretty sure he told me that back then Dave had his own bus and it was a much bigger scale than what we did. Dave was on the same bus with us on our tour. . . . Musically, it was fantastic."

With regard to DLR himself, Wikso sees him as "one of the most unique individuals I've ever met," adding, "he's very smart, but he can kind of go off in a million different directions. It's hard to know which one it's going to be." Wikso added, first noting that he had not spoken with Dave in "twenty-six years or whatever it's been" since they toured together, "his world is kind of like just like his world." He expanded further on that one: "He's not married, he doesn't have an immediate family, his sister used to come out with us occasionally. I don't know whether he really has a lot of close friends. I know he's got his entourage and stuff like that, but you know how we visit our friends and go have dinner or something like that? I don't know that Dave does that or not. . . . He's got a lot of time and he's got money, so you know he doesn't have to scrap around. His mortgage is paid, he can sit around and figure out calligraphy or speak languages or whatever because he's got the time. I mean, good for him."

As it turned out, Roth's studio players and touring band did know one another, per Wikso. "I actually saw Nile Rodgers not too long ago. He played in Omaha and I went there. Richard Hilton is one of his keyboard players he's worked with now since probably the '80s. Richard actually came and played some shows with us with Dave and that's where I met Richard. So I saw Richard at the gig and then I saw Nile and I said, 'Hey, by the way I played on that stuff you produced.' He goes, 'Oh you played "Big Train"?'"

Furthermore, aside from Terry Kilgore, Richard Hilton may have been the only musician to both play on *Your Filthy Little Mouth* and perform on the tour in support of it. "I did do two gigs with those guys . . . I sang background vocals. . . . In '94 in Florida. Very kind of him to invite me and I was thrilled to do it. They were very kind to me and very generous and I had a blast."

Yet Terry Gilgore, who grew up around Dave, played and wrote a lot of *Your Filthy Little Mouth*. But he appears to be the guitarist Roth references in the *Crazy from the Heat* memoir as sending home for asking for too much of a raise in the middle of a tour. Explained Rocket Ritchotte: "All of the sudden, they just dropped him off at the airport in England and said 'bye.' That's why I had to fly in the next day and take his place."

Rocket Ritchotte, who was referenced in the previous chapter as cowriting the song "Last Call," pulled no punches with talking about rehearsals for Roth. "After rehearsal, we'd be beat up. 'Cause like Kane said, you have to really perform. I don't do that. Usually for rehearsals. . . . I'm not going to be jumping around and sweating. I save my energy. He wants to see it. So you're working in that cellar for four or five hours and his cellar is a big safe, it's in his dad's old house that he bought from him in Pasadena. A big echo cement thing. It sounded horrible down there. After all that was done. . . . Everybody wants to split, but this is his talk time now. He starts talking and telling stories. . . . We're just looking around, going, 'We want to get out of here.'"

Pausing this story a bit, the "Kane" referred to here is Kane Ritchotte, who I interviewed alongside Rocket. Kane Ritchotte is the son of Rocket, an in-demand musician whose recent credits include Haim and Portugal. The Man. He also spent a few weeks rehearsing with David Lee Roth, nearly becoming his drummer for the 2020 Las Vegas residency. So yes, Eddie and Wolfgang Van Halen are not the only father/son combination to have played music with Diamond Dave.

Rocket Ritchotte did enjoy the time onstage on the *Your Filthy Little Mouth* tour. Sort of. "It was fun when you're doing it. Until you start really getting to know his attitude. We used to actually hide from him when we were in England. We had double decker buses and we see him coming down and he's all grumpy and didn't have any pot or whatever. You can see his face. We'd all run upstairs. 'Where's the guys?'. . . A lot of hiding."

After laughing, Ritchotte continued: "He was fun to go to a t***y bar with, he would give everybody a bunch of ones. 'Come on, guys, look sharp, we're going out.' He liked chaos. One show and it might've been England, we go to the soundcheck and he walks in and I can see his face is all grumpy. 'Bring the backline up twenty feet.' They already did all the lights. They already did everything, so everything was focused. We had like fifteen minutes to doors."

Another funny story from Ritchotte: "One time he came up to me, 'No, play right over here.' He points to a part of the neck to play. 'Dude, I'm in this key, the inversion's going to be all wrong.' 'Just play over here.' We laughed about that, me and the band."

Here's another: "I'm starting 'Ain't Talkin' 'Bout Love' one time, it's a muted guitar part, he grabs me and he goes, 'Don't ever dampen on me.' I said, 'What the fuck is dampen?'" He laughed. "'Don't even dampen.' The rest of the band, we just laughed so hard because listen, I don't know what 'dampen' means. 'You mean mute? Oh, okay.'"

Okay, one more for good measure: "When I was with him, after Bissonette complained like crazy, because Dave would like to speed up. . . . Gregg would just shake his head onstage 'no.' I've got drummers out there that are watching me. They're one of the biggest bands around right now, he'd say, 'I'm not rushing. I'm not going to do that.' So when he did, he started playing with a click, get Dave used to it. Somewhere between live speed and record speed, he got the click, so he got comfortable. . . . As soon as they did it live, he'd say,

'It's too slow.'" He laughed. "You get excited live, so you think everything's slow."

For Ritchotte, he felt Roth's musical issues with his musicians were often rooted in him not being a serious musician. "He plays a little guitar, 'Ice Cream Man' and stuff like that. You know, your basic chords, but not really. He doesn't really play any instrument. I remember one time at a session, he goes up to the engineer and he goes, 'Can you make that guitar sound like an organ.' I said, 'No, you mean a Leslie, but he didn't know what that word was.' It's like Cher trying to tell you 'Play over here.' She didn't play guitar, she didn't have the faintest. It's the same kind of thing, but they're both great in their way."

Richard Hilton had a slightly different take on DLR than Ritchotte: "Dave is a remarkably astute and talented person in a lot of different areas. So when you hear him saying 'I've spent so many hours' or whatever preparing myself in this way, I mean, he's a serious martial artist, he's a serious graphic artist, he's a serious musician as well as an amazing singer. Like most of the best rock and roll singers that I've worked with. He plays guitar pretty well. He's not just some guy who's sung in the shower, he's actually a musician, and he comes with the goods."

Whatever the case, *Your Filthy Little Mouth* came and went in 1994 with little hint as to what was coming next for David Lee Roth. But as you will soon read, plenty of activity would follow for Diamond Dave in 1995, 1996, and 1997.

Vegas

Part I

Chazz: Okay, lemme ask you a question: whose side did you take in the big David Lee Roth–Van Halen split?

Chris Moore: What?

Marcus: What kind of question is that?

Chazz: Who's side did you take: Van Halen or Roth?

Chris Moore: . . . Van Halen

Ian: HE'S A COP!

Such is actual dialogue from the 1994 movie *Airheads* that starred Brendan Fraser, Steve Buscemi, Adam Sandler, and Joe Mantegna. Released less than six months after David Lee Roth's *Your Filthy Little Mouth* album, it is telling that Roth was still viewed as being cool by a lot of people. Whether or not they wanted to hear his latest solo album was another story.

Rather than hiding out for a year or two after the commercial failure of *Your Filthy Little Mouth*, Diamond Dave doubled down with a residency in Las Vegas. Yes, a Vegas residency in 1995. An era when Las Vegas was a prime destination for boxing, sure, but it would still be more than a decade before Vegas would be a hub for residencies that would attract people under the age of forty; Roth himself was around forty years old when his Vegas residency launched.

For this residency, Roth was backed by a guitar-less fourteen-piece ensemble known as the Blues-Bustin' Mambo Slammers. Aside from some low-key warm-up gigs, the residency was set to kick off at Bally's Celebrity Showroom—a venue inside the Bally's Hotel that held fewer than 1,500 people—on October 19, 1995. Rehearsals were done in Miami. Wardrobe was a family affair of sorts, being designed by Roth's sister Allison. Per Roth's *Crazy from the Heat* memoir: "The show was designed to update Vegas to our sense of humor." But as the book also points out, "Vegas agents didn't get it."

The residency was promoted via a Roth appearance on *The Tonight Show with Jay Leno* that featured Roth, musicians, and dancers performing "California Girls," followed by a sit-down chat between Roth and Leno. To put it nicely, this was definitely not the Dave that Van Halen die-hards were dying to see, nor arguably fans of *Eat 'Em and Smile* or *Skyscraper*.

In our 2022 interview, Blues-Bustin' Mambo Slammer band member Edgar Winter looked back on Dave's 1995 Vegas residency fondly: "We had a blast doing that and it was interesting, the Vegas run. Something I never expected Dave to go there to go in that direction, but it was a very cool show. I enjoyed the heck out of it."

Per an interview Roth did with *Slawterhouse*—then his official newsletter and website of sorts—in 1997, as also alluded to in his *Crazy from the Heat* book, a scripted Michael Jackson joke in the show is what got it quickly canceled by two different Vegas hotels. Not poor ticket sales or negative reviews, of course.

Roth ultimately called the residency "a three, four month vacation" and would ultimately hire some of these same musicians to record an updated version of "Ice Cream Man" in 1995. As Roth noted in *Crazy from the Heat*, he spent around $250,000 of his own money on that recording, inclusive of a video, which he still has not released as of this book's early 2024 publishing. As of DLR's memoir's publishing in 1997, he had "easily a hundred songs like this that I've done over the years."

Frank Meyer was one of the journalists who gave Dave's 1995 Vegas show a glowing review. "Dave in the early nineties did a Vegas run that now is very typical of rock guys like him to do, but at that time it was sort of seen like, 'That's a cheesy thing.' He didn't do it as 'hard rock Dave,' he did it as sort of like a 'mambo orchestra, dancing disco Dave,'" began Meyer. "I always felt like it was the natural progression for Dave. . . . I thought it was amazing and perfect."

That review became sort of a career changer for Meyer. "I wrote this rave review in *Pork Chops & Applesauce*, it was a punk rock zine. So I never thought it would make its way to Dave, but it did and I got a call from his manager Eddie Anderson, his former bodyguard. . . . 'Dave loved your review. He wants to know if you'd be interested in writing a bio for this song he was doing on a soundtrack to the movie *Sgt. Bilko*.' He had a song ['Bad Habits'] in there that. . . . I guess his publicist at the time didn't even really want to bother making a thing out of it." That publicist, for the record, was Mitch Schneider, and Mitch, I don't think you were wrong about that one.

Continued Meyer: "So he hired me to write up the PR thing [for *Sgt. Bilko*] and then he essentially gave it to his publicist and said, 'Just put this out.' He liked that too, and suddenly I was writing a bunch of press releases and he kind of just brought me in as, like, the guy he thought was putting a better spin on things. But he had a publicity team at that time."

For Meyer, he believes that it was his fan-oriented view that drew Team Roth in. "I think he just liked the reverence. I also think that I was younger than most of the rock journalists he was dealing with. I think he was very hip to the underground scene and fanzines. He liked the idea. This is the time when fanzines pulled a lot of weight." Continued Meyer: "Like, the record companies were trying to get groups in fanzines. We were generally an indie fanzine covering more indie rock, but we all loved Dave. So we put him on the cover twice in a row because if he'll talk to us, he's on the cover."

Roth's preference for independent coverage may have had something to do with his record label situation, according to Meyer. "Dave was not on Warner Bros. anymore. . . . He was independent." Regardless of that freelance work he did for Roth, it was a while before Meyer met him in person. "Eddie [Anderson] loved me and Eddie and I had hung out a bunch of times at that point. So Eddie and I were tight and I was like, 'Oh, I can get a good sit-down in person with Dave.' So I went to *Pop Smear* [Magazine] and pitched it."

Fortunately, the assignment was promptly greenlit for Meyer, so long as he could bring a guest. "I ended up going over with my publisher from *Pop Smear*, who was a good friend of mine. Dave invited us over to his house and we went to the Pasadena mansion. . . . He gave us a full tour and we sat in his back house studio and he was playing us unreleased songs, jams, and just all this stuff. I spent probably eight hours at his place."

But Meyer nearly did not make it through eight hours at Dave's home. "Eddie had a stop on the way. We followed him, and he had a box of alcohol. ... We killed it all! Like I got so wasted that at one point I was in Dave's bathroom taking a pee and the whole room started spinning and I kind of had to focus, go like, 'Do not vomit in David Lee Roth's bathroom, keep it together.' I managed to keep it together and I drove out of there and my friend was a mess and Dave turns to me and he's like, 'Is he going to be alright?" And I'm like, 'Yeah, Dave, we're fine. Thanks so much. Great, hanging with you, man.' We split and I go down the driveway and the gates open and I turn the corner and I park, and then I open the door and I just vomited, and then drove my friend home."

And Frank Meyer's friend? "My friend got so wasted. He missed his flight the next morning too, so anyway, that was my first time with Dave."

In the meantime, more to come from Frank Meyer, in addition to three more Vegas residency attempts by DLR.

Reunion

Part I

On September 4, 1996, the four members who made the first six Van Halen studio albums—singer David Lee Roth, guitarist Eddie Van Halen, bassist Michael Anthony, and drummer Alex Van Halen—made their first public appearance together in more than eleven years. This took place on the stage of the 1996 MTV Video Music Awards at New York's Radio City Music Hall. For those in attendance, it was entirely a surprise. For those in the music industry and/or closely following Van Halen, this was an inevitability.

On the surface, this appearance at the 1996 VMAs was four musicians standing on a stage together to present an award. But in reality, this was all meant to throw attention toward *Best Of—Volume I*, Van Halen's first ever "greatest hits" album. The significance of this Warner Bros. Records release was that it would feature tracks from both the Roth and Hagar eras of Van Halen, and additionally two newly recorded Van Halen songs with Roth on lead vocals, "Can't Get This Stuff No More" and "Me Wise Magic."

What is printed in the previous two paragraphs are facts. Just about everything else from this era of DLR and Van Halen is a bit convoluted because the "facts" have not only changed over time, but Roth himself seems to have changed the timeline a few times . . .

In his book *Crazy from the Heat*, as published the following year in 1997, David Lee Roth said he contacted Eddie Van Halen after he finished the book's manuscript as a means of making amends. And this is what led him to recording the new Van Halen tracks for the "best of."

That narrative greatly varies from what Eddie Van Halen told reporters during the 1996 VMAs' press conference with Roth standing beside him. Eddie Van Halen's memory was Roth reaching out to him for more information when he heard that Warner Bros. would be releasing a Van Halen retrospective album, because it involved material Roth had cowritten. Then after finding that they got along fine, Eddie extended the invitation to Roth for the new songs.

That narrative varies from what Roth said during Kurt Loder's interview with the band at the VMAs—the same evening Eddie participated in a press conference—when he said the inspiration for him reuniting with the band for new music was his witnessing of a bike accident in Florida and him getting nostalgic. Roth then "made a call [to Eddie] and said 'Let's be at peace.'" And that sort of varies from what Howard Stern said to Roth during a 1996 on-air interview that he tried to reunite Van Halen to record new music for the *Private Parts* soundtrack.

Actual events aside, Roth and the Van Halens also offered up different facts when it came to how long this regrouping would be for. Per Eddie Van Halen, he told Dave to expect "baby steps," seeing how things went with those two songs. For Dave, they were getting back together, touring was a possibility, and he was ready for all of it. Regardless of all that, Michael Anthony confirmed during the previously mentioned interview with Kurt Loder that two music videos would be made for these two songs; those music videos ultimately did not happen, even though both songs were worked with radio campaigns.

Another point of contention with all of this is legendary songwriter Desmond Child, who has been responsible for countless hit songs, including anthems by KISS, Bon Jovi, Aerosmith, Ricky Martin, and Katy Perry. In both the *Crazy from the Heat* book—in which he calls him "Desmond Childs"—and a late 1990s interview with Howard Stern, Roth mocks the quality of Child's songwriting and Van Halen's consideration of using him to cowrite Van Halen material.

Yet when I interviewed Desmond Child in 2020, he told me a story of nearly working with Roth. "David Lee Roth had come to see if we could collaborate, and that's a great story," began Child. "He shows up and then midway through our meeting he says, 'Well do you want to really know what I'm all about?' And I go, 'Yeah.' So he puts this cassette in and it's, like, stripper music, and suddenly through the door walks these two girls in fedoras and overcoats and really high stilettos in my tiny little office. They take the coats off, completely naked underneath, and they're doing these kind of sexy pole-dancing moves and then all of the sudden he stops it and then they stand up. They go, 'Call us if you need any more inspiration.' I was dumbfounded. I thought it was the greatest gag of all time."

That is not the end of it, per Child: "So about a few months later I get a call to go and work with Van Halen. So I go up to, I think it was Eddie's house where the studio was and everything. . . . It was after they split from Sammy Hagar. So I'm up there trying to write and suddenly David Lee Roth shows up in a top-down convertible and like, 'Oh, Desmond Child is here.' Like, 'What's going on?' It completely killed the vibe and he completely bombed the writing session."

Tommy Nast, a long-time entertainment industry executive who was thanked in the credits of multiple Roth releases, also remembers things differently than Roth did. Siding with how the Van Halens remembered 1996's ill fated reunion, Nast wrote an "open letter" that was picked up by a variety of outlets. In it, he reinforced that Roth ignored the Van Halens' insistence that this was a temporary regrouping, and that Van Halen had also worked with other vocalists in this era; history has proven this to include not only Gary Cherone but also Mitch Malloy and Sass Jordan.

Mitch Schneider, who had been David Lee Roth's publicist since 1991's *A Little Ain't Enough*, remembers being at the MTV Awards in 1996. "It all happened so fast. I remember David Lee Roth was not happy that Eddie Van Halen onstage mentioned something about a hip operation and he brought that up in his book. He thought it was the most 'unrock and roll' thing to say, that here we are trying to get people back into us as a foursome, and it was like, 'What a buzzkill to talk about your hip operation.'"

Schneider and team, including Amanda Cagan, promptly had to go on the defense for Roth after it became apparent that Van Halen would not be working with him beyond those two new songs for *Best Of*. "David Lee Roth asked us to send out a fax because this is when there was faxes more than the Internet," began Schneider. "I think that David Lee Roth wanted it to go further, but it didn't and we sent out a missive via fax. It's probably on the

Internet, just stating from him how upset he was that it wasn't working out. . . . I just remember that morning Amanda and I standing in front of the fax machine going, 'Wow this is pretty heavy what he's written.'"

Cagan also remembers that one well: "That's another moment that will live in my career memory forever. The press release about his brief reunion in 1996 with Van Halen connected to his appearance at the MTV VMAs. From what I recall, Dave laid it all out on the table. He didn't hold back with his message. There was really nothing left for him to say about it. I'll never forget getting to my office extra early the morning we sent it out, earlier than usual whenever we sent out press releases, which was one month after the VMAs." She later added with a laugh: "Since I was Mitch's assistant and a fledgling junior publicist at the time, I had my very own fax machine."

As per Cagan, Roth seems not to have harped on the overall situation once the fax went out into the world: "Dave just moved on with his solo career and we continued on our way with him. He was always just so busy that we didn't have to do anything else about it after that press release went out. They were doing their thing and Dave was doing his thing." Cagan was ultimately listed in the "Cast of Characters" in Roth's autobiography, which she described as "a huge honor," noting that she "was so touched" to see her name in there.

When interviewing former MTV VJ Kennedy in late 2020, just weeks after the passing of Eddie Van Halen, I was coincidentally wearing an Eddie Van Halen shirt that she noticed. That led to a side conversation about the 1996 VMAs that I had never heard about previously. "We were all backstage in the green room and I was in a beautiful light pink ball gown with a little white collar and little white gloves and it was a beautiful dress. It truly looked like a Cinderella dress. And so I'm standing there with David Lee Roth and Eddie Van Halen, and David Lee Roth goes, 'That dress is beautiful. It'll look even better all crumpled up on my hotel room floor,' and Eddie looked like he wanted to kill him. He was so disgusted that he would say something like that and I'm laughing. I think it's great because I love cheesy pickup lines. . . . But Eddie Van Halen came up and apologized. He's like, 'I'm so sorry.' I'm like, 'It's really not a big deal.' But then they kicked him out of the band again."

I then joked to Kennedy that it may have been she who ended the 1996 Van Halen reunion. She responded before laughing, "I hope so, just because it would be nice to be the impetus for something." She then continued: "But he was so disgusted and he was so visibly aggravated, so that clearly was a moment. . . . That's funny, because a lot of people don't remember that they got back together then that year and I'm so glad you did."

And this led to Kennedy sharing an unrelated memory of hanging out with Roth and Henry Rollins on a separate occasion. "He and Henry Rollins had a very close friendship. And so Henry Rollins, back when you had to pass around The Jerky Boys and Red Tapes and all that stuff, he was playing some for David Lee Roth and Henry's laughing and David Lee Roth was like, 'I'm sorry but I don't think this is funny, because you're really taking advantage of someone. You're making fun of them and they're not a party to it, and I think there's something about it that's very cruel.'" Kennedy paused. "I was like, 'That's not the David Lee Roth I thought I knew.'"

Per a 1997 interview Roth did with Slawterhouse, the *Crazy from the Heat* memoir started off as 1,300 pages and was whittled down to "360 whatever pages." Roth noted that "we have several books." His cowriter was found by Henry Rollins, who then worked with editor Paul Scanlon from the "heyday" of *Rolling Stone.* An interview done that same year with MTV News noted that a twenty-three-city book tour was planned as part of its production.

The aforementioned Henry Rollins also directly worked with Roth on *Crazy from the Heat,* as he told me in a Q&A done over email in 2021. "I worked with DLR closely on that project. At one point, he expressed interest in being onstage and telling stories from the book, I think. As I remember, I suggested that he have someone onstage with him to ask him questions that would prompt the stories. I think the record idea sprang from the fact that he did the book out loud onto tape. Almost 100 hours, which I have listened through three times. The man has a blazing intellect. He is a multi-lingual, multidisciplined self-starter. He is a voracious reader and student of history. Mark Twain meets Groucho Marx, who's also a black belt. That's DLR." And Rollins confirmed what Roth said about the book being "only a fraction of what he put on tape."

I also asked Rollins about Kennedy's story regarding Roth not appreciating the humor of The Jerky Boys: "I think he's a warrior and in that, he wouldn't dig someone being disadvantaged and made sport of. If he showed up to a sword fight and the other guy didn't have a sword, DLR would wait for a sword to be brought in for the other guy and then commence. I don't remember the story, but I'm not surprised he wasn't into it."

In speaking to The Jerky Boys' Johnny Brennan, I recapped Kennedy's story to him, which gave him a laugh. "David Lee Roth, he's a character. I actually know Marshall Berle. Marshall Berle managed me around the year 2000, and so you know the whole story of Marshall Berle and Eddie Van Halen, so Eddie and Marshall were very good friends."

Brennan recalled a story of nearly meeting Eddie. "Marshall was on the phone with me and Eddie was there. He said, 'Eddie's like, "Yeah, tell him I said hello."' We never got a chance to talk though, but Van Halen was always huge Jerky Boys fans." And the feeling was mutual for Brennan. "I always thought Eddie was a tremendous innovator, and I've said many times I believe that David Lee Roth was probably the greatest frontman in rock and roll history as far as putting on a show. He had to deal with the greats that came before him like [Robert] Plant, Mick Jagger, [Roger] Daltrey, etc."

Also newsworthy for David Lee Roth in this era was the release of *The Best* via Warner Bros.' reissue label Rhino Entertainment in October 1997. *The Best* was a greatest hits album that compiled his solo work from 1985 to 1996, also featuring one song exclusive to the album, "Don't Piss Me Off." A blues shuffle of sorts, "Don't Piss Me Off" was cowritten with Roth by keyboardist Brett Tuggle, *A Little Ain't Enough* guitarist Steve Hunter, Jack White (no, not that Jack White), and Daniel "Freebo" Friedberg. A music video was not made for this track.

It is unclear whether Roth recorded other songs for consideration for *The Best*, or whether "Don't Piss Me Off" was simply an outtake from *Your Filthy Little Mouth*. Per a July 1997 interview with MTV News, it had been noted that Roth recorded a song called "Private Parts" for Stern's aforementioned soundtrack of the same name, but it did not make the final tracklisting. In turn, it was available for downloading via the Slawterhouse website. Yep, in 1997, DLR was offering music exclusively to the Internet.

Roth opted not to tour in support of *The Best*. As he told Slawterhouse in 1997: "I'm not gonna do any club tours, there's not gonna be any theater tours . . . somewhere at an arena or at an outdoor venue." However, that same interview included a reference to former bassist Billy Sheehan possibly rejoining his band as he noted that "Billy is ready to go hunting." When Howard Stern asked Roth in October 1997 whether a Van Halen reunion was still a possibility, he said, "it can still happen."

While revisionist history generally has Van Halen maintaining tremendous international success from 1978 forward, with Roth's career floundering after *Skyscraper*, Rob Lane remembers things quite differently. "I would say Dave managed to keep his US popularity over here and probably stayed at the level of Van Halen. The last VH Dave show in the UK was at the Donington Monsters of Rock in 1984, and after that Dave stayed pretty loyal to his British fans and returned on every tour. Unlike VH who didn't come back until 1993, Dave had been over every few years so his fans were still there." Added Lane: "A lot of people are stunned to learn that Van Halen were actually special guests to Bon Jovi on their stadium tour in 1995."

As if that were not enough action for Roth in 1997, he had to deal with a stalker by the name of Jo Ann Fonzone. Per a court filing: "For the past four years, Fonzone, acting as her own attorney, has been trying to divorce the former lead singer of Van Halen in Lehigh County Court." Yes, you read that correctly, and no Roth has never been married. But he was one of eighteen defendants targeted by Fonzone in close to two dozen lawsuits filed starting in 1997. Yet that is far from the weirdest court filing you will find including Roth—for that, enter the following into Google and grab some popcorn: "4:05-cv-05234-SDA." Just a little tidbit from that one, its plaintiff alleges that Roth "told me he gave the launch codes to the nuclear missiles to the Russians."

Nukes and restraining orders aside, 1998 was shaping up to be an exciting year in the life of David Lee Roth.

DLR Band

On March 28, 1998, radio host David Adelson asked callers on his KLSX program *C-Notes* to listen to an unnamed new song by an unnamed recording artist and guess who it was. That song was "Slam Dunk" and that artist was David Lee Roth. After a caller successfully guessed the artist, Adelson welcomed Roth on the air for an interview by phone.

"These two brand new songs were done in maybe three and a half days," explained Roth after noting there was to be more to listen to than "Slam Dunk." "They started off as demos. I said, 'Let's do this like the old days.' . . . If the single proved to hit a nerve, to strike that note in the audience's mind, well, then great. People would rush to get an album out. As it stands, we have written some twenty songs. If you like what you have in your hands right now, and I hope you're holding my CD in your hot little hands, then you're gonna love the rest of this."

Adelson ultimately opened up the phone lines to listeners, and as expected, some trolls were on hold. Caller Jim from Burbank asked when he would let go of Van Halen. Rather than letting loose with some insults, Roth waxed poetic at Jim: "There comes a point where if you get past what is a standard three and a half year career these days, up around ten, twenty hot and humid summers. . . . Then you become known for what you have done, as opposed to what you do and what you do in the future." DLR then compared that sort of longevity appeal to Beethoven and The Rolling Stones. "If you are lucky enough to join that very small pantheon of heroes who have created what essentially turns from a simple song into a soundtrack for someone's life, race it, man."

While Roth's last few releases—1994's *Your Filthy Little Mouth,* his contributions to Van Halen *Best Of* in 1996, and his *The Best* retrospective from 1997—were also released by Warner Bros., Roth did not have a clear answer for Adelson as to who would be putting out this new music. "I don't have to shop it around, they're pounding on the doors, big caliber stuff. . . . I can't decide if I want to get with a standard label or start my own and get a distributorship." Another listener asked Dave whether he had plans for a second book, which he ducked via a Rothism-type response. However, he did say that a tour was in the works.

Another highlight from this interview with the unannounced participation of Lonn Friend, magazine editor turned A&R executive; one of Friend's major label signings, oddly enough, was Nerf Herder, which had a minor hit in 1996 with the Roth-loving song known as "Van Halen." Friend told a story on air about Roth hanging out with Donald Trump at New York City's Spy Bar, which he later recounted with more details for an article: "It was after some big concert like U2 and there were all these really heavy people in the room. I think Rick Rubin was upstairs spinning. And I look down and at the VIP table in the front and I see Donald Trump and David Lee Roth. Like together with two hot chicks and I couldn't help but walk over to Dave and lean over to Dave and go, 'Dave, it's Lonn from *RIP Magazine,*' and he goes 'How's it going man, good to see ya.' I said, 'I have just one question, who made the call? You or Trump? How does this happen?' He didn't even have an answer. He just smiled at me."

Trump cameo aside, the byproduct of those "twenty songs" was the full-length album titled *DLR Band.* Put out into the world by Roth's own Wawazat!! record label, it was entirely made on Roth's own terms. In some interviews he said it was made in ten days and in other interviews he recalled it taking three and a half weeks to make, yet the two songs played on air by Adelson took "three and a half days." Further confusing in that timeline is that the songs feature three different lead guitarists, each of whom was a cowriter on his own tracks.

Enter guitarist number one of three: John Lowery. "I've been coming to California ever since I was a baby. My grandparents lived out here, my sister

Diamond Dave onstage during his tour with KISS.
Photo by Kevin Baldes.

Dave live with guitarists Jake Faun and Al Estrada.
Photo by Kevin Baldes.

Dave kicking higher in his sixties than most of us could ever kick in our youth.
Photo by Kevin Baldes.

Dave front and center, alongside bassist Ryan Wheeler and guitarists Jake Faun and Al Estrada.
Photo by Kevin Baldes.

Dave playing to the back of the room in Bakersfield.
Photo by Kevin Baldes.

Dave giving a direct look at photographer Kevin Baldes in March 2020.
Photo by Kevin Baldes.

Dave and Eddie Van Halen having a laugh onstage at the Hollywood Bowl.
Photo by Kevin Baldes.

Dave, Eddie, and Wolfgang Van Halen in
action, October 2015.
Photo by Kevin Baldes.

More of Dave, Eddie, and Wolfgang Van
Halen playing onstage together for the
last time.
Photo by Kevin Baldes.

Dave, Eddie, Wolfgang, and Alex loving life live.
Photo by Kevin Baldes.

Dave showing off some of the ink he had done by Horiyoshi III in Japan.
Photo by Kevin Baldes.

Dave live and beside guitarist Jake Faun in Bakersfield.
Photo by Kevin Baldes.

More of Dave, Eddie, and Dave's ink from October 2015 at the Hollywood Bowl.
Photo by Kevin Baldes.

Wolfgang looks on as Dave gives Eddie a well-deserved thumbs-up in concert.
Photo by Kevin Baldes.

Dave prevails, as seen beside bassist Ryan Wheeler and drummer Francis Valentino.
Photo by Kevin Baldes.

A crew member laminate
from Dave's 1994 European
tour.
Courtesy Matthew Speedings.

DAVID LEE ROTH

P.O. Box 93549 • Los Angeles, CA 90093
(213) 856-5449

"A LITTLE AIN'T ENOUGH"?
You Be The Judge - January 31, 1991

DAVID LEE ROTH

P.O. Box 93549 • Los Angeles, CA 90093
(213) 856-5449

THANKS FOR BEING SENSIBLE IN THE 90's

Showing the power of your telephone, a sensibly shod DAVID LEE ROTH is currently strolling up the Dial MTV Top Ten.

Yes, you've been calling MTV and MTV's been listening, and "Sensible Shoes" is walking up the charts. So is the journey over? Are you kidding?!? We're not at #1 yet!

Incidently, some of us here at Diamond Dave Headquarters have persuaded Warner Brothers Records to donate some goodies to show our appreciation for all your support. If you've been calling MTV, writing to magazines, getting your friends involved -- or if you're interested in being instrumental in promoting DAVE's career -- or if you just want to know what's going on backstage and behind the scenes -- let us know!

Keep your eyes on this space: Pretty soon, we'll be sending out updated "A LITTLE AIN'T ENOUGH" tour itineraries as well as letting you know what else is going on.

In the meantime, if you're thinking about calling to request "Sensible Shoes", take the advice of those other shoe people and "JUST DO IT!"

Also, here are a few request lines we'd like you to be sensible and call requesting "Sensible Shoes".

WDVE	Pittsburgh, PA	412/333-9303
WTUE	Dayton, OH	513/457-7625
WDHA	Dover, NJ	201/328-7625
KAZY	Denver, CO	303/759-1067
KXRX	Seattle, WA	206/421-9339
KXFX	Santa Rosa, CA	707/270-1369
WRIF	Detroit, MI	313/354-9743
WLLZ	Detroit, MI	313/298-6398
WLVQ	Columbus, OH	614/821-9696
WGIR	Manchester, NH	603/669-0610

Remember, Diamonds are forever.

Jennifer

DLR's fan club did what it could to get "Sensible Shoes" played on MTV in 1991.
Courtesy Steve Herold.

Lit bassist (and *DLR Book* photographer) Kevin Baldes with Dave in the early 2000s.
Photo by Kevin Baldes.

lived out here, and I had a lot of family in California," he told me during our second of three interviews, as taped in 2019. "I would always watch movies in the '70s and they were all filmed in California and even the TV shows like *CHiPS* and *The Brady Bunch*; I knew it was home for me."

Lowery moved out to Los Angeles from Michigan as a teacher with plans to be "just a session guy," as opposed to a touring artist. "I never really planned on being out front or being an instrumental touring guitarist. So many people were telling me, 'You've got to get out there and tour.'" And touring is something he has done extensively for decades, both as a solo artist and as the featured lead guitarist for major artists: "When I joined Marilyn Manson, the first thing Manson did was give me the name 'John 5.' After I left the band I thought, 'Well, a lot more people know the name "John 5" and they do not know "John Lowery," so I just kept it.' It was like Ace Frehley when he left KISS, he wasn't going to change his name to Paul Frehley."

John 5 literally found his way into the world of David Lee Roth through the previously mentioned *Crazy from the Heat* book. "I was sitting on the couch at my friend's house and I thought, 'I wonder what David Lee Roth is doing.' There was a number on the back of the book and I called it and said, 'Can I send Dave some songs? I think you'll really like them.' With incredible luck they agreed. In the end they did really enjoy them and I'm still friends with Dave to this day."

During another interview I taped with John 5, I brought this same topic up again, and fortunately he remembered it the same way as he had several years prior. "That's the true story. Nobody knew who I was and I just called out of nowhere and said, 'Are you guys looking for songs?' Pretty much the luck of the draw, I sent those songs 'Slam Dunk,' 'Relentless,' and 'Little Texas' in with no vocals, and then he really dug it. Then we just recorded them."

Credited alongside John 5 as a writer on those three songs and several others on *DLR Band* is Bob Marlette, whose credits also include titles by Alice Cooper, Black Sabbath, Rob Zombie, Tracy Chapman, Seether, and The Storm. Yes, the same "The Storm" that former Roth drummer Ron Wikso had been part of. I interviewed Marlette in 2022 and asked about how he came into the world of DLR. "I hate to say this to you, but I don't really know. I don't really know because at the end of the day, the most vivid memories I have of that whole time period was . . . I was doing something with Black Sabbath . . . I used to sort of be all the time at Henson Studios, the old A&M

Studios became Henson . . . I was working . . . but he would be across the street at Crazy Girls, the strip club, all the time. When he got bored over there, he'd buzz over like, 'Hey dude, can I come over and hang out?' And it's like, 'Sure, okay.'"

Continued Marlette: "So I'd be working and he'd come over and he'd just sit there and sort of talk to me while I'm, like, trying to mix this record and chit-chat about stuff and he was just such a hoot. It was always just so funny working with him 'cause he was a real character." While primarily known for his production and engineering work, Marlette contributed songwriting to *DLR Band*. "That whole thing started because John 5 has been one of my best friends for thirty years, and John was like, 'Hey, Dave called me up, and what do you think about doing this?' So we just started writing tunes and coming up with ideas and stuff, and that's how Dave and I started knowing each other through that, and then he would come visit the studio and stuff."

When speaking with Marlette, I brought up "Slam Dunk," the album's first and only radio single. I said that it reminded me of "Hot for Teacher," and Marlette explained that was with good reason. "That's probably the only song on that whole record that I actually remember anything about, and it's only because I remember John and I sorta sitting there, and I looked at him and I said, 'You know, I love that song "Hot for Teacher."' I thought what a cool song that is, that kind of shuffling thing. And I'm like, 'We should do a song like that.' . . . It was just sort of was born out of that. . . . 'Let's try this idea.'"

Another standout track on *DLR Band* is "Blacklight," track two, another Lowery/Marlette cowrite with Roth. Notably, this song features Diamond Dave singing in a higher register than any other recording of his I could think of. Reminding me of Roth doing a Robert Plant impression, I asked renowned choral teacher, composer, and podcaster (and brother) Adam Paltrowitz for his take on these vocals. "DLR definitely has an expansive range. The fact that he can sing so high and has low notes demonstrates the flexibility and control he has." Although the high notes are not Adam's cup of tea. "I believe DLR uses a chest-dominated mix. This means, he has a balance of both his chest voice and his falsetto. I believe he does this at the very top of his voice and the bottom as well. The bottom of his voice is a bit airy, showing that it is not heavily weighted. This, to me, demonstrates a mixture of falsetto in his low range."

Back to John 5, were there ever plans for John 5 to play in Roth's live show beyond the studio work? "Oh absolutely there was. I remember him saying, 'Come on over, we're going to work out stage moves. I'm going to do a kick over your head,' and all this stuff. I'm like, 'Alright, that's awesome.'" But then came an offer from Marilyn Manson's camp. "I got a call to join Marilyn Manson and told Dave and he was very supportive. He thought it was great."

Did he nearly rejoin Roth's band after his time with Marilyn Manson ended in the mid-2000s? "No, because I've always been working. But I'm very loyal to whoever I work with. I think it's a very important trait to have in the music business. The grass is not always greener and it's really good for artists to know that too, because a gig with the biggest artist in the world could only last a month or two, but who you're with could last a lifetime, you know? I've always been very, very, very loyal, unless I get fired or something, then I've gotta go. But other than that, I'll stick around."

Overall, John 5—who will appear again later as a studio collaborator for Roth—continues to think very highly of Roth as a person and a performer. He tied in a compliment with a quick yet mind-blowing anecdote related to the *DLR Band* album in our 2021 conversation. "Dave is a very smart guy and he was way, way, way, way, way ahead of his time. He made all of those CDs. So if you have a CD, they were making those in his back house. I think that's so smart because that's what everyone's doing today and he was just so ahead of his time and so smart."

Bob Marlette feels similarly about Diamond Dave as his friend John 5. "My takeaway from Dave was that he's a cool, interesting dude, and smart as a whip. He's very clever." But Marlette did not see working with DLR as being that especially different from a lot of other artists he had worked alongside. "He had a lot in common with a lot of artists of that time period with a certain measure of success. It honestly wasn't that much different than working with guys like Ozzy [Osbourne] and people like that. They are people who, their brains are sort of always like . . . exploding with ideas, and more times than not, a good portion of my job is, is saying, 'Okay, I see the synopsis . . . let's figure out how to turn all these gazillion ideas into something that is gonna work.' . . . You've kinda got to figure out how to turn it into something."

Enter guitarist number two of three: Mike Hartman. Two songs featured on *DLR Band* have the DNA of Hartman: "King of the Hill" (originally titled "Stomp") and "Indeedido" (originally titled "Southern Romp"). Hartman was slated to be Roth's touring guitarist, per an interview between Hartman and R. Scott Bolton in 1999. But tragically before touring started, Hartman and his wife Jeanie were hit by a drunk driver, and both of them sustained serious injuries; Jeanie broke her pelvis and leg, and Mike suffered a concussion and bruised ribs. In Bolton's words, "a bout with pneumonia and exhaustion put him back in the hospital shortly thereafter."

Possibly sensing déjà vu with what happened a half-decade earlier with *A Little Ain't Enough* album guitarist Jason Becker, Roth's camp was concerned with Hartman's ability to continue. In turn, Hartman was fired. Yet as Hartman recalled it to Bolton: "They didn't bother to pull me aside and say, 'What's going on? You said you were fine?' I would have said, 'Look, man, I can give you my two best hours of every day. Just give me the rest of the day to take care of myself and I can walk on any stage and play.' But they didn't give me that chance."

In the same interview with Bolton, Hartman recalled spending ten days recording *DLR Band*—for those keeping track, Hartman played on only two songs and that took ten days, while two of John 5's songs alone took three and a half days, making Dave's *DLR Band* timeline a little, well, off—and confirmed that he was the "B'urbon Bob" credited as playing bass on those two songs. "Stomp" and "Southern Romp" would appear on Hartman's solo album, *Black Glue*, which was released in April 1999 and featured the playing of Roth drummers Gregg Bissonette and Ray Luzier. Hartman, who tragically passed away in July 2000, also had the chance to spend time with former Roth guitarist Steve Vai. As described by Bolton, Hartman first met Vai when he was a teenager through the Make a Wish Foundation.

The previously mentioned Ray Luzier spoke with me by phone in 2019 when promoting his then-new album with the all-star band KXM. As it turns out, DLR was not his first gig with a hard rock notable. "Jake E. Lee from Ozzy Osbourne was one of the first kind of 'name people' I got the gig for, and that was my first tour. . . . So I started getting on a bus and I'm playing some Ozzy songs and Badlands songs of Jake's, and that was my first taste of it. . . . I was doing everything from teaching drum lessons to playing on sessions, movie soundtracks, TV commercials, all these people's records."

One of those sessions directly led to playing with Roth, even though Luzier had no idea that it would. "One of the sessions I did was with a guitar player who was working with David Lee Roth. He called me back and said, 'Hey,

Dave loved your playing, he wants to cut the songs again for vocals,' because it was an instrumental record. I went down and played two songs with Dave and got that gig and that led to eight years with Dave. I had no idea in a million years that I'd be playing with one of the singers of one of my favorite bands of all time."

Enter guitarist number three of three: Terry Kilgore. Or should I say reenter, because he was around for the recording of *Your Filthy Little Mouth* and some of its related touring. Kilgore cowrote and played on five songs on *DLR Band*. One of those songs, "Tight," as referenced earlier in this book, had been been unsuccessfully submitted as "Private Parts" for Howard Stern's *Private Parts* soundtrack. However, he did not appear onstage with Roth for any of the touring in support of *DLR Band*.

Touring duties instead went to Bart Walsh, whom Roth had recruited from The Atomic Punks. Reportedly the only Van Halen tribute band endorsed by Van Halen, The Atomic Punks are praised in the *Crazy from the Heat* book and were also shouted out by Roth during a 1998 appearance on *The Howard Stern Show*; it is unclear why he called them "Atomic Punk" in both mentions, however.

Aside from the bass guitar tracks played by John 5 and Mike Hartman on *DLR Band*, bass duties were performed on two songs by Tom Lilly, a longtime bassist for Beth Hart. Lilly and I traded a few Roth-related emails in 2021, and he confirmed that he got to do a little more with Roth than play on those two tracks. "I also had a chance to work with Dave behind the scenes helping out when Billy Sheehan was tied up and Dave was auditioning a drummer, and also when Dave was first starting to work with guitar player Michael Hartman." Added Lilly about Hartman: "Michael Hartman is someone I had met in a very unique and special way, long before he and Dave got together. It's a small world sometimes."

While *DLR Band* is not a project that Lilly often thinks about, he has positive memories attached to it: "I've always thought very fondly of Dave, as during my little bit of working with him he consistently made it fun and treated everyone respectfully." Bass duties for gigs in support of *DLR Band* would ultimately be handled by Todd Jensen, who was on the road with Roth for the *A Little Ain't Enough* tour.

"I certainly picked up the *DLR Band* album but it came out with little to no fanfare over here," UK-based musician and podcaster Rob Lane told me in

2022. "You had to be digging into the pages of rock magazines to learn about new releases like that."

With regard to radio fanfare, I reached out to Lenny Bronstein of Heavy Lenny Promotions—one of the first names thanked in the *DLR Band* album booklet—in 2021 to ask what he remembered about working with Roth. "Truthfully, I don't remember any unusual details about DLR, which I worked very hard and was proud of getting radio to support. No anecdotal stories that would aid you."

So to recap, *DLR Band* was independently released by David Lee Roth's own record label. Its CDs were printed at his house. It featured three different guitarists/cowriters, and none of them were slated to hit the road with Diamond Dave in support of the album. It did not have any accompanying music videos. And its radio promoter does not remember much about working with DLR.

Reenter Frank Meyer, who was well regarded by Team Dave around the time of *DLR Band*. "At that point I was just like, 'Well if Dave will talk to me, I'll pitch to everyone just as an excuse to keep hanging out with Dave.' So the next sort of in-person [interview], I remember being really cool was a rehearsal for the DLR Band who were essentially the Atomic Punks, and there's a Finland show, a big festival in Finland . . . I brought a woman that at that time, I don't think we were married, but she became the wife and mother of my children, we're since divorced. . . . I brought two friends of mine from the rock band, The B-Movie Rats. . . . They were Van Halen freaks like me."

Continued Meyer: "So there's only about fifteen people at this rehearsal besides the band and the crew and Eddie [Anderson]. So it's them rehearsing on a soundstage and we're just all sitting on the floor. . . . It's epic. . . . I always try to sort of [stay] in my lane and not overstay my welcome. . . . So I leave the rehearsal assuming Dave wants to cool down and talk to the band and not be bothered with the likes of me. So me and my wife-to-be go, 'Dave, such a pleasure, man, so great.' He's just sitting there in a chair. There was a behind the stage with sort of a room with a console, like a studio room. They probably recorded it. We're listening back to rehearsal at some point or whatever and Dave's just sitting there kind of toweling off. There's a bottle of Jack there, but it doesn't even look like he's tapped it yet. 'Alright, thanks Frank. Mrs. Meyer, always a pleasure.' We split."

And that is not the end of the story. "I call my friends the next day to say like, 'Man, how cool was that?' My friend answered [does a hungover voice] and I go, 'What's up, man? You guys go partying after the Dave rehearsal?' He goes, 'No, we partied with Dave all night. I just got back like two hours ago.' . . . I was about to leave right after you. I said, 'Dave, such a pleasure to meet you. I've got one wish in the whole wild world. Can I hit that bottle with you and do a shot?' Dave looked at me and said, 'Only if you boys are going to kill the bottle with me.' They stayed all night and killed the bottle with him and hit a second one and he just was talking and playing music and hosting for whoever stayed around. . . . I thought I was reading the room. Apparently, I was absolutely not reading the room."

That was not the only live DLR performance that Meyer had seen in this era, fortunately. "I saw Dave and Bad Company in San Diego around that time. Dave invited me to Club Dave backstage, which was a full Hawaiian-style party. It was great because he walked out with two twin strippers and he had a Hawaiian lei and he was putting leis on people."

Doing one of those "well, where was Van Halen at the time?" comparisons, in being released in June 1988, *DLR Band* hit stores about four months after *Van Halen III*. *Van Halen III* was the group's first and only album with Extreme's Gary Cherone fronting Van Halen. While Cherone declined to be interviewed for this book, I did speak with him in 2016 and had thrown in a Van Halen question. He responded: "If I were to do it all over again, I would have liked to tour with the band before we recorded the record. Looking back, I always thought there were some good songs on the record, but could have been more cohesive. We became more of a band when we were on tour."

Over the years, *Van Halen III* has been described as "an Eddie Van Halen solo album." It featured Eddie's sole take a singing lead—aside from a brief vocal on "Humans Being" from the *Twister* soundtrack—which Roth was highly critical of during a 1998 Howard Stern appearance. He said that Eddie Van Halen should never sing lead vocals, much like he should never play electric guitar. Then again, Eddie did sing lead in Van Halen before Roth joined, Roth has played electric guitar, and in 2019 Roth took credit for writing some of Eddie's guitar solos. So let's call that one a wash . . .

On the business side of things, the *DLR Band* era saw Roth retain legal representation on a few occasions. He would dismiss long-time associate Eddie Anderson in 1999, claiming that Anderson was selling Roth-related memorabilia without permission. He would have a financial dispute with the Slawterhouse team, leading them to sue him for nonpayment. Guitarist Bart Walsh would also sue Roth with relation to his dismissal.

With regard to the firing of Eddie Anderson, David Jellison still does not understand that one in 2022: "He was Dave's longest lasting employee and friend and I was quite surprised when he got the boot after several decades of absolutely loyal, nonstop, 'round the clock service." Including cowriting the Roth song "A Little Luck," which Rocket Ritchotte confirmed to me. Added Jellison: "The stories that he has on DLR would fill an encyclopedia, and I'm certain he will never tell a living soul!" Roth would also find himself in court several years later after Kieren McClelland, believed to be Anderson's management replacement, sued Roth after his professional dismissal.

Lawsuits, inconsistencies, and *Van Halen III* aside, Van Halen still had a loyal fanbase and its legacy had influenced people in a variety of entertainment fields. Some examples of that in the late 1990s:

- Chris Kattan portrayed David Lee Roth in multiple *Saturday Night Live* skits. When I asked him about this in person mid–photo op at The Plaza Hotel & Casino in Las Vegas in 2022, he described this as "fun."
- Phish covered "Runnin' with the Devil" at an Atlanta concert in 1998. Per *Attendance Bias* podcast host (and great drummer) Brian Weinstein, the song was played as an encore "to huge applause" and was "teased" decades later at a Madison Square Garden show of Phish.
- Ween began covering "Hot for Teacher" regularly in concert.
- Less Than Jake's Chris Demakes would identify himself as "Chris Van Halen" or "Chris Lee Roth" when doing interviews.

So in knowing that the world was ready for some classic Van Halen, what comes next from Diamond Dave? A self-directed, long-form music video filmed at his house: the *No Holds Bar-B-Que*. Get ready for a real head scratcher of a chapter . . .

No Holds Bar-B-Que

When David Lee Roth left Van Halen in 1985, he was set to direct and star in the film *Crazy from the Heat,* for which he cowrote the screenplay. This followed Roth's success from directing a string of hit music videos, including Van Halen's "Jump" and "Panama" (from the *1984* album) and his solo hits "California Girls" and "Just a Gigolo/I Ain't Got Nobody" (from the *Crazy from the Heat* EP). Roth would direct or codirect plenty of music videos for tracks he recorded for other Warner Bros. titles, but he did not attempt another film project for a long time. Until *No Holds Bar-B-Que* came along, that is.

"I try and describe it to people like, 'I put together a puzzle, and some puzzles are harder than others,'" began acclaimed film editor Marc Elmer, who helped edit *No Holds Bar-B-Que.* Describing his average editing job as taking "chunks of video and chunks of audio, music, people talking, visuals" and putting "them together to tell a story," this one would ultimately be one of Elmer's more challenging projects. "The puzzle with Dave was not an easy one because there was no story. There was never a 'through narrative' that I could grab on to and go, 'Okay, this is our train track. We're going from point A to point B.' There was no A, there was no B." He later explained in our 2022 conversation: "Good storytelling is a beginning, middle, and end. We didn't have two out of those three. We just had a middle."

Another difficulty for Elmer was that he was on hand for the filming of *No Holds Bar-B-Que*. He was there for ten weeks of editing, which we will come back to.

According to publicist Mitch Schneider, who had started working with David Lee Roth in 1991 around the *A Little Ain't Enough* album, *No Holds Bar-B-Que* was something Dave made independently without much of a game plan. "I remember laughing and thinking, 'This is really funny and it's very avant-garde in its own way,'" reflected Schneider after seeing the video for the first time. "Again, noting that he likes being in hip New York publications like *Paper*. . . . He asked about getting it out and I said, 'Well aside from putting a press release out about it, we should send it to people.' So there were like a hundred VHS copies made and we sent them out to the media and I remember like a couple weeks after people received it and had a chance to watch it, it was definitely a 'What's going on here?'"

Looking back at over a decade of working on Roth-related projects, Schneider still remains surprised their working relationship lasted so long. "It's amazing, looking back, that I'd lasted as long as I did because with David Lee Roth, it's all quick and it's like 'What's new? What's fresh?'" Schneider continued after a pause: "He liked me long enough to stay with me that long, and I was always very truthful. But to a certain degree, when someone is paying you, you have to be a bit of a 'yes guy.' I mean, I'm just being really honest about that. I think that as a publicist you can say the media may take umbrage with something, there's a way to tell an artist that 'This might not be right.' So it's always like that fine line to walk."

What Elmer and Schneider appear to have implied in our interviews without stating it directly is that *No Holds Bar-B-Que* is not among Roth's finest work. An hour-plus video filmed at Roth's Pasadena home, it is a mix of performances, speed-altered action sequences, skits, and pin-up models, often with previously unreleased cover songs playing underneath the non-performance scenes. While original and undoubtedly entertaining at times, it is also erratic, unfocused, and—in viewing it again twenty-plus years after its original release—insensitive at times. But if you are a DLR loyalist, a lot of the music is great, and most of it remains commercially unavailable all these years later.

"I've read about famous people saying they have a 'no assholes on set' policy. . . . I feel like Dave was someone that had that aesthetic," stated Melissa

Elena Reiner, a violinist who was on set as a performer for *No Holds Bar-B-Que.* "He definitely didn't suffer fools. . . . You have to be on your game. If you're on your game, I found him to be incredibly respectful and enthusiastic. People that faltered, he could lose his temper a bit, but as long as you're on top of your game, it didn't matter."

In turn, Reiner remembers *No Holds Bar-B-Que* as generally being fun to make. "It was a really positive atmosphere on the set, and Dave wanted everyone to participate." Referencing the hallway scene, she explained that he had "roped a couple of the makeup people to just be in that scene for a bit because he wanted to really fill it out and look like a party, and it was a party." However, like Marc Elmer had alluded to: "No one knew what it was supposed to be, or what it was about. I mean, I don't. I'm not sure Dave knew exactly what, except it was supposed to maybe represent a day in the life of David Lee Roth, maybe a slightly fantastical version of a day in the life."

For Reiner, a classically trained performer, most of the challenges related to her work with Roth had to do with the fact that the other musicians could improvise. "I'm used to being in the studio, but I'm not used to improvisation. . . . It's actually incredible that Dave didn't fire me on the first day," she began, before talking about how the gig became hers. "I can't remember how much notice I got, but it was a friend of mine who was also a violinist. . . . Someone found him and asked him to recommend someone. So he recommended me, which was extremely kind and I think I remember asking him like, 'Is there going to be any music?' Like, 'What do I do?' I think he said, 'Well, I don't know, just go there and wing it.' I don't remember that they sent me anything in advance."

Continued Reiner: "I may have been hired as kind of a last-minute addition because I know when I arrived the band had already rehearsed at least one day without me. . . . Some of those guys maybe didn't even really use [sheet] music. . . . So he hands me this chart, and it's like scribbled out, like, 'C7 diminished,' all these chords—and I barely got through music theory at my conservatory."

So why did DLR not fire Reiner, in her opinion? "I get there to the rehearsal, and I'm looking at the chart, and I'm thinking, 'Oh, I'm fucked.' . . . I'm just going to have to be really nice and smiley and really, really receptive and kind, which I am, and I'm not going to be a diva because it's not about me. . . . The rehearsal was just about to start and then Dave gets a call on his phone from his security guard at the front gate. The guy says, 'Oh, the keyboard player's here,' but it was past time for the rehearsal to start. Dave was like, 'Let him come in here and get his stuff, he's fired. He's done. I don't take lateness.'" The musician had pled his case, and Roth stood his ground, per Reiner. "He wouldn't even really let the guys speak, but he was like, 'Sorry, I'm not changing my mind. This is not professional. Let this be a lesson to you for future gigs.'"

Fast forward a couple of hours. "At the end of the rehearsal, Dave says to me, 'I can tell that this isn't what you're used to doing. And you could do better. But I can tell that you're a really great musician. You have a beautiful sound as a violinist, and let's just get you prepared.' . . . Talk to Bart [Walsh], whatever you need to get going for this, we'll get it to you. You need charts? You need music? We'll get it for you.'" Thus, her theory is that Roth had already "fired one person that day" and that was enough for her: "I was really young, I was in my mid-twenties, maybe early twenties at the time, and I was the only girl, and I was the youngest person and I think he was being nice."

Released more than a decade before *Tim & Eric* and other sorts of comedy where bad editing was part of the joke, there are moments in *No Holds Bar-B-Que* that one may find themselves questioning if what they were seeing was meant to make it into the final product. I asked Reiner if she recalls taping multiple takes for a lot of her scenes. "I feel like there were multiple takes, but I don't remember it being onerous . . . I think the camera was just rolling." Continued Reiner: "There's that one scene where all of us are in the hot tub. We're playing, or we're pretending to play because obviously some of it was recorded with sound and a lot of it was just the studio. . . . Most of our stuff, we were just set up, lots of different angles, just having a good time, and then the editor would go through and pick out what shots looked amazing."

Elmer agreed with Reiner's assessment on how many takes were generally filmed. "One or two, and he was happy with that. He usually nailed it, because I don't know if he rehearsed it before the camera started rolling or whatever, or if he's just that good. Maybe he is, and he nearly always nailed it." Added Elmer: "There were times when you have two takes and they'd both be right. And he'd say, 'I like this one because I like the way the clouds look in the background,' or 'I like the way that Jimmy had his finger up his nose.'" And sometimes mistakes were not only left in but repeated multiple times on purpose: "It's Neil Zlozower who actually says, 'Arnold, get the fuck up.' . . . That one, I was like, 'Hey Dave, look what I found.' It's just Neil yelling at this poor guy in a gorilla suit."

Elmer also agreed with Reiner's immediate assessment of Roth during that first day of shooting: "[She] said it so well, she said, 'Dave does not suffer fools gladly,' and he was definitely testing me on the first day about what I did know."

Aside from us not knowing who the fired keyboardist for *No Holds Bar-B-Que* was, another mystery from this release is who the harmonica player who plays with the band is; Roth's reposting of *No Holds Bar-B-Que* to his YouTube channel in 2016 cuts off suddenly and before the originally included credits roll. Roth named the harmonica player as "Sam," and I questioned Reiner if the musician was really named Sam or whether it was a dig at Sammy Hagar. "Dave knew everyone's name. . . . For all his kind of loosey-goosey stuff in the video, I think he really knew what he wanted. . . . He knew what was going on. He was very much in control."

So how did Marc Elmer—a big fan of Van Halen and Roth's solo work—wind up working on *No Holds Bar-B-Que*? "I did the making of *E.T. The Extra-Terrestrial*, I was, like, the 'all the DVD extras' guy. So one day I was also teaching at the time in between gigs, I would teach Avid classes. . . . I taught this guy named Peter Buell, who I have since lost touch with. But he and I became fast friends and he finished his classes and he went on to become an editor. And he called me one day and he was just like, 'Dude . . . I am kicking myself because I have this job and I can't take it, and you have to take it.' I was like, 'Alright, I appreciate that. . . . What is it?' He's like, 'No, no, I can't tell you.' . . . I'm thinking to myself, 'Is it some sort of, like, government, X-Files, CIA?' . . . He said, 'I'm going to have the guy call you.'"

That guy called about twenty minutes later and it was Roth's manager Matt Sencio, who was credited as "supervising producer" on the project: "He told me the rate and he said, 'We'll have you start on Monday and we'll have you come in. Here's the facility.' Here's the info and everything." But there was more for Elmer to have prepared. "You may want to invest in some unscented deodorant and don't wear any cologne. Don't wear anything that smells. And I was like, 'Okay, yeah, I can do that, no problem.' I think to myself, I remember all the stories about Van Halen and the brown M&Ms. . . . He's making demands like this, like before I'm even on the job, what else is coming?"

Earlier, David Jellison noted that when working on pre-production for *Crazy from the Heat*, Diamond Dave slept little but worked hard. That same sort of working schedule applied to *No Holds Bar-B-Que*, per Elmer. "Dave would kind of come in early in the morning with his sunglasses and his hat on and kind of go in the back." And people did take notice of Roth being in the building: "Without fail at least three times a week, we would have random people knocking on the door with a package like, 'I have a package.' . . . Alright, sure, buddy."

But per Elmer, Dave does do normal, "everyday people" sorts of things when in work mode: "One day we went to Subway, we'd get lunch every day. . . . He's got his hat on, his ponytail, and he's got his sunglasses on and he's ordering at Subway and I'm standing behind him in line and I'm like, 'Do you people not know who this is?' . . . It's just one of those scenarios that was so surreal. Here I am, with David Lee Roth at a Subway. It was a crazy experience all the way around. It was such a blast."

As noted earlier, Elmer's time spent in the editing bay for *No Holds Bar-B-Que* was ten weeks. As big of a fan of Dave as Elmer was, this was not an easy ten weeks. "We had a lot of amazing visuals with some great music, but it drove me bananas. He loved to crash into the middle of scenes and then never end anything. He wanted to start with something already in progress. His whole thing was like, 'Marc, we want to get into the action. We don't want to spend a lot of time bumping around trying to figure out what's happening.' He wants us to go right to the core of it. . . . Eventually I just got frustrated. I was like, 'Dave, can we just end one of these? These things, can we just take one song and just end it and then start a new one?' He's like, 'Marc, that's exactly what they're expecting us to do,' and he gave me that big Dave grin. . . . He never wanted anything that was conventional or expected or anything he had ever seen on TV before. He wanted something completely new, completely different, even if it was jarring, even if it was strange, he wanted jarring and strange."

While unclear what people were "expecting" from an unannounced, independently produced project, Elmer did have an overarching theme to work with. "Dave said his vision from the get-go, from the very beginning, 'I want it to feel like somebody sitting up late at night, flipping channels on TV, but that person's got ADD.'"

Debatable about David Lee Roth is whether he is a perfectionist, or someone who regularly likes to experiment and try new things, as my interviews have yielded anecdotes that lead to both of those conclusions. For Elmer on the *No Holds Bar-B-Que*, he found DLR to be more experimentation oriented. "I didn't feel perfectionism from him. There was just this sense of experimentation. . . . Like, 'How about we try this?'"

Per Elmer, some of that could have been influenced by the employees that Roth often kept around. "There were always two or three other people from his entourage there in the room with us. Every time he said something, 'What if we try this?' They'll be like, 'It's amazing, Dave. Let's do that.' My second or third day, I thought, 'This is not healthy for him,' because everything he said they thought was brilliant." Elmer took a breath before continuing. "So I took a chance early on and I made a vow to myself, I'm not going to blow smoke, even though I'm a huge Roth fan, I am loving being here. Here it is, day two and he's asking my opinion. So he'd be like, 'What do you guys think about this?' 'Oh, it's amazing, David. Wasn't that a great idea, Dave?' I'd be sitting there just editing, like, 'Don't ask me, don't ask me, don't ask me.' And he'd say, 'Marc, what do you think?' I'd be like, 'Well, Dave, here's what I think. I don't know if it's going to work because of X, Y, and Z. It feels like it maybe it will work if we tried it this way or whatever.' . . . He really respected that in the process, and I felt like that somehow won me some points with him because I was able to be honest."

Not that he necessarily listened to the editor, explained Elmer with a laugh. "Half the time he would just ignore what I said anyway and be like, 'Alright, well, let's just do it anyway.' . . . So it was a very collaborative process. Way more so than probably 90 percent of the work that I do. He was extremely collaborative and I was shocked."

One can argue that *No Holds Bar-B-Que* is more of a long-form music video than a proper film, based on there being minimal dialogue and a nearly continuous soundtrack. I asked Elmer whether he was editing to the music, or editing and then the music was being added later. "It was very music driven from go. . . . His first pitch to me when he came in the first day was like, 'Look, I made all this music and I need to put something to it. I need a visual treatment to it. I need to take it and put it in, present in some sort of a package that has video to it as well.' So he wanted to make this sort of like ADD, flipping-the-channel kind of package that sort of featured all of these tracks that he had spent time kind of working through. He was really happy with the music that he made." One of the tracks edited to was Roth's cover of "Mustang Sally," Elmer recalled, although that song did not make the final cut of *No Holds Bar-B-Que*; this recording was finally released by Roth over twenty years later in early 2023.

Elmer, who was only six years into his editing career at the time, did laugh at some of the things that wound up making the final cut. "He said, 'Can you take the mouth on the barbarian guy and move it up and down like a puppet? . . . I wanted to be like a ventriloquist puppet.' . . . So I cut out the bottom of the chin and moved it up and down to try and match. I was like, 'It doesn't quite match.' He's like, 'No, no, it's great. I love it.' You'll see a couple of places where things are out of synch. It makes me look like a terrible editor, but he wanted it."

Sure, this was all around twenty years ago, but does Elmer remember how much footage he had to work with editing down from? "It's really hard to say how much actual footage went into it. If I had to take a stab at it, maybe ten, twelve hours of footage." But that was not all he had to work with. "There's a lot of stills that he wanted animated. There are a lot of times when they were taking video of a photo shoot, which we were also using among the stills. There was a videographer who was there the whole time. There was a guy who was doing eight-millimeter film. . . . We did a lot of processing on stuff. There were a lot of layers and a lot of different things."

So about Sencio's request for Elmer to wear unscented deodorant, that would eventually play into things. "Probably five, six weeks into the project, we're working away. . . . We're doing good work and I felt good about it," began Elmer. "Because we were working minimum fourteen-hour days, sixteen-hour days, six days a week, and so I had no chance to do any laundry. So one day I was like, 'Screw it, I'm going to wear tennis shoes. I'll just wear flip flops,' because I'm an editor, like, who cares? Nobody cares what I put on my feet, you know?"

Continued Elmer: "So I go in and we're about an hour into the edit and they start sniffing . . . I'm thinking to myself, 'Here's my brown M&M moment. Everything's going to go south. I'm going to lose the gig.' He's like, 'You guys smell that?' and I'm like, 'I don't smell anything.' Everything else is like, 'No, I don't smell anything.' He's going around the room and he gets close, 'Well, it's your shoes.' I was like, 'Oh, man, I'm so sorry, Dave, I didn't have a chance to do the laundry. I don't have any socks. . . . Maybe it's my feet. My feet might smell.' 'No, no, no. Dude, it's your shoes.' And he's like,

'Lenny, go get Marc's shoes and put them outside and then go to my trunk. Get out a pair of socks I'm giving Marc and he'll put those on.'" Elmer's tone then changed. "So I edited the rest of the day with David Lee Roth's socks on. I still have that pair of socks somewhere in my drawer someplace and people are like, 'You should sell it on eBay.'"

Elmer recalled that Roth was intense about the majority of things, but often that can be misinterpreted. "He has an intensity about him, this real hawk-like intensity that I think people misinterpret as 'angry Dave' or whatever. But he gets really focused at times. And I think that if you interpret it incorrectly, you could feel like he's angry at you or whatever. But he is always very high energy, he's always cracking jokes."

As intense as Roth can be, Elmer had the perspective to know that was not full intensity for Dave. He confirmed that Roth did not fear marijuana. "I think he does it just to keep himself at a human level of energy. I think he needs it just to bring himself down so that he can interact with everybody else on a level that's not so frenetic." This echoes something DLR had written a few years earlier in his *Crazy from the Heat* memoir: "When I smoke pot, everything's cut by two-thirds speed." In that same chapter, Roth had described the differences between his "pot list" to-do list and his "non-pot list" to-do list.

Given how hard Roth worked on *No Holds Bar-B-Que*, there came a point in the editing process where he asked Elmer if he, beyond directing and starring in the project, should also have a credit as an editor: "He's like, 'Hey Marc, what do you think about, like, if for the end, for the credits, if we say, 'edited by Marc Elmer and David Lee Roth,' what do you think about that?' And I was like, 'Oh, well, Dave, usually the guy in my chair is the editor and the guy picking all the creative decisions and kind of doing the producing stuff is the producer, executive producer, or the director, even though they are making those creative decisions. I actually know the software and those things.' He was like, 'Alright, that's cool,' and that was it. That was the end of discussion."

So why did Elmer stop working on the project at the ten-week mark? "I think I had a job coming up at a certain point. . . . It was never stated as to what the length of it would be. It kind of kept going. . . . We did a nineteen-hour day at one point and it was just, honestly, the guy is a never-ending tsunami of energy. It's crazy how much energy he has. He would pace behind me while I was editing. . . . He only sleeps like two to three hours a night, three to four hours a night, something like that."

But yes, Elmer did have the option of continuing to work on *No Holds Bar-B-Que*. "I was invited for that second shoot and I couldn't make it for whatever reason and I'm kicking myself. That was one of my two regrets from the actual project." The second regret, you ask? "When I first came on, I was telling my friends about it. They're like, 'You've got to be cool. Don't ask for autographs, don't ask for pictures, but just be cool, alright?' . . . I didn't get a picture with him. I never got his autograph, and I'm kicking myself now. I would have loved to have had a picture with him and he totally would have been down for it."

Elmer then shared an anecdote about just how cool Roth could be to fans. "There was a girl who was in my theater company and she found out that I was working with Dave and she said, 'Look, my brother, his name is David. He's a massive David Lee Roth fan. He wore his hair like Dave in high school. . . . Is there any way you could get his autograph?' This is about five or six weeks in, I could tell he was fine with it at this point. He trusted me, and he knew I wasn't going to be weird about it."

A bit of a mensch himself, Elmer went out and bought the *1984* remaster and brought it in to the studio the next day. Roth listened to Elmer's story and said he would take care of it. "He set it down next to him, and I'm like, 'He's going to forget.' We got into editing and two hours go by. He taps me on the shoulder and he's like, 'Here you go.' He hands me the CD and I'm like, 'Thank you, man, I really, really appreciate it.' 'No, no, no. Open it up.' Alright, so I open it up and it's, like, look at this original artwork by David Lee Roth. He had drawn like a whole seascape with boats and palm trees. There's some space in the back of the album, there's some white space. He had taken a Sharpie and he had just covered it with art and then he signed it to 'David, my biggest fan,' something like that about David Lee Roth. I was like, 'Dude, this guy, he's going to blow an artery. This is amazing.' And he was so proud. . . . So now I'm kicking myself. I never got original art by David Lee Roth. I just would love to have it hanging around the house."

One of the Roth-related mysteries Elmer helped clear up for me was why the 2016 YouTube reposting of *No Holds Bar-B-Que* includes a musician with a blurred-out face. Or better yet, who was that? Elmer believes that was guitarist Bart Walsh, who did sue Roth in the early 2000s. He explained that the YouTube version of the video appears to have had some shots reframed to entirely cut out Walsh. In turn, Toshi Hiketa is the only backing guitarist clearly shown on camera in this "updated" version of *No Holds Bar-B-Que*.

So is Melissa Elena Reiner still in touch with any of the musicians she worked with on *No Holds Bar-B-Que*? "I stayed in touch with Ray because probably he was the other person that was closest to my age out of all the guys in the band. They were all really nice, honestly, everybody in the group was so nice, so respectful, including Dave himself. It really made me feel very welcome because they were obviously a band, like they'd all been working together for a while and I was just like coming in . . . I honestly felt like all the guys in the band were the opposite of sleazy. They were just really welcoming. And afterward Ray was just like, 'Hey, I play in this random band. You should bring your friends to come see us sometime.' It was Metal Shop." Metal Shop being the precursor to Steel Panther, whose singer comes up a few times in this book *and* was the frontman of The Atomic Punks.

She did have one more interaction with Team Roth after filming wrapped, and it was very positive. "Months after the fact, I think, I get this call from Matt, and he's like, 'Hey, hold for Dave.' I was like, 'Oh, okay, great.' I mean, it still amuses me, even though I lived in Hollywood, I wasn't talking to that many celebrities. . . . To be told to hold for someone just still makes me laugh."

Continued Reiner: "So Dave gets on the phone and, and he says, 'Hey Melissa, how are you?' 'Great.' 'Hope you're well.' . . . Then he's like, 'I've become, like, super into the violin. I want to know all about the violin, and I want you to teach me.' 'Yeah, well, how do you want me to teach you? Like, what are you looking for? That's great.' And he was like, 'I want you to go to Tower Records. Just buy all this different music for me to listen to, I want you to get me all these different albums that show the violin. Matt will give you whatever you want. There's no budget.' . . . So to get something like that after the fact from someone as famous as Dave, especially months after working with him, really made me feel good."

Around the time of *No Holds Bar-B-Que*, Diamond Dave had a few large-scale projects going, according to Frank Meyer. First of those projects? "I had at this point written a bunch of books. . . . So I reach out to Matt Sencio . . . and essentially kind of remind him like, 'Hey, I'm a writer. Dave and I had a little relationship going where I was writing a lot of stuff about him.' . . . I kind of came into this conversation with an agenda . . . I said, 'I want to do a book with David Lee Roth called *The Dao of Dave* that is rock and roll philosophy with David Lee Roth. It would be everything you'd want to know from Dave, like how to fire a guitar player, how to hire a manager, how to book a club, date, how to tip a stripper.' . . . All the things you would want from Dave's brain in sort of Zen-like quotes or something."

Meyer gave some context as to what the book was supposed to look like: "If you've ever seen those old tour programs that Dave used to design, I kind of had this idea of it being like the Van Halen *Fair Warning* tour program. . . . He loved the idea and we got started on that book and there's a version of the proposal I wrote that Dave signed off on and I was going over." Added Meyer: "I was talking on Dave on the phone, mainly for that stuff. Matt would get me on the phone with him and I just sort of rattle off ideas and get his feedback and he'd give me some ideas."

Continued Meyer, and later this one will lead to another major project that almost involved Roth: "At one point, and this was the day that Van Halen announced their [2004] reunion tour with Sammy . . . I'm over at Matt's house by coincidence . . . I worked in the Valley at that time and I would actually be driving by Matt's house from time to time. It sort of made it easy to get stuff happening with them. He was like, 'Hey, if you're going to be nearby, why don't you swing by? I want to talk to you about something.' He comes over and he hands me, I've got it right over here, this giant, super collectible— I'd heard about it, but never seen it—David Bowie, Mick Rock sort of photo art book that David and Mick put together. There's pages with different paper stock, that form pieces, it's the most $5,000 book. Only one limited pressing and the first batch. . . . A bunch of them came signed. He hands me the 'signed to David Lee Roth' book and says, 'Dave wants you to borrow this and look at it for inspiration for you guys.'"

With a laugh, Meyer added: "By the way, that was the last time I ever saw Dave or Matt, so I still have that book. One of these days, Dave's going to see one of the interviews where I've confessed to this and I'll get a call saying, 'Can I get my book back please?'"

Intermission

Crazy Girls and Other Dave Sightings

In speaking with over one hundred people for DLR Book, *there was no shortage of fun or interesting stories about David Lee Roth. But not all of those stories tied in well with the timeline of Diamond Dave's career. A "sidebar" is how Roth viewed the film* Crazy from the Heat, *with relation to his overall career, so how about a little "sidebar" before we resume the story in 2002?*

TRIXTER'S STEVE BROWN, NOVEMBER 11, 2021, INTERVIEW
What was your acceptance from being a fan of the band to being a peer of sorts and being able to know those guys? Because we all know the inner circle, you don't easily get into that with the Van Halens.

I got to meet Ed at the 1991 NAMM show at a private event he was doing to launch his new guitar, and my dear friend my brother Matt Bruck—who was one of Ed's best friends and right-hand men—Matt was new to the organization. I had met Matt the night before this event, Spinal Tap was playing this crazy event out at NAMM, the after party or whatever and it was just an incredible night. I was hanging out with Steve Lukather, Nuno [Bettencourt], Andy Timmons, and lo and behold I get introduced to Andy Johns, who was friends with Bill Wray, who produced the first Trixter record. I got introduced and Andy said, "Oh I hear you're a big Van Halen fan. You know, I'm producing the new Van Halen record. Congratulations on your success with Trixter." He was a really really cool guy . . .

I remember telling Andy how much I loved his work on the Cinderella records and then two seconds later I get introduced to this guy with long curly hair, who's Matt Brock, who goes to me, "Hey man, I just want to congratulate you. I'm from Philly," which is close to Jersey. "You guys seem really cool, your band is really cool, I know you're a big Ed fan and Ed was a big influence on you." I'm like, "Man, he's everything."

Fast forward to the next day at NAMM, where I see Matt again and he goes, "Hey man, if you can be out at the Marriott parking lot at five o'clock, meet me there. I've got something cool I want to show you." I met him there and I kind of had a feeling what it was. Lo and behold, I get walked into this private room where this stage is set up and it was a private event that Ed was doing with Albert Lee and Steve Morse and it was for Music Man Guitars. I'm standing there and Matt's showing me Ed's rig and it kind of dawned on me I'm finally gonna get to meet my idol, the guy that I owe everything to, pretty much, in my musical career. Sure enough, five minutes later, Ed walks in, he's got glasses on and a big oversized blue t-shirt . . . I didn't have a camera, but Ed comes in and what struck me immediately about Ed in that time—and I know this [interview] is about David Lee Roth—but Ed was just so nice to everybody he walked up to, every stagehand, "Hey, how you doing? I'm Ed." Anybody that has ever met Ed and really knew him knows what a humble, normal guy he was, and Alex for the same part. That just struck me immediately.

I was sitting there talking to Matt and Ed came over and they started chit-chatting and then Matt goes, "Hey Ed, I want you to meet my friend Steve. He's the guitar player in Trixter." Ed shakes my hand and goes, "Yeah, Trixter. Who you guys touring with?" I go, "We're going out with The Scorpions in a couple weeks." He goes, "Oh man, I just heard your commercial. Congratulations." The cool thing is we were #1 on MTV at that point, that was probably the peak of the record sales, we were selling like ten, fifteen thousand records a week. He was like, "I've heard a lot about you guys. I saw your video." Then Matt goes, "Hey man, he's only twenty years old." He goes, "Man you beat me to the punch, I was twenty-three when the first record came out." So it was just really cool and then I wound up telling him some dirty jokes and we were just laughing and we wound up spending the whole soundcheck together. We went to this private VIP room after soundcheck and we were talking and

Dweezil Zappa was there, Jeff Watson from Night Ranger, and it was just so cool and so chill. That was the introduction . . .

I tell the story all the time, Darren, that we all have heard the stories of "be careful about meeting your heroes because they're probably going to let you down." . . . I've gotta tell you, for me it was the most incredible thing and it was a lesson in humility. For me, Ed Van Halen was a god, he was a super-hero, but when I met him that day, he didn't come in with the red and white striped jumpsuit and doing scissor kicks, he was just a normal guy like I was. We hit it off because of humor and that was always what kept our relationship so fun and so cool, because I never talked about gear with Ed. He had his prototype 5150 amp and he showed it to me, he goes, "Oh man, you've got to check this out," and he had his blue Soldano amp. . . . It was just the beginning of a friendship that lasted close to thirty years. Sadly he's not here anymore, but all I can say is cherish every incredible moment. . . . That's how I got in and it was immediate.

Then fast forward to when Van Halen went out on tour for the *Unlawful Carnal Knowledge* tour that summer. A bunch of my friends were on the tour and I helped Scotty Ross, who became the tour manager for Van Halen for the next ten years. I helped him get the gig because he was Poison's tour manager and I was out a couple weeks after meeting Ed, I went out and did a week and a half of shows with Poison, our first arena shows in 1991. Scotty Ross was their tour manager and Scotty Ross treated us like royalty, as did the Poison guys. . . . Every night after the show we would have dinner with Scotty Ross. So fast forward a couple months later, I get a call from Ed and Matt Brock and they go to me, "Hey man, we're interviewing Scotty Ross to be our tour manager. What do you think?" I go, "Dude, he is the perfect guy to be Van Halen's new tour manager." Subsequently Scotty got the gig . . .

Then Van Halen's production manager grew up in Paramus, New Jersey, my town, Frank Stedtler went to Paramus High School, grew up a couple blocks away from where I grew up. My father was Frank Stedtler's English teacher in freshman year of high school, I guess 1967 or '68, along with Howard Ungerleider, who went on to be Rush's first tour manager and Rush's lighting guy and Van Halen's lighting guy on the *Balance* tour. There's so many connections in the Van Halen organization besides my friendship with Ed and Alex and everybody else. But it's just crazy stuff and Howard

Ungerleider, who is a legend in the Rush camp, he grew up a block away from my grandparents on Howland Avenue in Paramus. The first time I met Howard on the rehearsals for the *Balance* tour, I was there with Ed and Howard and he goes, "Hey, Steve Brown, Paramus, New Jersey, your father." . . . It was just all these crazy coincidences connected to Van Halen, so near and dear . . . I always tell people it was kind of fate that I got to meet Ed and become friends with them.

So with Roth, you mentioned getting to meet him around the time Trixter was taking off and having to turn down the *A Little Ain't Enough Tour*. At what point did you lose Roth as a fan?

I never lost Roth, and he still to me out of all the guys—and I think it's the truth in my heart and soul—I feel that when Van Halen came out '70s and especially in the '80s, David Lee Roth was the greatest rock and roll frontman in history. He was the most charismatic, the most unique and he basically was the architect for what became how to be an '80s rock frontman. Fashion, how to talk to an audience. . . . People rip on him a little bit because of how onstage he would hardly sing, but look man, when you're putting on a show of that caliber with the acrobatics and everything, something's gonna suffer. I just thought that his humor and everything that he did, it spoke to me like Van Halen did.

Look, I saw Van Halen, my second concert I ever went to, after KISS in 1979. It changed my life forever, seeing the original KISS on the *Dynasty Tour* at Madison Square Garden. Fast forward three years later, Van Halen, Madison Square Garden, same venue, on the *Diver Down* tour. In the first half-hour of the show, I knew by watching that band that's the type of band that I want to be in and that I'm going to form. It was everything and it just completely overcame me, my body, and I still get chills talking about it. It was the party atmosphere, the girls, the guys hugging each other, singing along to "Jamie's Crying" and "Dance the Night Away" and the debauchery of it all. It was like New Year's Eve and a rock and roll show brought to life, where KISS was like Halloween and maybe a space-age superhero movie and a horror movie all brought into one, much like Alice Cooper. It spoke to me, but Van Halen was something that was more believable and realistic to me, because I'm twelve years old now, I've been to parties, I've seen my older brothers party and this was everything you could ever imagine rolled into one, as far as an '80s wild party.

David Lee Roth just completely captivated me, and I think anybody that ever saw Van Halen in that timeframe—let's say from '78 through '84, and really to me from '80 through '84—Dave Roth was the G.O.A.T., the greatest of all time. There was no other frontman that was even on the same planet as him as far as I'm concerned. . . . Sadly there's not enough footage of Roth at that time, but if you watch the Largo 1982 show, Van Halen was at their prime, that was their greatest moment. *1984* was their peak but it was also the end of the band. So to see David Lee Roth at that time and getting to the music, which is most important I think, David Lee Roth was one of the most creative lyric writers in melodic hard rock. . . . His stuff even that he did in the '90s, I think that most people don't give him enough credit as a songwriter. But no one of that genre could write lyrics like David Lee Roth, you know? I think somebody who came sort of close was Nikki Sixx, because Nikki was so different as far as his lyrical writing ability, where he took sort of the Aerosmith nursery rhyme thing but also took it to another level.

David Lee Roth was just so unique, you never knew what he was talking about and that's what made him great. Ted Templeman was of course so responsible for David Lee Roth becoming a great singer—It's been documented, of course if you've read Ted's book by Greg Renoff, who's a good friend of mine—something a lot of people didn't know, and if you listen to the early Van Halen demos, it's very very apparent. Then when you hear *Van Halen I* and *Van Halen II*, you hear, "Wow this guy wrote some cool melodies." Well, from what I know, a lot of that was Ted Templeman who wrote those melodies, and Ted Templeman was sort of Mutt Lange before that became Mutt Lange's forte. What Mutt did even with AC/DC he doesn't get enough credit for, he was the guy who brought the pop sensibilities to AC/DC and then we all know what he did with Def Leppard. . . . Ted Templeman was so responsible for Dave's vocal melodic ability as far as writing those melodies to those unconventional lyrics, which I think are just groundbreaking and important again for the melodic hard rock, the '80s hard rock, the hair band stuff, whatever you want to call it—Dave coined it "big rock" . . .

Let's go to 1989, we just got a record deal, we go to LA September of 1990, we had two weeks before we were starting to record. We got out there, we were living in the St. James on Fuller Avenue, which was the corporate housing that Universal/MCA at the time put bands in. . . . It was kind of like, "Guys, go to LA, you have two weeks to have fun, see it, go to the Sunset Strip." Checking that out for the first time was incredible, mind blowing and I'm so glad I got to witness that . . .

We went to some clubs and we were able to go to a Thursday night, I'm sure you heard about Thursday nights in West Hollywood at the time, this club Bordello, which was world famous. . . . I went to Bordello with my manager Ken Makow at the time, George Drakoulias who went on to produce The Black Crowes and some other great bands, and Rick Rubin, because they went to NYU with my manager and we were all friends. So we went out one night, it was when I was interviewing producers for the first Trixter record we went to Bordello. I was there, my first time going to a real, like, hipster night in Hollywood and I was there with Rick Rubin who was rock royalty at the time, still is, such a cool dude. . . . We were just hanging out and I remember being there for like two minutes and Slash walks in and he comes over shakes my hand, gives me a hug, "What's up, dude? How you doing?" He didn't knew who the fuck I was. [laughs] It was just so cool and this was at the height of Guns N' Roses mania, then fast forward a couple months later, I'm there . . .

Next thing I know [Trixter drummer] Gus taps me on the shoulder. He goes, "Dude, David Lee Roth is here." I turn over my shoulder and there he is. He had on all leather, he was riding his motorcycle, he was on his Harley, he was there with a bunch of guys, and he had kind of the *Skyscraper* hairdo . . . I remember grabbing PJ and Pete and Gus just going, "Holy shit, there he is." . . . Here we were, a band from New Jersey, we got signed to MCA Records, we're out in California recording our first album, pretty much because of Van Halen because that's all we ever wanted to be, you know? Van Halen, Bon Jovi, Def Leppard, KISS, those were the bands that were our biggest influences. . . . We wore our influences on our sleeves and there was one of the guys who was responsible for that.

So I remember just getting up and going to say hi to him. I said, "Hey Dave, I just want to introduce myself." He was smoking a cigarette and he was so nice. I said, "Hey man, I just want to tell you I'm here with my band. We're here from New Jersey, we're recording our first record for MCA Records and I wanted to tell you that you and Van Halen were the reason that we wanted to do this." He was like, "Steve, congratulations, that's a great story and it was nice to meet you." It was really short and sweet, but he was just so down to earth and so cool and I could tell that he was very glad to hear that story. I can tell that he was touched by it. It just meant so much to me . . .

When our first Trixter record went gold, I sent Ed Van Halen a gold record and I wrote a really nice, long note to him. The end of it was, "Without you and your music I could have never achieved any of this, so thank you from the bottom of my heart, Steve Brown." After I gave him the gold record, I saw him a couple months later and he gave me a big hug and a kiss and he said, "What you wrote meant more to me than the gold record." I knew that a gold record's just a decoration on the wall for some people, especially when you're Ed Van Halen, you have fifty million records sold. But it was just a great experience with Dave and something I'll never forget. It's etched in my mind. I still remember it. . . . What I told you, the greatest rock and roll frontman of all time, and he's hanging out with a drink and a cigarette, he's exactly what you'd want to see him as. He was in all leather, he looked cool, and he was so nice.

THE STREETWALKIN' CHEETAHS' FRANK MEYER, JULY 2, 2021, INTERVIEW
So how about your next interview experience with Dave?

I had a gig that night with the Cheetahs at a club called Bar Deluxe, a small little bar, but one of my favorites, down the street from the Chateau Marmont. So I do the interview with Dave, but the whole time I'm kind of . . . rushing it. We went, like, three hours and I'm going, "What time are we on?" So, we wrap it up when we leave—Dave, by the way, walked in, in a full leather outfit, leather jacket, leather pants, like the chaps on the jeans, it was amazing . . . I said to Dave, because it went well. "Hey man, I'm playing a gig with my band right up the street if you want to come down." He goes, "Well, Frank, I'm headed to Crazy Girls to see the strippers. So, it's either your punk rock band or titties at Crazy Girls. What would you do?" I would obviously go to see the titties and he goes, "All right, man, but I'll be there all night if you want to hang out."

So I raced over to Bar Deluxe, ran up to the band, and said, "I've gotta go split and hang out with David Lee Roth, so we've got to rush the set. We're cutting three songs and I want to play this fast." And I did no talking. Then I jumped back in the car, brought Lyndsey Parker with me and my friend Jon Anderle, son of record executive David Anderle. . . . So Jon and Lindsey and

I roll over to Crazy Girls. We get there maybe around 1:00 or 1:30 and I'm thinking we're only going to catch Dave if he's even still there for a few minutes. But he kept the place open for us. Like when they were closing, he was like, "Mario, I'll stay here with my friends."

They kept a couple strippers and the bartender and we were there 'til like 4:30 in the morning and he had the strippers doing lap dances on each other for us, which I never even thought of before. He had the stripper technology.

LINUS OF HOLLYWOOD, JULY 7, 2020, INTERVIEW
I remember you telling me a story about hanging out with David Lee Roth in the mid-1990s. . . .

When I moved to LA in 1994, I was twenty-one years old and I got a job at a telemarketing place, which is where everyone worked when you first moved to LA. It was pretty funny because I grew up on hair metal and a lot of the guys that were in bands that I loved were also working at this job, because it was '94, hair metal was over.

So I was selling long-distance products. . . . If I would get a sale, I had to snap my finger and this other guy would come over with a tape recorder to verify the sale. They had to record the person saying they were gonna switch their long distance, but literally I would snap my fingers and then the guy from Roxx Gang would come over. . . . All these bands that I saw in *The Decline of Western Civilization*, they're all sitting next to you . . .

The manager at this place, how I could say this, he sold "amusement pharmaceuticals." He would get us into all the strip clubs and stuff because that's basically where his office was, so we would do our telemarketing and then afterward we would go to Crazy Girls, which is a strip club that's on La Brea. Lemmy would be there in his little Daisy Dukes shooting pool with his little butt hanging out, and then David Lee Roth was always hanging out with my manager at the telemarketing job, because of course he gets the free—what did I call it—"entertainment enhancers"? . . .

So a lot of times I would be sitting in the booth at Crazy Girls and someone would come in to do a business transaction and the person and my manager would go into the bathroom and I would be sitting at the booth with David Lee Roth, just me and him . . . I was just trying to be cool . . . I would just make small talk with him and just talk about random stuff. Of course he never made any sense at all. You would say something to him and he'd be like, "Yeah, it's kind of like when you're on the airplane and it starts to die down and you grabbed a little inflatable from under the chair and you're like 'Hold on, it's time for a ride.'" He literally is like that cartoon character guy or whatever. So anyway, yeah, I had a lot of moments.

Did you ever talk music with Dave?

I was in a band a long time ago called Size 14 . . . I wrote a song called "Old Van Halen." . . . Then Nerf Herder came out with their song "Van Halen" . . . I'm like, "Oh man, I've gotta change the lyrics." So that ended up being the song called "Let's Rob a Bank" that was on the first album. . . . When I was sitting next to David Lee Roth, I just go, "Hey man, you probably don't want to hear this, but I play in a band and we wrote a song like in tribute to you. It's called 'Old Van Halen.'" And he's like "Ah man, that's great. Just remember, if it's a hit song, I like expensive cars."

He starts like listing stuff that I needed to buy him when the song became a hit. That was the only time we talked music, but I spent many, many a night just sitting there trying to make idle conversation with David Lee Roth and not acknowledge that he was David Lee Roth.

THE SMASHING PUMPKINS' BILLY CORGAN, AUGUST 18, 2022, INTERVIEW
Have any David Lee Roth stories?

The last time I saw David Lee Roth in the flesh, I can't remember the name of the strip club but it's across the street from Henson Studios.

Crazy Girls?

Yes. . . . So I walk into Crazy Girls with some other rock stars—plural—and I look to my left and there's David Lee Roth with two blondes, one on each arm. He looks at me, and I had met him before, but it's dark and there's music and he looks and goes, "Billy!" He waves me over.

I mean, slow motion I'm walking over, I'm like, "Oh my god, I'm in a Van Halen video, this is fucking tremendous." So god bless David Lee Roth, one of the greatest of all time.

TUFF'S STEVE RACHELLE, JANUARY 21, 2022, INTERVIEW

In your case, have there been direct interactions between you and Dave over the years? I ask that because a lot of people will be like, "Yes, I was at this club this one night and Dave went in and I said, 'Hey.'"

Yeah, I've got a couple . . . I can tell you the stories . . .

So I'm at a Lakers game, this is in the '90s, I'm with Vince Kelly. Vinnie Kelly was the singer of a local band called Tommy Gunn out in LA, him and me were always good friends. We're at the game and during one of the time-outs, the Lakers Girls come out and they start doing their dance, the song was "Jump" by Van Halen. The girls are jumping around and my buddy just looks at me, he goes, "Dude, have you ever met Roth?" And I was like, "You know what? I never met him."

At this point the mid, late '90s, I've already been in LA ten years and there was all kinds of times where I'd walk into the Rainbow at like 11:30 on a Friday and everybody would be like "David Lee Roth was just here." I'm like, "Really?" "Yeah, he just left."

David Lee Roth was definitely one of my biggest influences. In 1984 I saw the *1984* tour that summer. I saw it a few months after seeing Mötley Crüe on the *Shout at the Devil* tour. Vince Neil and the Mötley Crüe tour in '84 and then Roth and Van Halen on the '84 tour, that just completely changed my path in life. I worked at a donut shop and I liked to ride skateboards and chase girls, so I'm going to be a fucking rock and roll singer, you know? I'd been in LA for ten years. I never met Roth. Of course everybody had their stories. So we were at the Lakers game and I'm like, "Nah, I've never met him." He's like, "Yeah, me neither." Whatever.

So the game goes on and we're people watching. There's Flea from Red Hot Chili Peppers, there's Jack Nicholson and typical LA Lakers celebrity stuff. When the game gets out, the guys were like, "Hey, we're going to go to the strip club." There's a porn star that's doing a feature, Jasmine St. Claire. I was like, "I don't even know who that is." "Oh, she's on Howard Stern, she's super hot." I was like, "Okay, let's go check it out." "It's in Pasadena." "Okay, let's go."

So now we get in the car, we leave The Forum; this is before the Staples Center was even built. We drive over to Pasadena. We walk into this club. . . . It's full of guys and I'm standing there and my buddy goes, "Dude, you're never going to believe this. Who were we just talking about?" . . . He's like,

"Turn around." I turned around and Roth is standing right behind me. . . . He's standing there talking to a couple people. I wanted to say hello, but I wasn't going to be "that guy."

I just kind of nonchalantly turned around, let him have his drink and talk to his buddies and I'm talking to my friends. There's girls moving around and at some point the room gets busy and he's no longer standing next to me. So I was like, "Okay, at some point I'll bump into him somehow." Forty-five minutes goes by, I've got to piss. I go to the bathroom. It's the typical small men's bathroom. One urinal, one stall, one sink, a garbage can. If you put four people in there, it's beyond capacity, no room.

So I walk in, I'm taking a piss, and I hear somebody in the stall, not thinking anything. . . . I hear him moving around, shuffling, the toilet flushes. I turn around, the door opens, who is it? It's fucking Roth. So now Dave's coming out of the stall, I'm zipping up my pants, and I'm like, "Excuse me." . . . Not probably the best time to go, "Hey Dave, so check it out." Like, I don't know if you just did a line or you wiped your ass, but you know, nice to meet you." [laughs] So I was like, "Excuse me, sir." You know? He shuffled around to the sink and rinsed his hands. . . . At this point, I'm 0 for 2 on bumping into Roth, next to a bar and next to a toilet.

Now the strippers are running around and everyone's excited, so now I'm kind of looking for him. I'm like, "Okay, I've got to say hi to this guy." At some point I see him, he's sitting in a chair and there's like a bunch of people around them and naked girls. I'm like, "Okay, not a good time to try to go, 'Hey Dave, I know there's four beautiful tits in your face, but so you want to meet the singer from Tuff.'" So that was my one and only direct confrontation with Roth. [laughs]

Who knows how he would have reacted, if he would've given me some kudos, "Hey, good luck to you kid," or "I've heard of your band." But other than that, a bunch of guys that I know played with him. I knew Bart Walsh, and I've known some other guys that played in his bands and obviously people that have toured with him and knew him and had some relations, but never got to hang with him.

You just pointed out Bart Walsh, he was interviewed for *Metal Sludge*. Ray Luzier I'm assuming you know as well, and of course all the Steel Panther guys are basically one degree removed from Roth in some facet. So even if

you weren't in a room with him, you were reporting on him over the years and so forth. Did Dave's management team ever feed you guys any news?

Now that you bring that up, there might've been a time or two that we got something. . . . As cool as we were, and as many people as we touched, and we did interviews with everybody. . . . I mean, we interviewed some serious iconic guys and legends. We interviewed Alice Cooper and Zakk Wilde and Nikki Sixx, Tommy Lee, Rikki Rockett, [Steven] Adler. . . . We interviewed a lot of rock royalty, per se, but we never interviewed Roth. We might've had maybe a webmaster that would send us something once in a while, but we never got Dave.

I would think that maybe Dave was probably thinking that we might've been a step below, which I understand that—he's a *Rolling Stone* guy, a *SPIN* guy, MTV, VH1. . . . He's obviously at a pretty high level. So when the Internet was new, and some little site that's goofing on people decided to go, "Hey, do you want to talk to us?" "We're not doing that."

That makes sense. But it's cool to hear that you're a fan and that you were around the whole thing. Did you stick with him through the solo career? For example, do you like "She's My Machine?"

I was a huge fan of *1984* and here's the thing . . . I was late to the game. I was born in '66, graduated in '84, grew up in Wisconsin, but I also grew up mainly as a skateboarder. I was obsessed with skateboarding. I had a half-pipe in my backyard, through the winter we would skate. There was a skate park in Milwaukee, so I grew up not only skating, but listening to new wave and The Clash, The Sex Pistols, The B-52's, Devo, Boomtown Rats, Oingo Boingo . . .

I was into all kinds of weird music and it wasn't until my senior year of high school, '83, '84, when I was seventeen, almost eighteen years old, that more of my friends were really listening to a lot of Def Leppard, Loverboy, Ozzy, Twisted Sister, Quiet Riot. . . . My friend said they were going to go see KISS in concert. Now I didn't know anything about KISS. I mean, I knew there were the guys that used to have the crazy makeup and sang those couple of songs. One guy would spit blood or spit fire or whatever. But if you would have asked me when I was seventeen years old, which guy in KISS . . . I wouldn't have known. I had no idea who they were . . .

Then my friend said, "We're going to go see Ozzy Osbourne." The only thing I knew about him was that was the guy that ate that bat, because that became, like a viral story, you know? I didn't know who Randy Rhodes was. I didn't know that he was killed. I didn't know anything about his guitarist. I didn't know he was the singer from Black Sabbath. I knew nothing about that, but my friends convinced me to go. So I saw KISS, *Lick It Up* [tour] in February '84, and I thought Vinnie Vincent was the coolest guy in the band. Everyone else looked old to me, and then at that point they kind of were.

Then I went to the Ozzy concert, waiting for him to eat that bat. When the opening band came out, I was like, "Who are these guys?" They looked really cool. Vince Neil, Nikki Sixx, *Shout at the Devil* clothes and when I left the Mötley Crüe concert, my life changed.

I heard the song "Jump" on the radio and saw the video and I was like, "Wow, that guy. He's just at the beach waiting to fuck girls." Like, what better life is there? Then I went, saw them in concert, and I saw a real frontman. Now, Vince Neil was a cool frontman and he looked the part, he had the hair and the clothes and the tan. He's never had any gab or any game or any shtick. Dave, literally they played two songs and he stopped the fucking show, and then he looked in the front row and said, "I'm going to fuck your girlfriend later." Eighteen thousand people just fucking wailed and I was like, "So this dude just comes out, sings the song, stops the show, looks at some guy and goes, 'Dude, I'm fucking your chick later,' . . . and the whole place is like 'Yeah!'" I was like, "Oh my god, this guy is fucking the king." I could see in the front row that those guys would be like, "Okay, you can fuck her, bro. Just, can I get a guitar pick?" [laughs] I left there thinking like that is the best performance I've ever seen in my life . . .

I'm late to the party. This is their sixth album. They're already fighting, it's ten-plus years deep and now at this point it's going to be over. But then I saw the *Crazy from the Heat* EP. "California Girls," of course, that was right up my alley. Then he did the solo record, which also was amazing. "Yankee Rose," "Shyboy," "Tobacco Road," and I was playing those songs with my cover bands around Wisconsin . . .

By the late eighties, meaning '89, '90, '91, now I'm in LA. In '89 I was twenty-three and '90 I was twenty-four, we signed [to Atlantic Records] in 1991, I was twenty-five. We were not only signed, but now I'm on MTV myself and in *Hit Parader* and *Circus* and touring and of course I had a grip on it. . . . I did start to have a different opinion of the guys that I grew up emulating or admiring, thinking were gods. Like, meeting Vince Neil and he's in flip-flops and chubby. Not that I thought he was going to show up in his fucking *Shout at the Devil* garb . . .

But yeah, the end of the '80s, early '90s, it started to make me, I don't want to say "second guess" them, but I started to realize that they were real people. They were not "they can do no wrong." . . . At that point is when I kind of started to lose them, per se, it just wasn't the same anymore.

TOTO'S STEVE LUKATHER, JUNE 25, 2021, INTERVIEW

One of the commendable things from my perspective about your career isn't just the great music, it isn't just the commercial success, it's the fact that you've kind of become this peacemaker that any band has two or three feuding factions and you seem to be cool with both of them. For example, you're still friends with Sammy Hagar, you were always friends with Eddie.

I'm friendly with Sam. We don't hang out all the time. I like the guy, I mean, he's never done anything to me. I like Mike too, Mike Anthony's a great guy. I don't get involved in other people's band business, man. I've got my own band with its own band problems, you know? [laughs] I'm Switzerland, I'm not a peacemaker.

Sammy called me to be on the [AXS TV] show. I did the show, it was fun, it was nice of him to do that for me, I really appreciated that it came out of nowhere. Jason Bonham and I are dear friends and he plays with Sammy and everybody knows everybody. I try to stay out of everybody's shit, man, you know what I mean?

But my loyalty obviously would be to Eddie. The loss of Ed has just destroyed me. I'm just gutted, you know? I've lost so many friends in the last few years it's insane. We lost our tour manager of twenty-five years, he went in for a hernia and found out he had stage four cancer and died two weeks later. This is the kind of shit you just can't plan for. Martin Cole was one of the greatest human beings of all time, we did some of the most insane things together. . . . He was one of the beautiful souls of life and I miss him and I'm just so sad. So many of my best friends that I've lost. I keep going to the doctor going, "Is it going to be me now?" He goes, "No man, unfortunately you're going to be around for a long time. You seem to be very healthy." Surprised me, too. He's been my doctor for thirty-five years . . . I haven't drank in almost twelve years, I don't do crazy shit anymore . . .

The long-term relationships you've held, I was curious if that and the "peacemaker" tag that I just put on you are rooted in the fact that you started off as a session guy, where you had to learn how to roll with the punches and that at a young age just gave you perspective to not sweat the small stuff.

I don't like to be in a tense room, man. I don't like to have people pissed off at me. . . . For whatever reason, I want to make it right. . . . Even if it was their fault, I just want to keep the peace. It's just easier to say "I'm sorry" than it is to hold a grudge. A lot of people hold grudges against me for reasons that they don't even understand or that aren't true, and some people have a right to do that. I don't know, I can't think for other people. I can only try to fix myself and there's lots to fix, believe me. I've got a shrink, I'm trying to work through my issues . . . I've been hurt by people and I've hurt people that I didn't mean to and/or been accused of things I didn't do.

If I did do something, I always apologize or try to make it right. I can admit fault in myself, but it's hard to be accused of things you didn't do. Then even when you're proved innocent, they won't let it go. So enough of that shit . . .

You're one of those people who, definitely there's a lot of untold stories, a lot of work you turned down that we will never find out about. You knew this person, they asked you to do it, you didn't have the time to do it . . .

Well, yeah, I was offered positions in Elton John's band, Joni Mitchell's band, Bob Seger, Miles Davis—I couldn't do them for the obvious reasons. I was already in a band and I had commitments. But it was such an honor to be asked.

[fast forward in the conversation after I had asked him about the passing of Eddie Van Halen]

For me it's the music I listen to every single day, for you it's the actual person.

Yeah. Everybody knows he's one of the greatest to ever pick up the guitar and know him as the artist, but I knew him as the person, forty-plus years. We'd been through it all together, the good, bad, and the ugly. I loved him as a friend and as a person. Of course I revered his playing and loved Van Halen as a band. They're one of the greatest of all time. I got a chance to play with him a couple of times, it was a great honor for me and record. I sang backgrounds on a couple of their records and stuff like that.

Wait, is that credited in anything?

I sang "On Top of the World" and some other song during the Sammy era.

Wow!

It's documented I did that. They didn't say on the record "background vocals," they've got "thanks to Luke" or whatever. I was just sitting around because I popped over [to 5150] often after I picked my kids up from school, it was up the hills and on the way home. I'd just buzzed myself in and showed up in the control room and Ted Templeman or someone was like, "Hey man, we need a third voice. Get out there." Just to do "oohs." I'd just go out there and did it for fun. Some people say, "You played guitar on a Van Halen album and I go why would I fucking play on a Van Halen album?" I offered a voice, a third part, on a "ooh" background part or something. But it was a kick to say that I did. [laughs]

THE TRAGICALLY HIP'S ROB BAKER, NOVEMBER 11, 2021, INTERVIEW
I always got the vibe that there were some Van Halen fans in the band, you just didn't publicly put that out there.

Yeah well, I like a good song. I was never a huge Van Halen fan and not a big fan of all the guitar histrionics and fireworks. But those guys wrote choruses, crazy good choruses. Just think about any one of their songs and you can go right to the chorus you can almost forget about the verse and the bridges and the guitar solos even to some extent. Not my thing, but the choruses are just so instantly identifiable, so hooky and that's the cash register right there—cha-ching.

BLUE OYSTER CULT'S ALBERT BOUCHARD, NOVEMBER 2, 2021, INTERVIEW

Are you aware that David Lee Roth had a graphic novel he put out digitally called *The Roth Project* that basically combined music and comics?

I was not aware of it, but I love David Lee Roth. He's fantastic. When I first met him I wanted him to be the singer of *Imaginos* and Sandy Pearlman's like, "What? No way, that would be a joke."

Did that actually get offered to him?

No. We were watching him sing with Van Halen from the side of the stage. I said, "Hey Sandy, I think this guy he should sing *Imaginos*, he's the character." He's saying, "No way, no."

So your band was on tour with Van Halen? I didn't realize that, or was that just a one-off festival?

We did about three or four dates, not a whole lot. I didn't really get to know any of those guys. It was more or less in passing, going from dressing room to dressing room, "Hey, great set." That kind of stuff.

Did you see any of David Lee Roth's shenanigans in person? Or was he out of character when not onstage?

Oh no, he was out of character. He didn't seem like he was pulling shenanigans. He seemed like a regular guy.

THE MOLDY PEACHES' ADAM GREEN AND KIMYA DAWSON, NOVEMBER 2, 2021, INTERVIEW

Were either of you Van Halen fans?

Van Halen fans? Bon Jovi, more. I could rock "Just a Gigolo" all the way through. I know that wasn't like their song, but I liked that video, I liked the "Jump" video, but I wasn't a fan. I like looking on YouTube and watching it. I don't even really remember it so much from growing up . . . I am a huge Bon Jovi fan, though. When I'm anxious I Google "Bon Jovi GIFs" and then I just look at a whole screen full of pictures of him just moving, it calms me.

LP, OCTOBER 22, 2021, INTERVIEW
I'll be spending three weeks in Vegas in a couple weeks and KISS is going to be there and David Lee Roth is going to be there . . .

Oh my god, David Lee Roth is going to be there?

I'm going to all five of his shows there.

Oh come on!

It starts off on New Year's Eve.

Oh my god . . . I want to celebrate with 80,000 straight men!

There you go. More like 1,100 crazy David Lee Roth fans and my wife.

I don't know man, and your wife. . . . She's a trooper.

Before I ask you another thing or two about yourself and then let you go, are you actually a Van Halen fan? I have no idea what your influences are.

Dude, I mean no offense to Sammy Hagar, I love Sammy Hagar and all that shit, I like a few of his songs. I think he did a great job because that's a hell of a thing to have to do, you know? But David Lee Roth, in the pantheon of frontmen, when it's really hard to be a shirtless long-haired guy, he made his own way. . . . The karate and all that stuff, he paved the way and here's some great songs. "I reach down between my legs . . . " I mean, come on, let's go!

HANNAH STORM, SEPTEMBER 29, 2021, INTERVIEW
Who is the better Van Halen frontman—Roth or Hagar?

David Lee Roth. I mean, anybody who has ever seen Van Halen in person, it was David Lee Roth. The magnetism that he had on the stage, because I do think with these bands, like you can't just go record, you have to go live. David Lee Roth, to see him perform was unlike anything. That energy, that charisma, it was something else. So, no, I am David Lee Roth all the way.

DREAM THEATER'S JORDAN RUDESS, OCTOBER 20, 2021, INTERVIEW
I've heard that half the band was rooted in KISS and Van Halen and the other hand does not love KISS and Van Halen. Is that true?

That's a funny question. I never heard that before and I never really spoke to the guys about KISS. I imagine that Mike Portnoy, being the rock icon. . . . He probably knows and appreciates all things about KISS . . . I don't think there's anybody else. I mean, maybe when Derek Sherinian was in the band years ago, he might have been into KISS and all that stuff. But I just never spoke to like John Myung or John Petrucci or James LaBrie about KISS. Van Halen, well of course. I mean, everybody loves Van Halen and the guitar playing was a huge influence on John Petrucci and all that. I hear more people asking about Rush and stuff like that, or Iron Maiden or Metallica, but not so often about KISS or Van Halen, so that's interesting.

ANDREW MCMAHON, SEPTEMBER 1, 2021, INTERVIEW
Do you have a favorite song by Van Halen?

I will pick a very probably unpopular song, but it's just because of when I grew up. It would be "Right Now."

Can you play "Right Now" on piano?

I haven't tried. I think I probably could. As a kid, I think I was probably in the second grade, those anthems were huge. Granted it was a much later era of Van Halen, but I love that jam.

THE STROKES' ALBERT HAMMOND JR., NOVEMBER 11, 2021, INTERVIEW
Has your craft been in any way inspired by Van Halen? Or anything you've ever done in life?

Never, not even the smallest amount.

So David Lee Roth, to you, is not the greatest frontman of all time?

I wouldn't want to put an opinion on it because I've never thought about it. If I say, "I don't think so," then I'm saying something that doesn't even . . . I was never moved by Led Zeppelin, either. I don't know them at all, so it's like, some bands affect you and some bands don't . . . I mean, I found The Misfits at like, thirty-one years old. I felt ridiculous. Certain Ozzy songs . . . I guess at that age I probably liked Phil Collins and Elton John more.

JASON ALDEAN, AUGUST 6, 2021, IN-PERSON CONVERSATION
Who's the best lead singer of Van Halen?

The best singer, or who was the best frontguy?

Good answer. I think I know what you're saying . . .

Roth is the best frontguy, but Sammy Hagar. Roth couldn't sing worth a damn. . . . If you want to get some good laughs, go to YouTube and check out some old videos of those guys when they were over in Europe playing, when they were wearing the spandex and all that. It is really, really important. Little kids in the front row and Roth is sitting there with his spandex pants on . . . right in this kid's face. I don't know how in the hell he got away with some of that stuff.

Future tour aspirations for you?

No, I can't pull the spandex off. Tight pants are about as close as I'm getting.

JASON ALDEAN, AUGUST 27, 2021, INTERVIEW VIA ZOOM
Looking at your stage show, I see the pyro of KISS, the three-microphone setup that maybe Paul Stanley may have done on some KISS tours. I hear some production influences from Mutt Lange. I see your pedal steel guitarist Jay wears an L.A. Guns shirt from time to time. Was hair metal a big part of your musical DNA?

Yeah, that '80s rock scene for me . . . I was born in '77, man, so by the time the '80s came around, all those '80s rock bands were a huge influence for me. For me it was more Def Leppard, Bon Jovi, Guns N' Roses. . . . Those bands were iconic for us. My lead guitar player, his favorite band was Van Halen, the other one was Aerosmith. My bass player, his was The Police.

I think there's a lot of mixture of that, and then obviously country music for me was a huge part of my background. I grew up listening to that stuff,

[Merle] Haggard, George Jones, Waylon [Jennings], Alabama, George Strait, and those guys. So that was also a huge part of it for me too. In our band I want the music to sound rock and roll, but I want the lyrics to be country, and I'm kind of the one that's always sort of tied it all together between my rock band and us playing country music. But yeah, that '80s rock. . . . That's been a huge part of our sound and influence.

DANA GOULD, OCTOBER 14, 2021, INTERVIEW
You recognized my Eddie Van Halen shirt, which I forgot I was wearing. David Lee Roth was known to be around The Comedy Store a lot. Did you ever run into him there?

Never, no. I was more of an Improv guy, I never went to The Comedy Store much. I don't think I've ever crossed paths with Diamond Dave, but I will say that there was a time when I had the same business manager as a member of Van Halen and he said to me in utter seriousness one day, "Dana, never get a plane."

KYARY PAMYU PAMYU, NOVEMBER 16, 2021, INTERVIEW VIA A TRANSLATOR
Do you have any rock influences as a singer? For example, were you ever a fan of Van Halen?

Rock has been a part of my journey through my musical life. I love the art and seeing rock performances, but I don't have the connection with Van Halen and classic rock.

THE BITCH WHO STOLE CHRISTMAS FILM ACTORS, NOVEMBER 17, 2021, PRESS JUNKET
Is anybody that I'm speaking with a fan of the band Van Halen?

Krista Rodriguez: Yeah, in theory. I don't have any point of reference, but I do know their music.

Andy Ridings: Van Halen was actually the first concert that I ever went to.

Ginger Minj: My first concert was Diana Ross.

Diana Ross is two degrees from Van Halen, because she dated Gene Simmons and Gene Simmons discovered Van Halen.

Ginger Minj: So the six degrees of Kevin Bacon!

AXS TV'S KATIE DARYL, DECEMBER 14, 2021
Is David Lee Roth the greatest frontman of all time?

What a loaded question! If we are talking high energy, high kicks, and high notes, DLR just might take the cake!

What is your favorite thing about David Lee Roth?

DLR oozes sex. I've never seen spandex look better and the way he tosses his hair while seducing the ladies with his eyes was just amazing.

At what point in David Lee Roth's career did you stop looking for new music? Or do you actually enjoy *Your Filthy Little Mouth*?

Van Halen by Van Halen was all I needed, everything else was just a bonus. I never want to be greedy. If an album satisfies me, I can stop right there and be thankful!

Do you think he is retiring after the last of his Las Vegas shows in January 2022?

Well as of now they already extended his stay to include more dates even though he had already "hung up his shoes." So I'd have to say if the money and moment are right, you'll be able to get anyone, including DLR, out of retirement.

PUBLICIST JASON CONSOLI INTERVIEW, NOVEMBER 11, 2021
Is David Lee Roth the greatest frontman of all time?

Admittedly I got into Van Halen very late being a twelve year old seeing the video for "Jump" on NBC's *Friday Night Videos* in 1984. But even though it was right at the end of VH's DLR era, holy shit, it seemed like this guy was just getting started. I must have been like, "Who the fuck is this dude doing extreme drop kicks and air splits?!" Simultaneously acting like hot shit while hamming it up with his brothers onstage.

The guy had everything you need to be the perfect frontman. That larger-than-life stage presence is one reason why people invoke "when giants roamed the earth"—I guess that started with Zeppelin—when referring to the classic Van Halen era.

Another great term I heard last year when Eddie died was that Van Halen was "the sound of a dog wearing sunglasses," and Dave being totally commanding and charismatic yet ridiculous and down to earth is a big reason for that. Is DLR the greatest frontman of all time? I'm not sure he is the tippy-top, but he is *way* the fuck up there. God bless David Lee Roth.

As a music business veteran, any encounters with David Lee Roth?

An amusing little Dave story that came to mind is sometime back in the late '90s I think—maybe this was when he was living in New York City doing the volunteer paramedic thing or a few years before—he was hanging out at that club Life, the old Village Gate, on Bleecker Street. He's holding court and drinking and winds up hitting it off with his cocktail waitress. He then takes her to some private spot in the club to have sex. After he finishes, like a total scumbag he pats the poor girl on the belly and says something to the effect of, "If you get pregnant, you can name the baby after me."

I think I'm remembering this fairly accurately and that it got written up in one of the gossip columns, probably *Page Six*, so it might be searchable. The only reason this stuck in my mind was that a year or so before on a New Year's Eve I had a drunken hookup in that same club's boiler room with a friend's cousin. So when I heard about Diamond Dave's "liaison" I was like, "For one night I was almost as much of a scoundrel as that guy!"

**AUTHOR AND COMEDIAN BOBBY SLAYTON,
OCTOBER 30, 2021, INTERVIEW**
I have nothing to say about David Lee Roth.

**QUIET RIOT, DIO, BLUE OYSTER CULT, AND WHITESNAKE'S RUDY
SARZO, JANUARY 17, 2021, INTERVIEW**
**The early days of Quiet Riot, the Starwood, and all, you must have seen
a hundred Van Halen shows. I've heard that before Van Halen was big,
that David Lee Roth had a different kind of onstage persona, where he was**

**telling more stand-up comedy one-liner kind of jokes, he's wearing overalls
and all that. Is that something that you remember at all?**

I became a resident of Los Angeles officially in 1978. . . . By then they were
signed, they were developed. I wasn't there for the early '80s part. I first
arrived in '76, came back in '77 and I spent almost a year and then I had to
leave because I ran out of money. Then I went and started doing some gigs,
came back with money and I've been here since 1978 steadily. So missed the
whole thing. I only saw Quiet Riot once at the Starwood, because Van Halen
was sold out at The Whiskey and I couldn't get in. This was, I believe '76, '77,
I was spending more time at The Rainbow because it was free to get in. . . .
"What if I could find somebody to give me a slice?" [laughs]

When you went into The Rainbow in the late '70s, each band had a booth.
The band Rainbow had a booth, the small one, not the big one. The big ones
were in the back, that was Led Zeppelin. Then in the middle you had Deep
Purple, you had The Who, and that was it. There was reverence. You did not
sit at that booth unless you were invited, and in my case, zero invitations.
[laughs] I know some people who were invited, but not me, because it's the
band and chicks. They want to invite some starving musician to sit at the
table? It gets cramped.

What some people call "the hair bands"—I call it "the MTV generation
of the Sunset Strip"—bands like Quiet Riot and Mötley Crüe and so on
we started getting big. Then everything changed, those booths became our
booths, but those same guys—including myself—we were the starving musicians walking around the aisles of The Rainbow in the hopes that somebody
would invite us to sit down and share with them a slice of pizza.

JASON BIGGS INTERVIEW, OCTOBER 4, 2021
Was Jason Biggs a big fan of Van Halen growing up?

That is a good question. Jason Biggs was and is a big fan of Van Halen. The
answer is yes. Losing Eddie, that was kind of brutal, I'm not gonna lie . . . I
have friends that are hardcore Van Halen fans. I am not that, but I have their
albums. I love them, Eddie in particular. I assume you're a Van Halen fan and
that's why you asked?

Die hard, going to five of the David Lee Roth shows in Vegas, but you gave off Van Halen vibes there.

Love, love them.

GLASSJAW'S JUSTIN BECK, FEBRUARY 4, 2022, INTERVIEW
So what was your first exposure to Van Halen? Was it the "Jump" and "Panama" videos on MTV when you were a kid?

Yeah, I don't remember which one came first. But I do remember having a cassette of "Runnin' with the Devil" and I'd just play it all the time on my parents' cassette player. . . . It was pretty tough and pretty evil. Just because it had "devil" in it. . . . But it was a little, I want to say, musically soft.

When I was in first grade, I was listening to M.O.D., S.O.D., Anthrax. . . . I've got kids now, you're talking like six, seven years old, and the lyrical content was completely unacceptable. . . . So I was into that. I remember getting the cassette, it might have been on a mixtape or something. . . . It wasn't scary, the music, but like the intro had a good groove to it, and that was probably my first memory of Van Halen . . .

I do recall the cassette first, then video second, because now I'm thinking about the videos coming on and being like, "What the fuck is this? Ninja guy? Blonde hair, fucking white guy? What the fuck is going on?" So I'd say it was cassette first, video second.

Being signed to Warner Bros., you were signed to the same label as Van Halen. Atlantic Records, the lights were kept on because of the Led Zeppelin back catalog. You could argue it's the same way with Warner Bros. and Van Halen. Were there any Van Halen–related interactions you had as a Warner Bros. roster member?

As a roster member? No. But to back it up and bring it back to East Meadow [Long Island]. . . . My best friend in elementary school, [later a successful actor and musician] Adam Busch. . . . He fucking loved Van Halen. . . . His brother, [later a top music industry manager] Matt Busch. . . . They'd always be exploring, like, the meanings of The [Grateful] Dead, and I didn't realize how "bad" the Dead was at the time. I just saw the pictures. And Adam would always tell me that there's like an evil, like, secret language . . .

I remember putting them in my CD player, being like, "What? They put the wrong CD, and this is bullshit." I couldn't reconcile that. . . . So a lot of my catalog of Van Halen came via Adam Busch, ironically enough. . . . Adam Busch has a very like David Lee Roth vibe. Adam was a very kind of eccentric, more of an introvert. I played music, but I'm not into being seen. Adam, he'd had the sunglasses on, playing the saxophone, doing solos in third, fourth grade. Like he was all about it. Hats off, Adam Busch.

My knowledge of Adam Busch just increased three-fold, and I thank you for that.

Yeah, very funny. So with Warner Bros. I never had any Van Halen interactions. But I did have a like a degree separation interaction with David Lee Roth, specifically. So you know, as you grow up, you realize there aren't too many cool Jewish people by nature. . . . We'd been in isolation for five thousand-plus years, we've morphed into our own creepy race of humanoids. . . . We evolved.

So when we step outside of our, our safety zone, it's always like, "That guy's fucking Jewish?" when you find out. . . . Because not every Jew needs to be a dorky fucking lawyer or doctor. So in my mind, I was like, "Oh, he's one of them. Like, that's fucking cool."

When I was in college, I was dating this Indonesian girl. I hung out with all Indonesians. . . . It was a cultural interesting point of my life. They would go to the city to clubs and stuff. I was in a hardcore band, I was like, "I'm not going to some fucking rave club, get the fuck out of here." They were always intrigued with Van Halen because Eddie Van Halen is half-Indonesian. They were obsessed with him.

My then-girlfriend comes home, and they're all speaking Indonesian. [speaking Indonesian phrases] "Van Halen," they keep on going. I'm like, "What the fuck? Van Halen?" They're like, "Oh, we just hung out with David Lee Roth." And I'm like, "Wait, what?" They're like, "Yeah, we just hang out with David Lee Roth." . . . I think they said at the time, unless my chronological mapping's off, he was in an EMT uniform, which I know he ended up doing. . . . They were bonding with him that they're Indonesian and that Eddie's half-Indonesian. I was so confused.

Where I thought that could have gone is you would have said, "Well, we have the same product manager at the record label as a Van Halen rerelease."

Yes, you are fucking right—Jeff Ayeroff. He headed up creative and stuff over there, and we had an interesting relationship. Because he was a Jew and we would always kind of bond on weird Semitic stupid shit. But I'm pretty sure he quoted me as being "the mini David Lee Roth." . . . I don't know if it's in an email.

Did you get to hear more of the Roth catalog? Like, do you know the song "Yankee Rose," for example?

I don't know "Yankee Rose," but I do remember once he broke off and went solo, I remember all the videos were definitely mesmerizing as a kid. . . . That was my first introduction to guys like Vai. . . . So to his credit, he definitely curated a nice bag of musicians that kind of brought the next phase.

And did that lead to a phase of you trying to learn how to play "Eruption?"

No, unfortunately, I suck on guitar . . . I'm not that good of a shredder. When I started playing guitar in sixth grade, I left my metal-thrash roots and entered hardcore. It was almost like if you were too good, you were corny . . . you'd be ostracized if you were too good. There was no soloing, so in the embryonic stage, when I could have maybe adopted the shred abilities skill set, I lost it because I was just learning about playing punk and post-punk grunge shit, you know?

ADAM BUSCH, FEBRUARY 21, 2022, INTERVIEW
What was your gateway into Van Halen fandom?

My older brother Matthew was my introduction to Van Halen. He had their records on vinyl and it all seemed larger than life. It didn't take long for me to hear that Eddie Van Halen was a genius. He was creating sounds I had never heard before. Textures and pulses that resonated like science fiction.

David Lee Roth reminded me of the Broadway stars I was exposed to at an early age. I was instantly comfortable with his pushy vibrato and careless athleticism. He appeared like Fred Astaire in music videos. For obvious reasons the idea of brothers making music appealed to me. My brother had a turntable and a drum kit, I had an alto-saxophone, my younger brother Justin played the bass, surely anything was possible. Plus, David Lee Roth's sense of humor was exactly as immature as I was as a nine year old.

You are the rare sort of person these days who likes both Van Hagar and original DLR. Has that always been the case?

I have a soft spot for rock ballads, so I didn't mind the switch. I didn't even think of it as the same band. It was a new band, making commercial music, with the same name and familiar elements. I can accept Genesis, Pink Floyd, or even Dead & Company the same way. I enjoy watching artists change and grow. I would buy all the guitar magazines that had Eddie on the cover. Then suddenly Eddie was on the cover of every keyboard/MIDI magazine so I bought those, too. It never occurred to me to resent Eddie Van Halen for growing and changing. It was not a threat to me as a fan.

I remember seeing Bob Dylan perform a few years back; I see him live as much as I can. The show, very much like the man, is always different and constantly evolving. There are usually a few people in the audience who have not seen him live before and only know his voice and music from older records. At this particular show, I witnessed a man dragging his friends out of the show midway through complaining that Dylan was "not a shadow of the man he used to be." I believe Bob would have taken that as a compliment. That's what he is going for. He is forever recreating himself and on this night, I was grateful to see the "gun-slinging, Vincent Price, mayor of a small town" character he was embodying. I would like to believe Eddie Van Halen had similar instincts and took pride in the new sound he had found and the new band he had created with his family.

As an excellent actor—my words, not yours—beyond your musicianship and singing, how would you rate David Lee Roth's acting chops? Are you able to see where the Diamond Dave character starts and ends when he is performing?

I can recognize when David Lee Roth was at the height of his powers, operating as the perfect conductor and physical embodiment of Eddie's sounds. There was a period when all of his instincts onstage were inspired and he could truly do no wrong. He offered that rare glimpse of danger, for better or worse you could not predict what he would do next, so you couldn't stop watching him.

I can also see when he ran out of material. He is not the world's greatest singer, dancer, comedian, or gymnast, but what he could accomplish with the combination is intoxicating. He honored his limitations and made the most of every gift he had. I feel he will be remembered mostly for his sense of humor. It remains unparalleled in rock and roll. I would like to believe musicians appreciate his unique contribution to music and on being the frontperson, that lack of self-awareness, the rhythmic sound of laughter in time. Very much like James Brown. It's the best he has to offer a song or a band. It doesn't necessarily translate outside of a music or rock context. But inside it, he truly is a diamond in the rough.

Finally, to you, where does DLR rank in the "greatest frontmen" of all time argument?

I currently believe the best way to enjoy the talents of David Lee Roth are with the use of the DLR Soundboard. You can push a button and instantly hear any of his famous catch phrases and use them to punctuate your own life.

PAUL NATKIN, DECEMBER 19, 2021, INTERVIEW
How does shooting David Lee Roth compare to other classic and legendary artists? Is it easier, because he's so animated? Or harder, because he himself has a lot of creative vision and has preferences as to how he likes to be shot?

I have never met him or talked to him, so I have no idea what his preferences are. He is a great showman who never stands still. Makes for great photographs!

When shooting Dave, do you take around the same number of photos as you would another artist? Or are fewer shots needed because you are likely to strike gold at any moment?

Same as any artist. I shoot as the artist does stuff onstage. He does more than most, which makes it easier to get great photographs.

Your website has a great story about shooting one of Van Halen's first shows with Sammy Hagar. Did doing that have any impact on your ability to pursue Dave-related photography?

I never photographed Dave after he quit Van Halen. Or when he returned.

Your credits also include Miles Davis, Frank Sinatra, Prince, The Rolling Stones, Tina Turner, countless other greats. Is there anyone you haven't yet shot that you are still hoping to get?

I have pretty much photographed everyone I ever wanted to, about 4,200 artists. Bands today don't really interest me that much, so I am pretty much retired. I only photograph when someone requests me, or if I am friends with the band these days.

Do you think Dave is retiring after the last of his five Las Vegas shows in January 2022?

No idea.

Finally, is David Lee Roth the greatest frontman of all time?

He is one of the good ones!

THE VERVE PIPE'S BRIAN VANDER ARK, AUGUST 21, 2019, INTERVIEW
I used to know your brother Brad. He had mentioned that at the peak of "The Freshmen" that David Lee Roth had just seen you guys in a club and bought you a bottle of champagne. Is that true?

That is true, yeah. I tell that same story because it was such a huge thing, you know? David Wells, the great [Yankees] pitcher, was there that night and a couple other actors. It was this really popular place in New York and Dave came over and said hi and bought us a bottle of champagne. But with that bottle of champagne comes three hours of nonstop talking from Dave. [laughs]

If you've ever spent time with David Lee Roth, or ever want to spend time, be prepared, the guy talks nonstop. You'll not get in a word in edgewise. Now that sounds like a complaint, and it is. There was *too much*. I was like, "I can't take this anymore." Brad and I looked at each other like, "Get him out of here, good god."

The Sam and Dave Tour

While the *No Holds Bar-B-Que* appeared to be David Lee Roth's attempt at evolving and trying to stay a step ahead of things, 2002 was arguably the beginning of David Lee Roth becoming a "classic artist." Rather than bringing a new studio album—at this point in time, his last full-length album was 1998's *DLR Band*—he opted to coheadline the *Song for Song, The Undisputed Heavyweight Champs of Rock & Roll* tour alongside Sammy Hagar. One of those tours that nobody ever thought would happen, Van Halen's first two vocalists were hitting the road together while Van Halen appeared to be inactive.

But according to Frank Meyer, per an early 2000s in-person conversation he had with David Lee Roth's then-manager Matt Sencio—on the day Van Halen announced it was reuniting with Hagar—Roth could have been back in Van Halen at this point in time. Joining mid-conversation, he was telling Sencio that it should have been Roth back with the Van Halens. "He goes, 'Yeah man, we tried so hard so many times, the whole MTV Awards thing. . . . Then, you know, back in 2000, they went in the studio and recorded all those songs.' I went, 'Whoa, whoa, what?' And he goes, 'Yeah, I guess a lot of people don't know this . . . in 2000, again, three years after MTV, seven years before the reunion, Dave went up to 5150 and they recorded most of a new album, a bunch of original songs, and recorded them live at 5150.'" Added Meyer: "I've never heard this before, and I'm a super freak."

Sencio then asked Meyer one of the best things a Van Halen diehard fan could ever hear: "'I've got the tape of it. Want to hear it?'" Reflected Meyer: "He played it for me, the whole thing. It wasn't the remake songs. It wasn't 'Tattoo,' because that's 'Down in Flames,' and it wasn't 'She's the Woman.' It was 'As Is,' it was 'Honeybaby,' and it was 'Trouble with Never,' it was 'Blood & Fire.' Each one, it was a soundboard tape from 5150, all four of them. So presumably it was Mike Anthony. . . . Each song stopped dead in the middle, like the band. That's how I know it was live, because you could hear count-offs and you could hear them stop a little bit of noise and then he'd go to the next song."

After hearing these songs, Meyer pried a little bit further on what he had heard: "I was like, 'What's the deal with them stopping somewhere right around the solo?' He goes, 'Well, that was Dave's thing. Dave knew that he was in Eddie's studio on Eddie's tapes and that once he walked out the door, who knew what was going to happen to that stuff?' He didn't want it all to show up as bonus tracks at some point without his permission. So he told Eddie the only way he'd go in and do these sorts of live demos are if they didn't have full recordings of them until they cut the deal to put it out as an album as Van Halen, which didn't happen for another several years." Added Meyer: "But those tapes exist and I've heard them and they were awesome . . . Matt's like, 'You can't tell anyone that you heard this.' And I didn't tell anyone, only in the last like year as I've been doing so many interviews, because . . . it's a good story and there's enough distance and Eddie's not around anymore."

To launch the *Undisputed Heavyweight* tour, Hagar and Roth were part of a joint press conference in front of the media. The two, who were definitely not friends beforehand and were said not to have met in person previously, took turns taking verbal jabs at the Van Halens and one another. Simply put, the tour sounded like a win-win for the fans, who would be hearing Van Halen classics and solo classics; interestingly, Hagar's 2002 release *Not 4 Sale* was not in US stores prior to the tour launch.

Backing Roth onstage would be drummer Ray Luzier (who began playing with Roth around five years prior), bassist James LoMenzo (as seen in the *No Holds Bar-B-Que* video), and guitarist Brian Young (as recruited from The Atomic Punks). No keyboardist. No second guitarist.

Brian Young did not come into the Roth fold thinking it was a long-term arrangement, as he told me in 2021. "When he hired me it was originally for two shows. So when I got the call to play with Dave it was for two festivals and that was all that was asked. 'Can you play these two festivals with David Lee Roth?' I said sure and then a few months later I get a call, 'We're going to tour with Sammy Hagar for the whole summer.'"

The backstory of Young is a lot more complex than him just being "the guy from The Atomic Punks." He explained: "Well I don't think there was ever a turning point in my career, because unlike some people who go from playing in a bar band when they're twenty to being in a signed band when they're twenty-two and famous and buying mansions . . . I guess getting a record deal [with Beau Nasty] was a big thing at the time. But if I look back on what I was doing, it turned out to be just another gig, and in the end I really made no more money than I made doing cover gigs."

I inquired a bit more about that money, of course. "We got a lump sum, but you get nothing for a year and then you get some royalties. It was nice to get a $10,000 check at one time like, 'Wow, this is big money.' I was used to making fifty bucks a night but then when you spread it over the living expenses for the whole year, it really turned out to be about fifty bucks a night. It wasn't like my ship came in or anything like that." Added Young: "I wasn't really happy in that band and I actually left that band to play with my brother's band that was doing original music, but more wild and wacky stuff."

At the time Young thought he was only playing two shows with Diamond Dave, that also was not something he viewed as a big break: "At the time I was really happy with what I was doing. I was teaching on Tuesdays and Wednesdays, playing with Perfect World on Thursday doing a disco thing or whatever, and then I was doing The Atomic Punks on Fridays and Saturdays. My week was full. . . . I surf every day and I'm playing music for a living. I've got no complaints." His initial reaction to finding out about Dave's tour with Sammy? As said with a laugh, of course: "That was the end of my surfing all the time."

Surprisingly, Young's bandmates in The Atomic Punks did not want him to take the Dave gig: "They actually offered to pay me more money to turn down David Lee Roth, so I thought about it. I go, 'Well, there's no way I'm going to turn down Dave.' . . . I thought, 'If I audition and don't get the gig, now I could just say I turned it down and get a raise.'" After laughing, he continued: "It was a little scary because I had to give up the teaching and all these things. I know I'm gonna lose all my students and so if the Dave thing only lasted three months and ended, I was gonna be back scraping for work again. Even though it was kind of like a 'dream come true' kind of thing, it wasn't anything to where I was going, 'I'm set for the rest of my life.' I knew that this guy could go back to Van Halen any day. I was just hoping it lasted six months, and that turned out to be six years."

The tour—which many refer to as the *Sam & Dave Tour*, rather than the aforementioned *Undisputed Heavyweights* moniker—would ultimately be documented with a VH1 special that took a look at Van Halen, Roth, and Hagar's histories, mostly utilizing archival footage. I asked long-time Hagar keyboardist Jesse Harms—who had also played on Roth's *Eat 'Em and Smile*—whether he had seen the special during our interview. "I don't know if I ever watched it, but I was there for the whole thing. . . . There was a lot of stuff that went down on that whole tour. I could really write a book about it. It was one of the most fascinating experiences in my whole musical life. It was way, by far, the most interesting Sammy tour we ever did."

According to Harms, there is plenty more than meets the eye not only when it comes to that special but also the tour itself. "They were filming that special and the original plan was for Sam and Dave to do a show together on MTV. I don't know, they were gonna share experiences? But both of those guys are very competitive." Continued Harms: "I really know Sammy better than I know Dave, but Sammy was very competitive with Dave, especially as time went on. There was a lot of maneuvering, and Dave is a really smart guy. He probably was more media savvy, as far as MTV went, than Sammy was at the time. He really got in some good licks there as they started filming the show."

In turn, per Harms, "the whole thing really blew up." The keyboardist reflected further on what went down, tour included: "I think it was more that when two people go into an arrangement, each person is thinking how it's going to end up in their favor. . . . When it didn't develop that way, I think, for either one of them, that's what caused the tour to blow up. I don't think that they ever really liked each other, but you know both of them are smart guys and I think they saw a good business arrangement developing. But they couldn't get past the personal stuff."

Harms remembers the shows themselves going well, however. "It looked like the amphitheaters were packed every night, that business was good, that everyone was happy with the shows, whether they were a Dave guy or a Sam guy. Tour vibes at least were good on that end. The money wasn't a mess and the attendance was good and all that." He confirmed that it was "Sammy that canceled the tour" and explained further: "We were supposed to go take it to Japan and Europe, but Sammy cut it off. We had a huge crew, like four semis out there and five, six buses, it was just a big tour. It hurt a lot of people but the one person that didn't hurt is Sammy, because he had the most money out of anybody."

Roth's temper casually came up during my conversation with Brian Young, although he understood how to navigate it with time. "He's gonna be upset, he's gonna yell, he's gotta blow off steam, and then everything's gonna be fine. It thickens your skin and you learn. . . . In the six years, of the hundreds of explosions I heard with him, I was only the target about two or three times . . . I just let it bounce off me."

But Young recalled that as being much less the case with sound guys for Roth: "Most people within the first few months, they find out if they're right for that gig. I saw so many monitor guys come and go in that first tour that we finally just started calling them by numbers. I'm like, 'Okay this is #5.' What's funny is the guy that we called #5 ended up staying around for five years, so forever he was named #5 and his name is actually Doug Short."

Prior to Short joining Team Roth, there was a series of techs who each lasted around a week. How exactly did they usually wind up blowing it? "I remember telling one of the guys, I remember exactly the conversation. What's happening is these guys aren't watching Dave, they're looking at the board. Dave's looking, he's trying to get their attention and they're not looking. So I said, 'You've got to keep your eye on Dave all the time.' He goes, 'What if there's a problem on the board?' I say, 'Keep your eye on Dave.' He goes, 'What if something spills?' I go, 'Keep your eye on Dave.' He goes, 'What if the board's on fire?' I go, 'Keep your eye on Dave.' Well, two days later, he was fired because he didn't keep his eye on Dave."

After letting out a laugh, Young explained that Short was exactly who Dave needed while onstage: "#5 was good. When Dave would point at his microphone, then the monitor guy would hit up a dB then Dave doesn't notice another dB. Five times later it's finally getting somewhere. . . . When Dave says, 'I want it louder,' you gotta make a big enough move to where he really hears you get louder, or he thinks you're not doing anything."

"Generally, I'm a front of house engineer," began Doug Short during our 2022 conversation. "Dave moved through, like, four monitor guys in a week or two. Basically, he would call them out in front of the audience by name, which I don't think was really cool. So Michael Mulet, god bless him, called me and says, 'Dave Roth needs a monitor guy,' and I was Michael's assistant tech for monitors on numerous tours. He goes, 'Hey, you want to give this a shot? The pay is good.' . . . So he threw my name in the hat and they hired me. When they gave me my laminate with the picture and the name on it, I just taped over with green tape and put a big '5' on it." So he had given himself that nickname officially? "Well, yeah, I guess I did."

As it turns out, plenty of people thought Short would be gone quickly. "When I joined in Tulsa, Oklahoma, I ran into the band and Sammy's band, Hagar's bunch, and Michael, [Anthony] who I've run into a few times, he goes, 'Can I buy you a drink?' 'Yeah.' He goes, 'Let's get a couple of drinks because you won't be here long.'" After letting out a big laugh, Short continued: "Mikey is one of the nicest guys in the world. He's completely down to earth and grounded. He will hang with anybody that seems like they're staying. Mikey's fucking great." I then asked about the rumors that Anthony offered to jam with Roth onstage during shows, but that Roth had declined that offer. Short agreed and added: "I think Dave wanted to keep his stuff in his circle."

I threw that same topic at Michael Anthony in our 2022 interview: "When I did my first show on that tour and guested with Sammy, Sammy and I were both kind of pounding on the door to his dressing room door, saying, 'Come on, Dave, come on.' So we'd all go out there and do 'You Really Got Me.'" Added Anthony: "Dave, I think got a little bit shy about doing it at that point. So we never were able to get him out there to join us onstage."

Doug Short also confirmed what Harms had said about the tour's end: "Sam quit, as far as I know. We only did fifty-five shows and it could have been much more." But Short added something that I did not recall hearing elsewhere: "Actually, what I understand about the *Sam & Dave* tour was originally it was going to be a Van Halen tour with both singers. Both guys doing an hour or ninety minutes, and then Ed and Al pulled out. . . . So underneath our breath, we were called 'The Non Halen Tour' and both guys brought out their side guys." Reflected Short: "If they did the dual Van Halen thing, that could have gone two years and made I don't know how much money."

Looking back at the *Sam & Dave Tour*, Brian Young enjoyed being part of a power trio backing band. "It was the only one that I was the only guitar player on, which I liked. That was because it was a thing with Van Halen that you want that sound." The majority of the tour's setlist would be rooted in the first Van Halen albums. "When we added the second guitar [via Toshi Hiketa], we had to really work to try to make it sound right with two guitars."

Continued Young: "The 2002 setlist was definitely the heaviest setlist. That was the setlist with 'I'm the One,' 'D.O.A.,' 'Atomic Punk,' all this stuff. Then every year . . . 'Atomic Punk' would leave and 'Just a Gigolo' would come in. Then 'D.O.A.' would go away and some of the lighter tunes, 'California Girls.'" He enjoyed all of these songs, but as a performer "really enjoyed the heavy stuff the best, because that's the prime."

After the tour had gone bust, Roth made a September 2002 performance on Carson Daly's NBC talk show. He would sit down for an interview with Daly, beyond performing with a full band. The interview included the following quote from Roth: "The way I stay ahead of the wave is I don't read anything about myself. Nothing could possibly be good, nothing. Anything even slightly bad ruins my week. So there's not even a piece of paper with my picture on it [in my home], there's nothing with my name on it. If I see it on TV, I ask the cats and say, 'Hey, everybody had a good time? Okay, everybody was sober? Close enough.'" He capped that one off with a laugh before Daly could get one out, as you would imagine.

Having watched that performance on YouTube many times, I complimented Young on the performance of "Mean Street" from Daly's show as the band was not only in top form but also very aware of where to stand to avoid one of Diamond Dave's spin kicks. "We knew when to run," he laughed. Young then followed that up with an anecdote that is sort of the thing one would expect from someone playing classic Van Halen: "If you watch any videos of us from that tour, or pretty much any tour, watch when he gets to 'Jump.' When he gets that middle keyboard section where he starts spinning that bar, we all run. I go behind my amp." Continued Young: "My routine was my tech would have a can of Budweiser, a nice cold can of Budweiser, and then right when I get around the speakers he'd pop it and I would down the whole thing because it's the end of the show. My thing was to try to drink the whole beer before you finish that part and run back out. That's a little secret no one knew about. I was drinking a beer." To confirm, none of that is visible in *Live in Hartford 2002*, an officially filmed yet never commercially released concert of Roth's, as directed by Virgil E. Hammond III; of note is that the performance often cuts away to visuals from the previously discussed *No Holds Bar-B-Que* video.

The *Sam & Dave Tour* turned out to be among Jesse Harms' last work with Sammy Hagar. "I made money with Sammy but I also made money doing other songwriting and other things, so it wasn't the 'end all' of my career," he began. "I'm very, very proud of my career . . . I got to be a teenager for an extra twenty years of my life, really incredible. . . . Both of my kids have college degrees, they have advanced degrees and I'm proud of that. I didn't make the music business be my entire life."

While things were winding down for Harms, they were still on the rise for Lit bassist Kevin Baldes. "I went and partied next to his bus at the Gibson Amphitheater here in Universal City, it was on the Sammy and Dave tour. . . . That was really cool and I actually got my photo with him. It actually became a full-page pin-up in *Metal Edge Magazine*, of all things." Baldes, who continues to play in Lit, has also found success as a photographer. On the small world end of things, he shot one of Eddie Van Halen's last photo shoots and also photographed one of Roth's last gigs before the COVID-19 pandemic hit.

The year 2002 may not have gone how Dave had planned for it to go, but it would turn out to be the beginning of a very productive period for him personally and professionally. And also from where many of our still-unanswered DLR questions arise.

2003–2006

(and Vegas: Part II)

As discussed in the previous chapter, David Lee Roth guitarist Brian Young never got too comfortable when working for DLR. "Ray Luzier was playing with Dave for a few years before I was, and I knew they'd go on tour and then I'd see Ray on his day off doing a drum clinic or doing a gig," began Young. "I remember thinking to myself, 'I thought when you land one of those gigs that's your gig, and when you're home, you're home and you don't have to work on your days off.'"

Continued Young: "I like that work ethic, where if I'm home and there's a gig, I'll do it. I kind of copied that work ethic and, in fact, Ray and I did a lot of the gigs together because we were both with Dave, so we both have the same days off. We were able to come home and do other gigs."

Doug Short, who eventually worked his way up to tour manager duties for Roth, confirmed that it was a surprisingly flexible schedule: "When I was with Dave, as I remember, if he was off, he was off and you got sent home. But we were kind of weekend warriors. Fly out Thursday, Friday, Saturday, Sunday, and go home Monday."

So while David Lee Roth toured regularly from 2003 through 2006, Brian Young did not take a lot of time off: "We actually did a thing where we did a Thursday with Dave, a Friday with a cover band, Saturday with Dave, Sunday with a cover band, Monday with Dave. It was fun to be that busy and it doesn't give you time to get bored, obviously. You just do it. . . . You just look at the next gig. . . . Just go, 'Okay, all I've got to do is get from here to the airport.' 'Okay, I can do that.' 'Get to the gig and then I get back home.' So if you chop it into little pieces, it's suddenly not that big of a deal."

But that gave way to a fun anecdote about Young overbooking himself in that era: "One of the craziest ones I ever did was when I was still with The Atomic Punks. We were playing at a place in Santa Monica: it's called 14 Below, it was a small club on 14th Street. We were playing the next day at the Pepsi Center in Colorado. We had a gig at the Mile High Stadium playing during the hockey game and we were playing at 11:00 in the morning in Denver. I remember being onstage at midnight in Santa Monica thinking to myself, 'In less than twelve hours I'm going to be playing a show in Denver, Colorado, and something's going to go wrong.' Sure enough, after the gig basically I went home to take a shower, go over to the airport, got on the plane, flew, got in the car, drove, the gear's there, tune our stuff up, next thing you know we're playing away. It all worked."

For Young, it was not the money driving him to stay so busy but more out of understanding what real work felt like. "My thing was saying yes to every gig because I had a day job back in the day and I hated it. I started playing with this top 40 band and it was for fifty bucks a night and I played five forty-five-minute sets for $50, which is really chump change now. But at the time that's $250 a week, I was paying my bills. I was living on that salary, but I really hated it because we were playing the same stuff over and over. I was twenty-one years old and I wanted to be in a real original rock band."

Continued Young: "I remember playing 'Sweet Home Alabama' for the thousandth time and then I actually quit the band and got a job back at my old day job place, the record place that I worked at and I remember after a month thinking, 'What was I thinking? This is terrible.' So after that I always said, 'I don't care what song I'm playing. The worst gig ever is better than a day job.' I never ever wished my way out of any gig no matter how crappy it was after that."

The previously mentioned John Blenn, who has interviewed Roth as a journalist, found his way into a career as general manager of legendary Long Island, New York, venue Westbury Music Fair in the early 2000s. In turn, he oversaw a Roth gig in 2003. "There was a different kind of energy when Dave was there. Most people think of the Westbury Music Fair as the land of Frank Sinatra and Tony Bennett. A theater in the round was different for Dave and the farthest seat in the building was sixty-five feet from the stage. People were buzzing about how close he seemed."

This was a bigger venue than Roth had played in the same market about a decade earlier, per Blenn: "I saw him years earlier at the even more intimate Malibu [in Lido Beach], but I thought it was neat to see his spectacle up close."

As someone who has encountered Roth both as an interviewer and a behind-the-scenes venue manager, how does Blenn think of Dave? "If David Lee is out in public, David Lee's *on*. As an interview subject, he's one of the best in the business—a walking, talking quote machine. You basically need 'hello' to get a full interview, he'll go everywhere you need to without even asking basic questions. Backstage, Dave's charming everyone in sight, from catering to tech crew. Any savvy performer knows you'll get far more out of the people you work with using sugar instead of vinegar."

Steve Brown—who had turned down a DLR tour in the early 1990s as a member of Trixter—finally got to open for Roth in the early 2000s as a member of 40 Foot Ringo. "We did The Chance in Poughkeepsie and we did the WDHA Christmas party, the first ever show at the Starland Ballroom in Sayreville, New Jersey, opening up for David Lee Roth. That was another great time because we were friends with all the guys in Dave's band, Ray Luzier, Brian Young, and some of the crew guys. Opening up the shows for Dave was great." Added Brown: "We didn't get to hang out with him, but it was just great to be there. No matter what, I always have a huge soft spot for Dave. I think he could be like the biggest dick to me and I'd still take it just because it's Dave."

In this era, Roth was touring—and doing lots of interviews and appearances—in support of an album titled *Diamond Dave*. While widely billed as a "covers album," *Diamond Dave* actually has a handful of original tracks on it, including the John 5 cowritten "Thug Pop." A proper music video does not appear to have been made for this album, even though Roth's last creative endeavor, *No Holds Bar-B-Que*, was essentially one long music video, and his *Crazy from the Heat* memoir had referenced him filming a music video for "Ice Cream Man" at Sony Studios in New York.

As John 5 is not believed to have worked with Roth while playing in Marilyn Manson's band, the tracks feature a variety of musicians and producers, and "Ice Cream Man" was noted in the *Crazy from the Heat* book to have been recorded in the mid-1990s, general consensus is that *Diamond Dave* was

compiled from a variety of sessions. Most of these songs were not featured in
No Holds Bar-B-Que, which was helmed after the *Crazy from the Heat* book
was written. Gentle reminder that in *Crazy from the Heat* from 1997, Roth
had bragged that he had "easily a hundred songs" that were unreleased at the
time.

This era of Roth's career saw him do a lot of things previously not done. He
made a cameo in a 2003 episode of *Late Night with Conan O'Brien,* running
on and off screen quickly in a blue skintight catsuit. He played himself in a
2004 episode of *The Sopranos,* having a good number of lines during a poker
game. He performed live with The Boston Pops as a July 4 celebration in 2004.

In the midst of all that, Van Halen did a reunion tour with Sammy Hagar
in 2004. In time for that came a double-disc compilation titled *The Best of
Both Worlds,* which featured both Roth- and Hagar-era tracks. The release
notably included three new songs recorded with Hagar—for which Michael
Anthony sang background vocals along with Toto's Steve Lukather—with
Eddie Van Halen on bass duties. As a result of the new songs, songs featuring
Roth were less than half of the thirty-six songs included.

Around this same time, Roth had opted to sue both Warner Bros. Records
and his former Van Halen bandmates. This was rooted in feeling that he was
underpaid royalties because the band had renegotiated its deal with Warner
in 1996, inclusive of a better royalty rate—likely tied in with 1996's *Best of*
album discussed earlier—without Roth privy to negotiations. He had felt that
he deserved 25 percent of Van Halen's royalties rather than the share he was
receiving. He ultimately asked for the case to be dismissed, hinting at an out-
of-court settlement.

A near happening for Diamond Dave in 2004—nine years after his Bally's
Las Vegas debut—was another Las Vegas residency. An article published by
the *Las Vegas Sun* noted Roth to be "creating a whole new show" with adult
revue *X* coproducer Angela Sampras and producer partner Bobby Boling.
With regard to Roth's Bally's show, Sampras was quoted as saying that it
"was not the right time for David to appear on the Strip" in 1995, but with
her team's "creative genius and his talent for comedy, I think we can have yet
another hit show."

In 2021, I attempted to speak with both Sampras—now going by Angela
Sampras-Stabile—and Boling to find out how far along plans for the show
came. Boling pointed out that he had not worked with Sampras-Stabile "in

fifteen to twenty years" and didn't "have any details" to offer. Sampras-Stabile responded: "Bobby hasn't been a part of the X shows since 2004. What publication are you with specifically?" Let's chalk that one up to producers leaking details before anything was concrete.

Another creative risk taken by Roth was his participation in a tribute album titled *Strummin' with the Devil: The Southern Side of Van Halen*. Released in 2006 by CMH Records—a label that has released all of Lisa Roth's *Rockabye Baby!* titles to date—it was a tribute album featuring bluegrass-inspired takes on Van Halen favorites. Roth himself sang lead on "Jump" and "Jamie's Cryin'," the first two songs on the album. He ultimately made the media rounds with a bluegrass band.

Brian Young was the only member of Roth's band who played live with the *Strummin' with the Devil* musicians. "Oh, I did a bunch of the TV shows," he explained. "The only one I missed was the Conan O'Brien show, and the reason I missed that was because we were also playing a gig in New York City and Dave was going to do the *Conan* show, which is filmed at four or five o'clock, then with the bluegrass band, and then head straight over to the gig. I just felt like I didn't want the stress of having it, because I knew that if I did the *Conan* show, the whole time I'd be thinking, 'The gig's coming up and I've got to rush over there.' So I skipped that one just to soundcheck and be with the band and be ready to go when Dave walked in." Added Young: "Now I look back, I should have just done the Conan show, because that's a pretty cool TV show."

By the time the *Conan* and New York City show referenced by Young had happened, Ray Luzier was out of the Roth band, replaced by drummer Jimmy Degrasso. During our interview to plug KXM, Luzier told me: "Towards the end of that I was not feeling that creatively fulfilled with Dave because I was a huge fan of *Eat 'Em and Smile* and a bunch of his original records, and he just was doing cover records and I felt like I was in a Van Halen cover band with David Lee Roth. I have too much music in me, I write too much."

And of course things would work out very well for Luzier, as the Roth gig was promptly followed by a variety of great projects: "I'd done a couple Billy Sheehan solo records, and Billy and I played the NAMM show in 2005. I met the DeLeo brothers there and that led me to Army of Anyone, and Army of Anyone was Robert and Dean DeLeo from Stone Temple Pilots and Richard Patrick from Filter. I fell head over heels, you know, because I really wanted that band to do multiple records and all that, and it was short lived, unfortunately. I'm very proud of that record."

Fortunately, the Army of Anyone gig got Luzier's foot into the right door. "They were managed by Korn's management company, so I kept asking our manager, 'Hey, what's up with Korn?' They're using Joey [Jordison] from Slipknot on this tour, Terry Bozzio on the record, Brooks Wackerman, and all these different people. They said, 'Yeah, they're looking for a steady drummer, you should go check it out.'" He paused before continuing: "I have blonde hair, no tattoos, and never did a drug in my life and they didn't seem to care. I went up to audition for them at Joey's last gig in Seattle and they said, 'Welcome to Korn, we'll see you in Dublin.'" That was October '07. As of this book's writing, Luzier remains a member of Korn more than fifteen years later.

Still with Roth after Luzier's departure was Doug Short, who few expected to last for more than a month. "It's a matter of knowing your place and doing your job. That's really what it is. . . . You have to adjust to what we call 'Rothisms.' What was fun too is that all of us in the crew, in the band, would do great impersonations of him. You can ask Ray and Brian about that." He let out a laugh, then did a spot-on DLR impression.

In the midst of our conversation, I asked Doug Short why we tend to regularly hear stories about Roth being quirky and hard to work for. He initially answered with relation to another former boss of his, Prince: "There's nothing publicized about Prince donating a couple of million dollars to music schools. Or him helping me buy my first house in Minneapolis because I couldn't get a loan. . . . Being generous and helpful doesn't make good press, does it?"

Dave the EMT

Remember how David Lee Roth was on tour in 2004, in support of 2003's *Diamond Dave* album? Well, as it turns out, there was plenty more happening in the world of DLR around this time. Like, Diamond Dave getting certified by the New York State Department of Health's Bureau of EMS to be a licensed EMT. Yes, seriously.

Per Roth's instructor Linda Reissman, his quest to become a licensed EMT actually goes back prior to 2004. "It was definitely after 9/11 . . . I would say end of 2003, 2004," Reissman told me by phone in 2021. Employed by the New York State Department of Health bureau of EMS for nearly a decade, Reissman's background included working 9-1-1 ambulances and being an instructor at the New York City EMS Academy. "I had applied back in like 1993 or 1994 to become the EMS Inspector for New York City and I got the job. I was the first woman in New York City ever to have that job."

After 9/11, Reissman was part of a federal response team, doing work around New York City's Ground Zero. But she was still teaching and very active in the EMS community as a consultant and instructor. Given her distinguished background, the powers that be sought her out when word came through that Roth wanted to undergo the coursework for EMT certification. While there was concern about Roth pursuing this certification, it did not have to do with his perceived level of ability.

"The State Health Department was a little concerned that if Dave was in a regular classroom it would bring the media and all that. . . . They gave one of his assistants or his manager a couple of phone numbers to call to find an EMS training institute," began Reissman. "When he said, 'I'm going to use this institute,'" the state had called him and said, 'Maybe this could be more of a private class.' Because the training institute knew me and the state knew me, they recommended me."

Before saying yes, Reissman wanted to make sure that Diamond Dave was going to take all of this seriously. "At first I thought it was a joke, but it really wasn't. . . . After I had spoken to his manager and I spoke to Dave, I felt that the level of sincerity was really there, and after I got to know Dave, I really respected why he wanted to become an EMT. It wasn't just a fad or anything."

So where exactly did those private classes take place? "The state gave us permission to travel to his apartment—I won't say exactly where it was, but he loved living on the Lower East Side, loved the vibe there, really he loved the community, loved the music down there, loved the grit." Continued Reissman: "I had equipment that I would bring to his apartment a couple of days a week. He would do his assignment. . . . He would always have his homework ready, completed his tasks, always made his rotations. The intelligence level and understanding of it, it wasn't just good enough for Dave to pass the test, Dave wanted to pass really well. It wasn't good enough for Dave to know the basics, he wanted to know even more, so we kind of really beefed up the class for him because of his quest for knowledge. There's just a level of professionalism that he's not going to go out there if he didn't want to go out there or embarrass himself, hurt a patient or his partners. . . . He made sure that he was good."

According to Reissman, Roth really did learn how to do everything and then some. "I would actually bring in a couple of experts, whether it be a police officer or someone who specialized in paramedic stuff, he even learned how to help the medic. He learned how to set up the EKG machines, things that normally you don't teach in an EMT class, but Dave was like, 'I don't want to stand around with my hands in my pocket and just be an observer. I want to be able to contribute.'"

In terms of contributing, Reissman remembers Roth's explanation of what got him interested in the pursuit of EMT training. "Basically what Dave said to me is, 'Hey listen, I've been on multiple tours where roadies and people have been hurt. I want to be able to help them if something happens. I think it's important to know this skill set. I think it's important for me to really learn from the best if I can.'" Impressively, Reissman was able to connect that to a famous Van Halen story. "That kind of ties into a lot of things, because when you read about Dave's contracts, you know about the brown M&Ms. It was really true and it was like, 'If they're not reading that, how do I know that they built the stage correctly? Or did they do the reinforcements correctly? Or listen to how we wanted things set up?'" She added: "He said he's seen people get hurt due to poor stage construction and things like that, and he's the kind of guy that wants to be prepared. Also tying into his concept of, 'Fame has just given me a passport to the world.'"

I asked Roth's first cousin Dr. Jack A. Roth whether he had been consulted by Dave in the EMT era of his life. "I didn't really get the details on that. I read a lot, I heard a bit about it on podcasts and so forth."

Beyond his home-based classes, Reissman recalls placing Roth all over the place for his training. "Even in his refresher classes, he made sure he made his way up to Rockland where I was living and we actually hid him out at the Rockland County Emergency Medical Training Center in Pomona. That's where he did a couple of his refresher classes . . . I had him at quite a few facilities around the Bronx, Manhattan, down in Brownsville [Brooklyn]." And the story he has told in interviews about resuscitating someone on a call after a local Ozzfest gig checks out. "He resuscitated folks, he was on trauma calls. We also sent him to specialized tactical training, so that if he ever was on a scene with the police, he knew how to tactically operate in that type of environment. He was gung ho."

Apparently, per Reissman, a New York State EMS license was not the only license pursued by Dave in this era. "I don't know if a lot of people know that he's a helicopter pilot. He learned from one of the guys from ESU who had retired, a former police officer." Sure enough, an FAA database search confirmed this for me, as Roth appears to have earned his "private pilot" license as of December 12, 2006, although "must have available glasses for vision"; for the record, the FAA will not be providing me with Roth's full pilot's file until he authorizes such, per FOIA regulations.

Per Roth's EMS Certification documentation from New York State via a FOIA request, his initial certification went into effect on November 18, 2004. Within two weeks after gigs performed in Canada and Minnesota. This means that the guy was touring, doing interviews, and otherwise pursuing his career as a performer *while* fulfilling his EMT training–relating responsibilities.

In retrospect, Reissman does not remember Dave doing his EMT training with any ulterior motives. "He didn't want any fanfare, he didn't want any attention about it, he didn't want to take away from the integrity of what he was doing from his partners and who he was riding with. I had such a level of respect for him. . . . He was very well respected by the EMS community and still is." She added: "People still say, 'Have you seen Dave? Have you spoken to Dave?'" Fortunately for Reissman, her work with Diamond Dave would continue into the next professional chapter of his life.

Dave the Radio Host

A recurring pattern in the life and career of David Lee Roth is that when he wants to do something, odds are that he is going to try it a few times. The webcasts that Roth was doing via his website—among the domains he owned were Dave-TV.com and RothRadio.com—in the late 1990s as *Dave TV* were arguably an early incarnation of the *No Holds Bar-B-Que* project; all episodes of *Dave TV* may have vanished from the Internet, but *Roth Army* member David Vincent is among the DLR fanbase who has digitally preserved this content. "Dave TV" itself was a concept that appeared in the music video for "Just a Gigolo/I Ain't Got Nobody" from the *Crazy from the Heat* EP. And Roth was never shy when it came to guest hosting for MTV or radio shows.

When Howard Stern announced that he was leaving terrestrial radio in 2004—simultaneously announcing a five-year deal with Sirius Satellite Radio—that left CBS Radio scrambling to find a proper replacement for the syndicated host known as "the King of All Media." While it's still not known exactly how Roth's name got thrown into contention to take over some of Stern's morning radio markets, things started to take shape in early 2005, as Roth was asked to do a week of "test shows" in the Boston area.

"I was the board operator and studio producer with him," began radio industry veteran John "Hutch" Hutchinson to me in 2022. "I was on mic with him as much as I needed to be, and he loved it. We had five days. That was during the St. Patrick's Week. We did a live meet-and-greet at a bar on

Commonwealth Avenue during that week, and we got on very well. All five shows went great for the most part. We had a good time that entire week."

Who else does Hutch remember worked with him and Dave on the show? "It was basically me, him, and Sencio in the studio for that week at WZLX in Boston, and one of the producers Braden Moriarty, who was wrangling the phone calls with a chalkboard and who was on the lines and stuff." Added Hutch about Moriarty: "He was a good old friend in Boston." Per Boston-based comedian and writer Gary Marino on an episode of *The DLR Cast*, he had been asked to provide some consulting and feedback on these test shows.

Altogether, preparation for the Boston test shows was loose but organized, Hutch remembered. "Basically Dave and Matt were standing opposite me. Matt was reading the *National Enquirer* or something, so they'd have a couple of things to talk about. Dave was telling stories and it was great. We played songs, played music, classic rock, some Van Halen and some other stuff. It went very, very well. We had a ball."

Fortunately, that was not the end for Hutch. "At the end of the week, Rob Barnett—I believe he was CBS National PD at that time—took me aside after the last show was finished. And he said, the first words if I remember correctly, 'Well, I guess I'm going to have to pay you too then.'" He paused. "I said, 'What are you talking about?' Anyway, long story short, they said, 'Dave wants you to come down to New York to work on the show down there.' . . . I said, 'Give me some time to think it over. That's kind of an adventure, I wouldn't mind having a bash at that.' I spoke to my wife about it and she said, 'Yeah, go for it.'" That conversation happened in April 2005.

But Hutch remembers having to stay mysterious about why Dave was doing test shows. "We had to keep everything quiet because nobody at that point knew what was going to happen with Stern. And then when Stern formally announced that he was heading to Sirius, and that it all came out that they were splitting his terrestrial radio syndication—Rover was taking the Midwest, Adam Carolla was the West Coast, Dave was taking on seven stations . . . New York, West Palm Beach, Dallas, Pittsburgh, Philadelphia, Cleveland, and Boston on WBCN." Added Hutch: "During those few months, I worked on what I needed to with him, not with Dave directly, but mostly with Matt, Dave's manager. At this point, everything was very secretive."

Did the prep work ramp up as they got closer to the show going on air in January 2006? Not exactly, as Hutch recalls. "When it came to pre-production, there really wasn't a hell of a lot. There could have been a bit more planning. Additionally, I think there was a bit of resentment about me being there." Hutch paused before explaining what he meant: "Dave, through Matt Sencio, told me to ask for a chunky salary. I mean, for God's sake, I was paying a mortgage on my house in Boston, I had to rent a place in Manhattan to be there, so I needed some money." He noted before laughing: "And they paid it in the end."

Part of the reason why pre-production was so limited may have been the lack of facilities made available to Dave and team, Hutch explained. "They were stripping out the studio, putting in a new studio, and we were supposed to work in there. Everybody was supposed to work from that studio. Dave didn't like it for various reasons, and so we worked in the little studio at the side, which got incredibly hot."

Hutch officially moved to New York in November 2005, taking some time to arrange for "a little efficiency apartment" on the Upper West Side. But he remembers behind-the-scenes strife with the show even before it premiered. "It became obvious that something wasn't quite right between CBS and Dave, mostly over what they expected of him and what he had in mind. There was a point when some of the CBS folks thought that Dave was going to quit before launch date on January 3. I was even questioned about that but, at that point, we were going to go ahead and do the show and go for it and do what we could with rehearsals. But there really wasn't a whole lot of that."

So what was a typical day at the office like for Hutch once the show got underway? "I would get into the studio at around 4:00 a.m. and do whatever setup I had to do and about. And then about 4:30, quarter to 5:00, I would walk down and have a cigarette down outside the building and meet Dave and Matt." Continued Hutch: "Matt used to pick him up in a limo and bring him over and we'd go over to the bagel shop and a little bodega and get a bagel and a couple of bottles of water and whatever. On the way back, I'd roll a cigarette—I roll my own cigarettes—and he'd say, 'Roll me one, Hutch,' and I'd roll him a cigarette. We'd have a smoke on the way back to the building, up the elevator, and get started."

And after the show, Hutch? "He'd hang out for a while and get his shit together. And at times he would disappear into a side office to meet with some of the CBS folks who were supposed to be running the show . . . because there were concerns." He noted: "It became an almost everyday

occurrence, which must have put pressure on Dave and Matt, for that matter. I never was in any of those meetings. I really didn't want to be, to be
honest with you, but I would love to have been a fly on the wall. Then he
would usually leave."

Of course *The David Lee Roth Show* was a lot more than Dave, Hutch, and
Matt. Its cast of characters—comparable to the makeup of *The Howard Stern
Show*—included actual employees of Dave's, like his security guard Harvey
"Animal" Stephenson and his guitarist Brian Young. Their schedules were
not necessarily identical to Dave's, as Hutch remembers. "Brian would hang
out. Sometimes Animal would hang out a little longer. Sometimes we'd all
meet up an hour or so later for lunch, to go to a bar for lunch or something.
And there were times when we went out with Dave in the evening." He
paused. "We went for sushi a couple of times, we went to a gentlemen's club,
he treated us all to a gentlemen's club with him one night, which was very
nice, nothing sleazy." Naturally, Hutch ended that one with a laugh.

While speaking with Brian Young, I referred to him as being the show's
"Paul Shaffer," which he agreed with. "I was Paul Shaffer, exactly. So they'd
call on me, I'd play out of the commercial, play back into the show, yeah. . . .
Dave called it 'track blasting.'" Young then explained what that term meant,
as I was not familiar. "Dave goes to the CD store back then, and he'd come
home with twenty CDs and then he would listen to them and he would pick
out his favorite songs and have his guy make him these CDs of just the songs
he liked. So he'd take twenty CDs and get it down to three CDs of 'the greatest
hits' and he had hundreds of his 'greatest hits CDs.' Then what he did with
those before the radio show, he took cool sections of a song, a little funky jam
or whatever without singing, and he would have these guys loop that for like
ten minutes. They were just a musical loop that lasted ten minutes long and
he made hundreds of those."

Hundreds of those? Yeah, I heard Young correctly. "Yes, the giant Animal
would carry these cases full of these CDs and they were just grooves and
grooves and grooves of different genres, different keys." Sometimes the fact
that Dave liked so many different styles of music could be problematic when
it came to Young improvising on top of them on air. "Some of them weren't
tuned to A440, so a few of them I couldn't play along with them because I'd be
out-of-tune sounding, they were between A and A-flat. . . . The music comes
on, I've gotta find the key and start soloing and he liked me to keep it kind of

bluesy, funky, so he didn't really want me to go wild or anything." He added with positivity: "It was definitely a neat experience, that show."

The occasional lunch aside, Hutch recalled Dave being "very private" during the show's run. "He had an apartment on the Lower East Side at that point. I never saw it, but I heard how he likes to sleep rough now and again. He'd put a whole bunch of astroturf on the roof of this apartment, because he had the top floor and he put a tent up there. Now and again I heard that he'd go sleep in the tent." Hutch, of course, let out a laugh with that last sentence.

Doug Short, one of Roth's longer-tenured tour crew members, was also in New York at the time of DLR's radio show. "I lived about four blocks away from him. He lived at 81st and I lived on 73rd. His place looked over Central Park and the Library. . . . He had three places. . . . He also had a place, I believe, near what used to be the World Trade Center. He never actually set foot in it all." Around this era, per Short: "There were a lot of pokes and prods for a [Van Halen] reunion."

Linda Reissman, who helped oversee Dave's EMT training, was also around for the CBS Radio show. "I was one of the sidekicks. I was on a few episodes with them because they kind of wanted to build sidekicks like Howard Stern had. I had a very good relationship and a good rapport with Dave, so his manager and the K-Rock folks felt it would be a good idea to have the occasional guests that would come and visit." Summing up the overall experience for her: "It was a really good experience, so out of my wheelhouse, but a really good experience."

Was Reissman part of the show prep besides being on-air talent? "I had to be up at 3:00 in the morning, down by K-Rock early, by 10:00 in the morning your day is over." She continued: "There wasn't as much Internet, so I had to have magazines delivered to my house. We had set the boards up to what he wanted to speak about, whether it was Britney Spears or this or that. It was very manual at the time and Dave had his own concepts of how he wanted to do that."

She remembered things similarly to Hutch as far as how things were behind the scenes on *The David Lee Roth Show*: "There was a lot of politics behind the scenes that I was around, but I kept out of it with the folks at K-Rock." Reissman offered some context that the CBS people perhaps should have considered further: "When you really think about it, when you think about who he replaced, let's think about that. That's probably the best radio guy in the history of radio. . . . They were on regular radio for how many years. . . . It was a lot of shoes to fill. Other folks felt that they should have gotten the job, so Dave was up against a lot. . . . There's a corporate perspective to things and then there's the artist's perspective and sometimes it doesn't mesh."

Apparently, Dave was not the only person being forced to change things up. "When I was in Manhattan, we were doing the show, they really reduced my function to just board op," began Hutch. "They didn't even want me to be on the air or up on the mic . . . I don't know whether it was the English accent. . . . So I basically was just a board op." He later joked, although perhaps not a joke: "I was probably the highest paid board op in the history of radio."

Fundamentally, Hutch knew outright that the kind of radio show that David Lee Roth planned on doing was not too similar to what CBS had envisioned. "Dave wanted to be different, and wanted the show to go a different way, and I was quite prepared to go along with him using music beds and some of the things he was doing and playing music. I don't know why CBS objected to that." He added: "But they wanted Free FM to be a talk show medium, and Dave wanted it to be more of a talk and entertainment kind of thing. . . . So we went along with it, some shows were great, some shows weren't so great. We had some great guests, we had some really, I thought not so great guests."

As a fan of both David Lee Roth and Howard Stern, I was surprised that Dave's radio show never featured an appearance by New York–based comedian and singer Billy Mira, who was a man Howard Stern often used on air to impersonate David Lee Roth. Roth was indeed familiar with Mira. "I remember he brought me up on Stern before in an interview," explained Mira to me in a 2021 interview. "We had mutual friends. I had heard that he had loved and he had hated me at the same time, because of the way that I had portrayed him, but he thought it was funny as hell. He was trying to really shake that kind of image because Dave is a really smart, intelligent guy." Added Mira: "I'm actually a huge fan of Dave, whatever he's doing for many reasons . . . I wish I had worked with him."

And that may have happened, had Roth's show stayed on the air long term, per Mira: "I don't know if it's true or not. . . . That they were gonna take me in there to work with him, possibly either as a sidekick or work with him as a personality or a writer with him on the show, which they thought would have been a great 'F.U.' to Howard. . . . They were trying desperately to keep that world in there." Expanded Mira: "I never asked Dave personally, like I said, but I heard it from pretty reliable sources that that was the case, and that would have been an honor."

Now a decade and a half removed from *The David Lee Roth Show*, Hutch does not think Roth takes the failure of the show personally. "Yeah, there was incident after incident after incident. And it was a wonderful ride, Darren." He laughed after finishing that sentence. "I think he was aware, but I don't think he cared. . . . I don't think it was that upsetting for him, he was going to come out fine."

Hutch, too, came out fine from the show. "I made a year contract out of it. I got my family attorney in Boston to draw up the contract, check it out, send it back to them, it came back, sent it back. A year's contract with a proviso in there that if something happened, which it did, that I'd get a decent severance. So I came out of there with a bit of money, but not a whole lot. It was really only six, seven months of work, you know?"

Although there is more to that story. "When we were coming to the end, and it was obvious that frustrations with growing and things weren't going to pan out completely. I'd come down after the show and call my wife and say, 'Hey, pay off the cars as quick as possible. Pay as many debts down as possible, because this might not go as long as we think it might.'" Of course that one yielded a laugh from Hutch. "When I made the decision to go and work with him, it was like, 'Oh, wow, man. Why the fuck not?' I kind of realized that it may be the last big thing that I did in radio . . . I kind of stored it away in my radio memories as a nice gig that I did for a few months with a great team of people, made some lovely friends, and I had a good time."

But Hutch, like Linda Reissman, does still think CBS Radio had it wrong when it came to its vision for Dave's show. "I remember walking down the corridor, with [Tom] Chiusano, because he was concerned about advertising, ratings, and revenue. I said to him, 'Tom, I don't think you know how long I've been in this business. Listen to this. . . . You lost the biggest voice in radio at that point, Howard, and you changed the call letters *and* the format. What the hell do you expect to have but a drop in ratings until they pick up again? It's going to take more than just a few weeks, it's going to take a year. You've got to build it.' . . . I was not impressed with the management team at CBS in New York. . . . So anyway, that may have been one of my parting comments to CBS. And yes, we did pay off both cars. So that's the end of the interview."

Ultimately, David Lee Roth did not close the chapter on *The David Lee Roth Show* with its final broadcast on April 21, 2006. Instead, he closed the chapter by successfully taking CBS Radio to court. Although settlement fees were confidential and court documents cannot be easily obtained, he reportedly walked away with a seven-figure fee.

While all of this was going on for DLR, things were relatively quiet in the Van Halen camp following its 2004 tour with Sammy Hagar. In mid-2006, Eddie Van Halen's first new music since the band's three new songs for the *Best of Both Worlds* collection was a pair of instrumental songs for an adult film—yes, you read that right—directed by Michael Ninn. The connection between Eddie Van Halen and that project was believed to be his then-girlfriend Janie's work in the "adult" industry as a publicist.

In celebration of the film *Sacred Sin*, Eddie Van Halen held an "open house" party, for which he performed a few songs with a backing band. Eric Dover—a musician whose credits include Jellyfish, Slash's Snakepit, Imperial Drag, and Alice Cooper—is a diehard Van Halen fan and was part of that band alongside former Mötley Crüe frontman John Corabi. In a 2022 interview, I asked Dover if he had known that event was going to be such a talked-about happening. "I didn't until I got there that day, actually. I really didn't understand the scope of how big the party was until it came time for us to play and I look out and there's all of these people in the backyard and there's a lot of famous people that I recognize. I'm like, 'Oh boy this is gonna really be something, isn't it?' 'Infamous' is the correct word for that party, because I've never experienced anything like that in my life."

Within a year of *The David Lee Roth Show* going off air, David Lee Roth would be inducted into the Rock & Roll Hall of Fame as a member of Van Halen in early 2007. However, both Roth and the Van Halen brothers declined to attend the induction ceremony, leaving Michael Anthony and Sammy Hagar to perform Van Halen hits alongside Paul Shaffer's band. No, not Brian Young, the real Paul Shaffer.

Speaking of Brian Young, he stopped working with Roth around the time of the end of *The David Lee Roth Show*. I pointed out to him that he is likely Roth's second-longest-tenured guitarist, behind Eddie Van Halen. He noted that to be "kind of cool" and then continued: "Dave's one of those guys who kind of sticks with what he knows," and you will likely keep your gig "as long as you don't do anything stupid."

Presently, *The David Lee Roth Show* is out of print and largely unlistenable at the moment, beyond some fan-reposted YouTube links. But some of its listeners from 2006 still look back on it fondly. "Before hearing DLR's K-Rock radio show, I had no idea about his personality," began Adam Paltrowitz. "I absolutely loved his show. He was so intelligent and engaging. He mediated and fostered healthy social, political, and societal debates and dialogs with his listeners. His intelligence as a radio host demonstrated the level of clarity, thought, and preparation he likely gave to every aspect of his vocal choices. Someone of that intelligence level doesn't half-ass what they are doing on the grand stage."

Van Halen Reunion

When David Lee Roth left Van Halen in 1985, he had already helmed two MTV music video hits and had a screenplay in production for CBS Pictures. When Roth recorded two new songs with Van Halen in 1996, he did not have an active major label recording deal and he was only a year or so fresh from a failed Las Vegas residency. When Roth attempted to regroup with Van Halen in the early 2000s, songs were written and demoed, but his bandmates opted to work with Sammy Hagar instead. And that is without factoring in their inability to reunite for 2007's Rock & Roll Hall of Fame induction.

While the announcement of a Van Halen reunion with David Lee Roth preceded March 2007's Rock & Roll Hall of Fame induction ceremony, most fans were not holding their breath that it was going to happen as planned. Fortunately, an official press conference came in August 2007 to announce a reunion tour, serving as the band's first public appearance with Roth since the 1996 MTV Video Music Awards.

Reporters had the chance to field questions to the band, and in that Q&A, DLR noted that they had already had "more rehearsal than in the last twenty summers" and that "this is not a reunion, this is a new band." Unlike the 1996 VMA interviews done by the band, Roth and Eddie Van Halen appeared to be on the same page overall as Eddie called their regrouping "a whole new beginning." Dave declared that they were already "plotting" the next album, saying "this is not like The Police," referring to the legendary trio's reunion never delivering new music. But for those keeping score, Roth had similarly slagged The Stones when referencing his regrouping with Van Halen at the 1996 VMAs press conference. He also would make a Michael Jackson joke, which is why he was allegedly fired from his 1995 Vegas residency. Thus, Vintage Dave was in full effect.

When speaking with The Police's Stewart Copeland in 2022, rather than asking him how he felt about Roth's 2007 press conference quip, I directed a question about whether he had ever met Roth before. "There was one [time]. I think it was the first MTV Awards, the first one they did where I think he was there, and I've always had a very high opinion of him. I thought his attitude was just so rock and roll." Continued Copeland: "The rest of us are all just trying to pretend to be rock stars, he was the real deal and you've got to love him. Not entirely sane, not entirely rational, but you know when it comes to being a rock star—and Tommy Lee as well, by the way—that's how you do it."

Widely known as the *Van Halen 2007–2008 North American Tour*, the seventy-six-show run kicked off in September 2007. Reportedly grossing over $93 million, it was of course Van Halen's highest-grossing tour to date. Featuring a scaled-down production, the onstage show did not feature extra musicians, special guests, or a whole lot of stage props. The setlist was rooted in Van Halen material recorded between 1978 and 1984. No Van Hagar, no DLR solo material, just classic Van Halen—only with Eddie's son Wolfgang Van Halen on bass and backing vocals; reports have emerged over the years that canned backing vocals were used on this tour, as originally sung by Michael Anthony. Touring wrapped in July 2008.

A little over a year later, Van Halen capitalized on gaming trends via the release of *Guitar Hero: Van Halen*, following other *Guitar Hero* editions starring Aerosmith and Metallica. Released to all major North American gaming consoles in December 2009, the game included twenty-five Van Halen songs and nineteen songs that were said to have been chosen by the members of Van Halen; Activision's then-head of music licensing Tim Riley said that most of the songs were chosen by Wolfgang Van Halen. While the game was commercially successful and undoubtedly helped raise awareness of Van Halen to a lot of potential new fans, it was criticized for having no mention of Michael Anthony, Gary Cherone, *or* Sammy Hagar.

Van Halen's next activity with David Lee Roth would be the *A Different Kind of Truth Tour*, as launched in early 2012 with a trio of warm-up shows.

Unique about this tour was that its namesake, *A Different Kind of Truth*, matched that of Van Halen's first studio album with Roth in nearly thirty years; that album also happened to be Van Halen's first (and only) studio album recorded for Interscope Records.

Once described by Roth "a sort of collaboration with Van Halen's past," a lot of the material heard on *A Different Kind of Truth* stemmed from old demos. One of the songs, "Honeybabysweetiedoll," resembles a song Roth debuted via the *No Holds Bar-B-Que* project called "Flex," which Lords of Acid fans may feel resembles "The Crablouse." While the most difficult part of making an album for artists is often creating great material for it, that was not the case with *A Different Kind of Truth*, as engineer Ross Hogarth told me in 2019.

"I have an amazingly beautiful relationship with Eddie, Alex, Wolf, the Van Halens. I love Ed like a brother and Al and I love Wolfie. They're like a wolfpack, pardon the pun on that," he laughed. "So that part of the recording was amazing. . . . Now, David Lee Roth, not so much." After laughing a bit more, he continued: "I just find him a very difficult person to deal with, and I think I'm not the only one. I think narcissism is an interesting thing. It's not the easiest thing to be around and I have a lot of respect for his intellect. I think he's absolutely brilliant."

Continued Hogarth: "But the making of this record had more to do with Wolf and the chemistry between him and his dad and his uncle, and the fact that if they really didn't need a singer they probably would have not done it with Dave. But they wanted to go back and create that Van Halen original [album] with Wolf in the band. Wolf had a huge part in making that record and inspiring his dad to wanna make music." After talking a bit more about how great it was to see a father and son working together as the Van Halens did, Hogarth added: "What a great thing for me to be able to shepherd this record through the winding path and across the finish line. It was an honor and a lot of it a pleasure, and there were definitely some tough times. For me, to this day I'm proud of the fact that I pulled it across the finish line, the first record with David Lee Roth since the '80s. . . . There's something to be said for finishing something, completion."

While John Shanks was the producer of *A Different Kind of Truth*, it was apparently not easy for the band to find a producer. Rick Rubin, a friend of Roth's, was said to be one of the producers initially talking with Van Halen.

When speaking with legendary producer (and Garbage drummer) Butch Vig in 2020, soon after Eddie's passing, I threw out a generic question as to whether or not he had any run-ins with Van Halen. Turns out, he did.

"I was contacted to work with Van Halen when I was doing *Wasting Light* with the Foo Fighters. I think they'd been working on a record for a long time, if this story holds right. They found a bunch of jams that they had done back in the day that Ted Templeman produced. . . . They had all these reel tape reels they were working on." He paused. "I was curious and interested and then I called a couple people and they said, 'You don't want to go down that path, it's a nightmare trying to get Eddie to focus. It's going to be a thankless job. You do not want to do that.' So I passed on it."

Continued Vig: "But Dave [Grohl] and Taylor [Hawkins] were kind of like, 'Maybe you should, dude. Maybe you should do it.' Then they're like, 'Maybe you shouldn't. Just let them do their thing.' I'm so sad now that Eddie is gone. He was such a brilliant musician, brilliant guitar player."

In support of *A Different Kind of Truth*, two music videos were released: "Tattoo" and "She's the Woman." The music for "Tattoo," the album's lead-off track and first single, is not far off from the video for "Jump," as it finds the band miming the song on a rehearsal stage. "She's the Woman," on the other hand, appears to be a mix of live footage, rehearsal footage, B-roll, and stills. Footage from an underplay concert that Van Halen performed at New York City's Cafe Wha?—yes, the same club run by Roth's previously mentioned Uncle Manny—appears in the "She's the Woman" video. Some trivia for "Tattoo," you ask? It is the only Van Halen studio recording on which Roth is credited as keyboardist.

Aside from the two music videos filmed, the band also created some unique content for YouTube via VEVO. One video, titled *The Downtown Sessions*, features Roth and the Van Halens—Wolfgang included—performing "Panama," "You and Your Blues" (from *A Different Kind of Truth*), and "Beautiful Girls" acoustically at Henson Recording Studios; this appears to be Van Halen's only commercially available acoustic appearance with Roth. Another video, titled *The Van Halen Interview*, has Roth, Eddie, and Alex talking among themselves without a moderator about the olden days. In that conversation, Roth discussed David Bowie and Mick Jagger being major influences on him as a singer, noting: "I consciously try to sound like other people to this day, and laugh when nobody gets it . . . nobody ever caught me." He also gets Eddie to tell a story about why the band never returned to Scotland after the late 1970s, which Roth appears to not have known the true reason for.

Many of the songs from *A Different Kind of Truth* would find their way into the tour's setlist on different nights, including "Tattoo," "She's the Woman," "China Town," "The Trouble with Never," "Bullethead," "Stay Frosty," and "Blood & Fire"; Roth told *USA Today* in 2013 that "Stay Frosty" was an entirely new song he had written fully and played guitar on. While performed as part of *The Downtown Sessions*, album track "You and Your Blues"—for which Roth filmed a "Song by Song" video explanation, as published to YouTube—appears to never have been played during the tour. Unlike the quartet's previous tour, *A Different Kind of Truth* brought Van Halen to Australia and Japan, ultimately grossing close to $50 million and ranking among the top ten grossing US tours of 2012.

Also of note about the *A Different Kind of Truth* tour was that most of its shows featured support from Kool & The Gang as an opening act. In 2019, I interviewed band leader Robert "Kool" Bell and asked whether he had been a big fan of Van Halen prior to the tour kickoff. "To be honest with you, I didn't know too much about Van Halen when that happened," he began. "They were going out on tour and we had just played in London, and David was there, and that festival had Coldplay and a lot of rock bands. We really rocked that crowd, so he called back to Eddie and Alex, 'Man, I've got the perfect group to do our tour: Kool & The Gang.'" He paused. "They said, 'Kool & The Gang? Dave, what've you been smoking?'"

Bell laughed and continued his story: "He said, 'Man, I just saw these guys rock this rock crowd. . . . They would be sharing the bill with us, like when Tina Turner went out with The Stones.' He told me, 'Most of my audience, 50 percent, is ladies. You guys wrote "Ladies Night," we had the big record "Jump," you guys had "Celebration," let's go out and do a party.' The rest is history. We did forty-eight shows with them."

After some time off for the band—not Dave, of course—Van Halen announced another tour in March 2015 via its website. Widely known as the *Van Halen 2015 Tour*, the group's forty-one shows ran between July and October 2015. While the band appeared on *American Bandstand* and regularly filmed promotional clips for local European markets in the late 1970s and early 1980s, the *Van Halen 2015 Tour* marked the first time that the

Roth-fronted Van Halen had performed on US television in decades. *Jimmy Kimmel Live*, *Ellen*, and the *Billboard Awards* were all blessed with performances by the mighty Van Halen; Roth notably busted his nose open while performing during the Kimmel performance.

The setlist for the tour was much closer to the band's performances in 2007 and 2008 than those of 2012 and 2013, sometimes not featuring any songs from *A Different Kind of Truth*. However, the setlist sometimes included songs that the band had not performed live since Roth left the band in the 1980s. In turn, these 2015 shows—as mostly opened by The Kenny Wayne Shepherd Band—were a return to form of sorts for Van Halen.

Evanescence drummer Will Hunt—who famously filled in for Tommy Lee for several Mötley Crüe shows—told me about seeing this tour during a conversation in 2022, with a story that resembles what engineer Ross Hogarth told me. "I knew Wolfgang via mutual friends. He was really good friends with Clint [Lowery], the Sevendust guys, and we kind of had the same some of circle of friends. At one point in Evanescence, our tour manager was this guy Marty Hom. . . . Marty was going to leave to go do the Van Halen tour, the last tour they did. . . . We had played the Golden Gods Awards out in LA and I flew home really early the next morning because Van Halen was playing in Orlando that night. . . . Marty and Wolfie were like, 'Come say hello, man.' I'd love to say hello and hang out for a little bit before the show."

Continued Hunt: "So we get there a little bit early, I go backstage with my wife, and we're hanging out with Wolfgang and just having an awesome conversation, this really cool thing. Then out of the blue, Eddie walks in and Eddie's got his guitar on and he's just doing a simple warm-up, just hanging out, and then it becomes this whole conversation." Hunt briefly paused. "Just to see those two guys, a father and son like that interact, they were like best friends and it reminded me of my father and me. . . . They had a golf game scheduled the next day here in Orlando. . . . They're talking to me about the tour, it was just normal shit, it was just a really incredible experience."

I asked Hunt if Dave was around, or if it was more of the commonly told story about Dave keeping his distance backstage. "Eddie mentioned it and he started kind of going into some things that at one point I'm like, 'Man, I'm not sure if I should be hearing this,' you know? . . . Dave is a tough nut to crack, man." Rumor has it that Dave's tour manager on this run was his former bassist Todd Jensen, who politely declined to be interviewed for this book.

Also unique about the *Van Halen 2015 Tour* was that it coincided with a live album, *Tokyo Dome Live in Concert*, released in March 2015. This title holds the significance of being Van Halen's first live album with Roth, its second live album overall—1993 saw the release of *Live: Right Here, Right Now* with Sammy Hagar—and the last official Van Halen release before Eddie Van Halen's passing in October 2020. Per Eddie, the band originally wanted to remix twenty-five demos that Van Halen had done before signing with Warner Bros., but the original tapes could not be found. A compilation of early club performances had also been considered, but sound quality was not up to his standards. In turn, we got *Tokyo Dome Live in Concert*—as recorded during the *A Different Kind of Truth* tour in June 2013—instead.

Remember earlier how David Lee Roth earned his New York State EMS Certification as of November 18, 2004? Well, the license obtained showed him to have renewed his certificate as of November 30, 2008—passing an exam in the process—keeping it active through December 31, 2011. In other words, Diamond Dave was still studying to be an EMT while part of Van Halen.

This was confirmed by Linda Reissman, who explained that he had kept ties with the EMS community even back on top with Van Halen: "When he was back with Van Halen or even doing some of his private concerts, he would hand me a boatload of tickets and tell me, 'Get the guys down here from St. Finney's or from Mary Immaculate.' . . . He took care of the EMS community, he was very caring about how they were perceived and he was perceived and the industry was perceived so."

Tokyo Dave

If you are looking through the discography of David Lee Roth, you will not see a full-length solo album released since 2003's *Diamond Dave* nor a Van Halen studio album with Roth for nearly thirty years beyond 2012's *A Different Kind of Truth*. Going through Van Halen's touring history with Roth, you will see big concerts done in 2007, 2008, 2012, 2013, and 2015. Yet the reality is that Roth has been a very busy man since the *David Lee Roth Show* ended in 2006.

In a 1986 *SPIN* cover story on Roth, he addressed the fact that Van Halen wanted to slow down after the *1984* tour, yet he did not: "I have money. I want to play, tour, go everywhere. Last time I was in Japan was 1979. Why can't we go to Japan? Because we don't make enough money. It's not 'We don't make money.' It's 'We don't make enough.' I always figured I got this gig partly because I want to travel, and if I don't make no scratch in Japan, fine. I don't make my money in New York, and if it's not New York, I'll make it in South America. It'll just go up and down, up and down, as my career goes on. You're not going to be popular in all countries all the time unless you're Julio Iglesias."

Perhaps the Julio Iglesias reference is a bit dated, but Diamond Dave did find his way back to Japan in 1988 via the *Skyscraper Tour*. He did go back to Japan on future tours as a solo artist and did finally make it back with Van Halen in 2013. The previously discussed 2015 *Tokyo Dome Live in Concert* live release documents one of those Van Halen return shows and actually finds Dave bantering in Japanese.

In an interview featured in Brad Tolinski and Chris Gill's book *Eruption: Conversations with Eddie Van Halen*, the guitarist makes light of Roth's Japanese skills, saying that a local said that he could not understand Roth's pronunciation of the language. I asked producer Kazuharu "Kaz" Shinagawa, who I was connected to via Tokyo-based author and historian Roland Kelts, about Roth's fluency. "He's not 100 percent fluent, but he knows some words and he always wanted to speak. . . . The man put a lot of effort into those kinds of things."

On episode 27 of *The Roth Show*—more on that series later—Roth discusses living in Japan for two years. While some Tokyo-based locals who knew Dave in that era said that he was there for "six months," an anonymous former Roth employee "who was there" provided a timeline for me: "He seemed to go over there right after the end of that 2012 tour. Maybe even that same summer. And he was still going there in 2015 as far as I know." So that person's explanation of the "six months" part? "It's possible that one group of people he engaged with for six months and then moved on to work with another group. . . . He'd go for a few months, then come back to California and then travel back to Japan. He was there to get his rather elaborate tattoo done."

While Roth definitely was there in Japan for some heavy-duty tattooing, one of his undertakings in that period was a short film known as *Tokyo Story*, as released in 2013. In addition to producer Kazuharu "Kaz" Shinagawa, I spoke with director Takurô Ishizaka and editor Aki Mizutani in 2022. The backstory of this one may remind you of how Marc Elmer described the creative process behind 2002's *No Holds Bar-B-Que*.

"Basically, I got a call from his assistant telling me he loves a film that I shot," began Takurô Ishizaka. "He wanted to meet me and then he was asking me whether I can meet him in Japan, because he was in Japan at the time. So I agree. My sister was a big fan of him, so I knew him, I didn't know him that well at that time. I research[ed] him and Van Halen, how big he is." Continued Ishizaka: "Where should we meet? He said just in front of Tower Records, so that's where I went. He had this big backpack with a hat on, he was standing right in front of the store and nobody noticed him because he was kind of disguised. . . . He told me, 'Let's go, let's eat and talk.'"

The story does not end there by any means. "He took me to this kinda izakaya bar place. . . . We sat down and we started talking about the movie and then why he was in Japan. . . . Then he basically started to tell me all that, what he wants to do, and then he was like, 'You want to do it or not?' That's basically, the beginning of the whole thing. He started telling me what he wants to do. . . . I have to listen to him and then kind of remember it at that time. I thought he's going to be writing something and then give it to me later."

Ishizaka then called Kazuharu "Kaz" Shinagawa about the project. "So I call Kaz and then see if he is interested to join. . . . That's the start of the production. I kind of wrote down what he said, and then I give it to him and then gradually he's changing the details into that, what we shot." So there was no script? "It wasn't even scripted, it's just a memo." That sentiment was echoed to me in 2022 by legendary sumo wrestler Konishiki, who appears in the film: "No script. . . . He just tells me, 'I want you to say this. I want you to do this.'"

Back to Ishizaka. "The first day I met him, there was a big snowstorm and I was late, like, two minutes. . . He yelled at me at the lobby, an 'I don't trust you' kind of thing, really close to my face. . . . 'Oh, I lost the job.'" Harkening back to Melissa Elena Reiner's recollection of the not-on-time keyboardist to the *No Holds Bar-B-Que* shoot, that seriously could have been the case. But fortunately they patched things up, and Ishizaka helped Roth understand some problems related to staffing and budget. "He's really easy to work with. . . . He seems like a really big star, big ego, whatever. But once it started, not really that much. He listened to us."

While Ishizaka confirmed that *Tokyo Story* was all filmed in one day, editor Aki Mizutani—like *No Holds Bar-B-Que* editor Marc Elmer—found herself in the editing bay a whole lot longer than the film shoot took. "It took me more than two weeks." She recalled Roth wanting specific music for the film. Shinagawa also recalled this. "I asked Dave, 'Hey, we may need more money for the music.' He agreed a hundred percent.' Ishizaka added, "He never negotiated. It's like, 'Okay, I'll pay.'"

Mizutani found him easy to work with when editing *Tokyo Story*, in spite of the long editing process. "One time he saw it and he was like, 'Oh, I like it.' He didn't give us much feedback. . . . Then we did the color sessions."

While Roth did not appear to do any promotion related to the film—which this author recalls being posted only to YouTube—Shinagawa remembers Roth having high hopes for it. "He explained to me that our movie was going to be kind of like a business card for him." He kept in touch with Roth even after the film was done. "I tried to hook him up with some of my friends, like a TV producer. . . . I really don't know what happened, but he just decided to go back to LA."

Ishizaka weighed in further on Roth's time in Japan. "I think when we met him, he really wanted to get his business going on in Japan. He was very energetic, thinking about doing something here." He then told a story about Roth auditioning for a film, possibly to play a role as a samurai, which he did not get. "That role has to be fluent [in Japanese]. So they went with somebody else."

Shortly after that, Ishizaka ran into Roth on the street in Tokyo and Roth definitely did not have his Diamond Dave smile on. "I could tell by the way I met him right before the day he was leaving for LA. . . . He was complaining about Tokyo. . . . Like, 'It's an unfair country.'" Added Shinagawa: "He just gave up on living here." Although as Ishizaka would note: "I can tell he's very good at making his own ground, wherever he goes."

The aforementioned Konishiki (aka Konishiki Yasokichi, Saleva'a Fuauli Atisano'e)—a mainstream Japanese celebrity for close to forty years—knew Dave before being cast in *Tokyo Story*. "The actual apartment he was renting was a place where I used to go and help . . . do volunteer work." He paused. "The big earthquake that happened, like, eleven years ago . . . I used to go and gather people to develop ways to go out and cook for people. We started a Koni Santa project and he was in the lobby and it wasn't me that approached him, because I didn't notice him, he didn't have the long hair anymore, he cut his hair. . . . He stopped me and said, 'Hey Konishiki,' he said it really like a real Japanese, he has a great accent. . . . He says it really clear as a Japanese accent. So I sat down, 'Hey, nice to meet you.'"

It was a mutual appreciation society. "He knew the [sumo] stable I was in and from there we became real, real close. He kept in touch with me and I thought, 'Let's take you to sumo.' I took him to a sumo stable, went to a couple of friends' dinners and stuff. He's a very, very, very intelligent man." He added: "He talks a lot. . . . He's so funny, he's got so much energy, man." But the reason Konishiki recalled Dave coming to Tokyo was not necessarily for tattooing. "He was a student of one of the best swordsmen."

Konishiki said that DLR did try to help him with business. "He was telling me how the business is all merchandising stuff. He does everything. . . . 'When you go to Texas, you cannot market the way you're marketing in LA because the groove is different, the movement is different, the looks are different.'" This advice was welcomed by Konishiki, who has also found success over the years as an actor, musician, television host, and live event promoter. "This guy knows what he's doing . . . I love his videos." After all, in more than one Roth interview he has referred to tour programs and merchandising as "communication" and "no different than writing lyrics." But Konishiki said their friendship was "more him asking me questions about sumo" as "he's so into the history of sumo."

So how exactly did Konishiki wind up in *Tokyo Story*? "He called me up, 'Hey, I have this little movie thing that I want to do. You want to be in it? Just let me know.'" And he brought other people into the project, per Dave's request. "'I need some guys that look kind of yakuza, can you get all these guys?' . . . They're friends of mine, so I got them to be part of the video." But Konishiki had no idea what Roth had envisioned for the film, or where it would appear: "I didn't know that was going to be part of the [Van Halen] tour, people were watching and people would call me, 'Hey, I saw you at the Tokyo Dome . . . I cannot believe you're part of it.'"

Earlier in the chapter, *The Roth Show* was mentioned. A video series published to Roth's YouTube channel, episodes of the show generally consisted of Roth discussing a topic of interest (for example, sumo, martial arts, tattoos, sarcasm), as paired with archival clips and background music. It was arguably somewhere in between *No Holds Bar-B-Que*, *Dave TV*, and *The David Lee Roth Show*.

Oftentimes, the background music on *The Roth Show* was music you could not hear anywhere else. In one episode, there was an acapella cover of Pharrell Williams' "Happy," which he was noted to have recorded in 2014 at Onkio Haus in Ginza, Tokyo. The end of the published video features Dave backstage singing "Happy" with acapella group Naturally 7.

But *The Roth Show* and *Tokyo Story* were not Roth's only creative endeavors while in Tokyo. In this era, Roth sometimes hosted the *Tokyo High Power Style* program on a local Tokyo radio station alongside his assistant Etsuko. He promoted this series in some interviews, hosting audio of it on DavidLeeRoth.com. However, these broadcasts have since been removed from that website.

In a 2013 interview with *USA Today*, Roth mentioned that he had not yet given up his homes in Pasadena or New York and was eager to do more with

Van Halen. He also aired some dirty laundry, however: "I'm not sure what's in Ed's mind at this point. . . . Truth be told, Edward and I haven't written a new song in twenty years." Strangely, in the same interview he referred to speaking with Alex Van Halen on a daily basis and that the aforementioned Konishiki would "lend me his house in Hawaii" for Van Halen to write in.

Instead, Roth told *USA Today* about keeping creative via material he had written and recorded with John 5; he had neglected to mention John 5 as being the "John Lowery" he had cowritten much of 1997's *DLR Band* album with. He intended these songs for a "jukebox musical" after seeing what the creators of *South Park* did via *The Book of Mormon*. The songs named in this article from that collection were "Somewhere Over the Rainbow Bar & Grill," "Giddy Up," "Alligator Pants," and "The Shit that Killed Elvis." Roth also clarified that these songs had been offered to the Van Halens and subsequently declined.

Bringing things full circle, a 2013 episode of *South Park* titled "Ginger Cow" features an animated Van Halen performing in Jerusalem at the unification rally of Christianity, Islam, and Judaism. Before a packed stadium full of followers of all three religions, the symbols of each faith melded together on a projected screen to form the Van Halen "wings" band logo. In the episode, the animated Van Halen performs "Ain't Talkin' 'Bout Love" and a CNN reporter then proclaims a ten-year peace agreement between the faiths.

While Kazuharu "Kaz" Shinagawa, Takurô Ishizaka, and Aki Mizutani have not heard from David Lee Roth in recent years, Shinagawa remains fond of Roth: "He did support me getting my green card. I think I'm the only one that has a support letter from David Lee Roth." I repeated that back to make sure I heard that correctly, and I did. "I put the letter on the top of the application, of course, for sure. Then all the embassy people were asking me, 'How do you know him?' That was a fun moment for me."

Before, During, and After "Tokyo Dave"

While David Lee Roth spent a lot of time in Japan between 2012 and 2015 and was also on tour a bunch during those years, he also kept pretty active in and around New York and California. The sort of stuff that keeps you wondering how one person manages to keep so active.

Muffs bassist Ronnie Barnett was introduced to me by Tsar drummer Steve Lauden (aka prolific author S. W. Lauden) in 2022. "I was working in a store in Pasadena called Penny Lane . . . I was there one Sunday morning. I was the only one there, this guy comes in with a baseball hat. There was a new Rolling Stone mono box set that had come out and he's like, 'You have that new Rolling Stones box set?' I'm like, 'No, we didn't order it. We didn't want to invest in a $200 item that somebody might not buy. He was like, 'Well, where's the section? Can you show me the section?' So I show him the section."

Continues Barnett: "He shops for like ten minutes and then comes up with some CDs. There was a Stones CD . . . and a Stevie Wonder CD. He puts down his credit card, puts down his ID. I pick up the ID, I've even gone as far as asking if he wants a bag at this point, I look at the ID, 'David Lee Roth.' I didn't recognize him. . . . In my head, I'm like, 'Holy shit.' I said, 'I'm sorry I didn't recognize you. I love you. Can I get a hug?' I stretched out my arms and he hugged me, and I started telling him how the reunion tour was one of the best nights of my life, because it truly was. I thought they were really good on that tour. I remember high-fiving the usher as I left at the end of the show."

Roth surprisingly kept the conversation going. "So I told him all this and he's like, 'Oh thanks. We're going in next week to start a record.' . . . I'm like, 'Can I get a picture?' and he's like, 'Sure.' I did it selfie style and it came out kind of crooked, but I'm like, 'Thank you.' He was like, 'How'd it come out? Is it okay?' 'It'll work. It's fine.' He's like, 'No, no, no, let's get it right.' There's one other customer in the store, so I asked him to take the photo. We took the photo and parted ways. He could not have been nicer."

Based on the timeline of DLR recording *A Different Kind of Truth* "next week," that story appears to have taken place in 2010. But Barnett would encounter Diamond Dave again just a few years later. "'DavidLeeRothRocks' was already my email address for a long time. . . . [On Instagram] I just picked '@DavidLeeRoth.' It was available. So that was my name for a good six years until one day I woke up . . . I got an email at the [Muffs] band's email address. It was a very formal letter and it, and it said, 'We represent'— and I'll quote here—'the famous author, a singer, songwriter, author and actor, David Lee Roth.' . . . 'You have this name, our client can't do business on Instagram with it.' But basically the tone of the letter was like, 'What do you want for it?' So my initial reaction is like, 'Look, I will give my idol his name.' This is in my head. I'm like, 'How about we meet, we sign the paperwork together, we take a photo together. We start our respective Instagram accounts from there.'"

Unfortunately that interaction was just in Barnett's head, apparently. "The very next day I got a lawyer from them where they were being such pricks, that I called my lawyer friend. I'm like, 'Look, can you help me with this?' Basically it was said that the follow-up letter was just like, 'Look, we can take this name from you and we can do all this to you.' So my friend, he's a music lawyer, he actually knew the people that were representing them and worked out this thing." Barnett signed some contracts and got paid. "I signed these contracts. . . . In the contract I had to delete every photo, this was like 1,500 photos, and at that point, it was one by one . . . I give him my password, which was 'panama,' and I didn't start a new account for a while."

Not the end of the story, though. "But I remember the day, a couple months went by, and the first David Lee Roth Instagram posting came out and I felt a little weird about it, to be honest. It was obviously his people. It was like a studio shot, 'Welcome to the Mojo Dojo,' or whatever. If you go back in his account and look and go all the way back for a brief moment in time, I was more popular than David Lee Roth on his Instagram account. Like the comments are still there, 'Where's Ronnie? You're not Ronnie?'"

Also in this era, episodes of *The Roth Show* sometimes included unreleased music in the background. One case being episode 3 featuring a song called "One Piece Thermo-Molded Country Plastic Chair," as cowritten with top-tier country songwriter Scotty Emerick. I connected with Emerick by phone in 2021 and asked how exactly that collaboration happened.

"Meeting him was wild. I was friends with his bus driver, a lady named Valerie, and she used to drive the bus for Blake Shelton. . . . They called me one day and David Lee Roth wanted some really good cowboy boots. Well, she called me knowing that I would probably know where to get some, and inadvertently she played him some of my songs and stuff," began Emerick.

Emerick continued: "He asked if he could fly me out to LA and record and he wanted me to bring a couple guitars . . . I didn't know what to expect and I met him and he just was like, 'Go out there on the studio floor and just play whatever.' So I just played off the top of my head a guitar chord progression and I saw he had these lyrics . . . that he had printed out and he was sifting through and that's what he came up with." How long did this all take to write and record? "It was just one day." Literally recorded in one take, he recalls.

Yet it is far from one of Emerick's career highlights: "To be honest with you I didn't even listen to it again . . . I just played the chord progression and he put whatever he had to it." He retained publishing? "I think he paid me for the day and after that I have my end of the publishing." Emerick added with a laugh: "But there was no money to be had from it." The song remains posted to Roth's YouTube channel, but not for sale or streaming via any traditional music retail outlets, much like "Ain't No Christmas," another *Roth Show* exclusive that some think is about him leaving Van Halen again in 2015.

In rewatching some episodes of the *Roth Show* as research for *DLR Book*, I noticed that the John 5–written "Giddy Up"—which did not get an official release until 2021—actually appeared as background instrumental music in an episode. I asked a former Roth staffer about this, whether his editors chose any of the music used in *Roth Show*, or he himself was picking things from his archives. "As for 'Giddy Up,' that was definitely a Dave decision. With something unreleased like that there was *no way* I was going to just plop that song into a timeline. . . . While I worked for DLR no one made decisions for Dave except for Dave." That same individual was asked whether Roth has as much unreleased material as he claimed in the *Crazy from the Heat* memoir. "He does have hundreds of things that are unreleased, I've heard copies of some of them, there are masters kept somewhere safe but not on his property."

When speaking with John 5 in 2019, prior to "Somewhere Over the Rainbow Bar & Grill" being released as a one-off in 2020, I asked about the status of the songs he had written with Roth in the 2010s. He answered: "I don't know when that record will come out." I had referred to it as a concept record, in having read Roth's "jukebox musical" comments, yet he had a different recollection of the sessions: "I don't think it was a concept record, it doesn't sound like a concept record to me, but it does sound like an amazing David Lee Roth record."

A few years later, after a few songs from the sessions had come out, I brought up the album to John 5 in 2021. I posed a question about whether he finds out in advance that the songs are going to come out. "I don't get a notice, which is funny. I just find out on Blabbermouth or something." He then discussed another song, which Roth did not name in the 2013 *USA Today* article. "There's a song that I just can't wait for Dave to release, it's called 'Nothing Could Have Stopped Us.' . . . It's my favorite song that I've ever done with Dave. It is beautiful, I don't know why he's not releasing that one yet, and I just can't wait for people to hear that one because it's about Van Halen . . . I'm really looking forward to him releasing that one." Eventually released as "Nothing Could Have Stopped Us Back Then Anyway," the song would eventually get an official digital release and accompanying music video in July 2022; Internet-based rumors have dated the recording sessions for this song as far as back as 2007.

Overall, John 5 remains enthusiastic about those sessions, which reportedly also included drummer Gregg Bissonette, keyboardist Brett Tuggle, and percussionist Luis Conte. "We had a blast, a lot of laughs, a lot of fun. I'm just so happy that I had that cool working vibe with Dave. We could just jump into the studio any time and knock out some songs." Continued John 5 with a tone of gratitude: "I'm very lucky because not a lot of people did get a chance to do that with Dave . . . I remember we were just all in there together and we were all just doing it together. Kind of like the old days and he wanted to do it like that. . . . We had so much fun doing it and it's one of my fondest memories." When I inquired about when exactly all of this went down, he clarified that they were "an amalgamation of different years and different times." Strangely, when approaching John 5 for another interview in 2022 after the release of "Nothing Could Have Stopped Us Back Then Anyway," this author's request was denied via Roth's management, who is not known to handle John 5 as a client.

Speaking of Gregg Bissonette and Brett Tuggle, history was nearly made in November 2015 as the "Yankee Rose Band"—including Bissonette, Tuggle, Steve Vai, and Billy Sheehan—nearly reunited then. At a jam night at a Lucky Strike bowling alley in Los Angeles. Steel Panther's Michael Starr (Ralph Saenz from The Atomic Punks) was set to sing lead vocals, but when word got out to Roth about this happening, he then wanted to take over for Starr.

Explained Starr, who still showed up: "There was supposed to be a reunion of the *Eat 'Em and Smile* band and they were going to get ready to go onstage and I knew somebody back there. I got back there and I started talking to Dave and his accountant was an accountant that I used to use. That sounds so douchey." He laughed and then continued: "Basically it was some woman that was smarter than me that paid bills for me and I paid her for it, and I'm like, 'Oh my god, you're working with David Lee Roth, that's crazy." She goes, "Yeah, here's my card, and Dave really would like to get up and jam with you guys.' I was like, 'Holy shit.' I reached out and he said, 'No.' So I think she was full of shit."

Reenter Frank Meyer, who was also there that night. "[Journalist and author] Lyndsey Parker, because she's like, that's my ride or die, she's my partner in crime, my friend for life. She heard about it and was like, 'We're going, right?' I'm like, 'Yes, we are.' She pulled her journalist strings and got us in." Continued Meyer: "As I was standing outside waiting for Lyndsey, Dave's limo pulled up and he got up and a bunch of reporters and stuff swarmed him and I just sort of didn't want to bother him. But he walked by and he looked at me and he goes, 'Mr. Meyer.' . . . He does have a good memory, I'll tell you that."

Television and film composer Jeff Cardoni had planned on being there for the reunion. "I was so pissed because I had to go out of town for it . . . I was just texting my friend who was in line the whole time."

Meyer did find his way inside Lucky Strike, as expected: "We saw them checking instruments and tuning [under a curtain]. Then we saw a bunch of guys in firemen's boots walk out, then everyone left the stage. Then the house lights went up and the show was over. . . . It was seconds away from happening." While Roth never attempted to reschedule this, Vai, Bissonette, Sheehan, and Tuggle did perform together in January 2019 at a NAMM event, performing "Shyboy" and having Durga McBroom perform her line from the "Yankee Rose" video before the band played.

Per my 2021 interview with Billy Sheehan—which occurred prior to the tragic passing of Brett Tuggle—the door is and was always open for Roth to play with him and band. "I'd love to play together again too, but who knows? It's Dave's gig. If he wants to, I know myself, Steve, and Gregg, we've expressed many times we'd love to. We just had a get-together. The last Winery Dogs session, I took a night off and went to Steve's house and met Gregg and we made some pizzas and talked, told stories. We get together often and tell stories from the old days. It's a riot, it's so much fun, we have a blast." And Sheehan does believe he has a "pro-shot" *Eat 'Em and Smile* live concert video in his collection still: "I've got to double check. . . . When we get off [the call] I'm gonna double check and make sure it's there."

As If Dave Needed More to Do

To recap, David Lee Roth did a lot of touring with Van Halen between 2007 and 2015. He recorded a well-received studio album with Van Halen in 2010 and 2011. He lived in Japan for around two years between 2012 and 2015. He recorded a batch of songs with former guitarist John 5. He made a short film. He started up a radio show. He launched a YouTube series. He recorded other stuff. And that is far from everything he had going on.

Per the United States Patent & Trademark Office, Roth trademarked his own name for recording purposes in 2016. However, his 2016 trademarking of "Road Tested by David Lee Roth"—via "Russ World, LLC," a corporation named after his dog Russ—was abandoned the following year. Similar fate for the numerous trademarks, which were registered and ultimately abandoned, including the following: "Sunquito," "The East River Surf Shop, "The Daily Catastrophe," "Dark Ocean Society," "Dries Tight," "Bug Shot," "Ink Nation," "Ink Tattoo Wipes," and "El Roth." Many of Roth's trademarks appear to have been related to INK The Original, a tattoo skincare company believed to have been launched by Roth with entrepreneur Ami James in 2018. The trademark for "Wawazat!! Records" was also abandoned in 2022—even though new music was released to digital streaming services with "Wawazat" in the copyright line—while that same year "The Soggy Bottom" was trademarked by Team Roth.

Speaking of Russ, Roth's beloved dog—as briefly heard on *A Different Kind of Truth*—who had passed in 2019, there were plenty of sightings of Roth around Pasadena in the 2010s with relation to Russ. As covered by the *Los Angeles Times* in 2012, Roth's "dog world videos" showed him and his "sheep-dogs" doing "herding dog moves." Roth told the publication: "We compete nationally with these dogs. . . . We got invited to the Nationals, but we didn't quite make it; we were making the Van Halen record."

Throughout Diamond Dave's tenure with Van Halen, he played guitar onstage during only one song: "Ice Cream Man." This led many to specu-late that he knew only a few chords on the guitar. However, recordings did emerge—presumed to have been recorded somewhere between 2004 and 2011—with Roth playing alongside his long-time guitar teacher Jeff Falkowski. This included a take on "Take Sarava," which DLR sang in Portu-guese; frequent language lessons were referenced during my 2003 interview with the singer.

Roth also popped up at a variety of benefit shows, performing free of cost for charitable reasons. One of them was at the 2018 Houston Grand Opera Ball, as requested by Roth's first cousin Dr. Jack A. Roth and wife Dr. Kath-erine Roth. "He's just really a nice guy. . . . It was just amazing and the ball was highly successful. We raised $1.2 million, we had about five hundred in attendance. . . . Everybody rushed the stage. We were very fortunate to have him and he was terrific. We spent some time with him there."

Getting a little more color on DLR from his cousin Jack, the family is defi-nitely proud of the Rock & Roll Hall of Famer's accomplishments. "David was clearly the most talented, no question about that. He's had a terrific career." Added Jack: "I always had the fantasy of being a rock singer, but I didn't get anywhere because I didn't have any talents." He laughed at that one, although to his credit, Jack was a member of the American Federation of Musicians as a trumpet player in his high school days.

While many financially stable, Hall of Fame–inducted musicians in their sixties would have slowed down at this point in their life, that was never for the plan for Diamond Dave. Instead, what was about to follow would be a massive undertaking: his third attempt at a Las Vegas residency.

Vegas

Part III

As noted in episode 27 of *The Roth Show*—published in late 2019—referencing his then-upcoming Las Vegas residency at the House of Blues, David Lee Roth had run "eighty rehearsals for Vegas." Yet in speaking with many of the players involved, that number of band rehearsals is far lower than what actually took place.

When speaking with Roth's former guitarist Rocket Ritchotte, he included his son Kane in the conversation. Kane Ritchotte is a successful actor and musician, and in recent years he has toured with Portugal. The Man and Haim. In 2018, he was slated to be part of the DLR band for some shows in Vegas.

"I think if we didn't do this [interview], it would be entirely undocumented," began Kane Ritchotte. "This was before the pandemic when Brett Tuggle was musical director. Dave was wanting to do gigs. . . . My friend Chris Greatti was hired as the guitar player. He wanted to hire a young band. . . . Chris recommended me for the gig, not knowing that not only had my dad previously played with Dave, but I'm really good friends with Brett Tuggle, who was MD'ing and playing keyboards and stuff. So I came to a soft audition. Those auditions kind of turned into a couple of weeks of rehearsal."

So did Ritchotte know a lot about the gig, as far as how long it was set to go for? "We didn't really know what we were rehearsing for. . . . So I did like two weeks of rehearsals and then the management came and they're like, 'Cool, so we're going to do this residency in Vegas. It's going to be from this time to this time.' And I had conflicts, I couldn't do it. So I was like, 'I can't do it.'" Added Ritchotte with a laugh: "I essentially played with Dave for a couple of weeks and entirely in private."

Per Kane, an email came from the management about how to act. "'We want you guys to come to rehearsal an hour before Dave. Just get warm, get loose, whatever. Then Dave will come up.' This is day one. I haven't met him yet. So we come down, we're playing with sounding great, whatever. Then his manager goes, 'Okay, cool, guys. So Dave is going to be here in about five minutes. He'd like you to start a song. He'll listen from outside. If he likes it, he'll come in.'" Added Rocket: "That's what he used to do. He just stays upstairs and listen to us downstairs."

Turns out that Dave showed up earlier than expected, as Kane remembers it: "We slammed into a song with a lot of steam behind it. I can't remember what it was. Literally like two seconds, we didn't even get beyond the intro. Dave busts the door open, comes in, gets us to stop. He goes, 'Alright, so you guys can play.' Then he just started talking about his philosophy on life and where he came from, all that stuff for the rest of the rehearsal." Continued Kane: "We didn't play another note. That was day one. And it was about three hours. It was like a TED Talk, but it was fascinating."

So the thing about "eighty rehearsals" from DLR, as it turns out, may not have included him singing with the band, per Kane: "He never sang. I never heard him sing one time, not for the two weeks. . . . He would jump in with a bit. . . . We'd get a little glimpse, but he would just walk around onstage to each musician and just watch what you were doing. . . . If it didn't faze you, you'd kind of get him to smile and walk to the next guy, and just do that all day long."

Kane recalled the band rehearsing in a power trio setup, plus Dave: "It was only Chris Greatti [on guitar]. So when he would take a solo, it would be bass and drums like a record. It was so cool. It had this, like, a Hendrix Experience feel to it. It was pretty raucous and rad."

Apparently Kane was not the only Ritchotte approached about this gig, per Rocket Ritchotte: "Tug called me about Kane and he said, 'Rock, are you interested?' Absolutely not. I'm not doing that again." Another gig of note for Rocket Ritchotte was his work on the television show *Friends*, which he did alongside fellow DLR band alumni Matt and Gregg Bissonette: "That's the best gig I ever, ever got. I did that for nine years, nine seasons. The residuals are fantastic. It's like the best thing, mailbox money."

Kane was not the only casualty from those rehearsals, as it turns out. "I think the only person who played those shows, who was in the initial rehearsals with us was this guy, Ryan Wheeler, who was playing bass. I think it was entirely different. Everybody else. I think Chris got fired." More on Ryan Wheeler to follow. "It was the first day of rehearsal, I was kind of told by Chris. . . . 'Try to learn this stuff pretty verbatim, nobody wants to hear it any different, just do it the way it's on the record.'"

A little more perspective as to why the band's lineup may have changed a lot of times: "He was really specific about endings of songs, like wanting them to be this big kind of dramatic big band ending. He was really specific about counting songs off with a lot of gusto, even though, even in rehearsal." In the course of the conversation, he explained that Roth could be "hard" on the drummer at times. "It was just a top count, but if you didn't give him a lot of energy upfront with the song, it would not start and we would do it again."

Altogether, Kane looks back on the rehearsals favorably, laughing at the quirks. "I love Van Halen because my dad loves Van Halen. Who doesn't love Van Halen? . . . All the same nuttiness that my dad always described to me, it was there." He added: "I got such a kick out of it. But I can imagine that if it was a contemporary of mine or something like that, not this rock legend who was not of my generation. . . . If he was an equal to me, he would probably drive me crazy. But because he's Dave Roth, the rock icon, and he made so much music I love so much, there's so many great stories about him that I loved that whole thing. I loved that experience."

Next on the drum throne for Diamond Dave after Kane was Michael Musselman, who had studied under Gregg Bissonette. "Gregg Bissonette is the nicest guy on the planet. He remembers you if you haven't seen him in seven years and you show up to the NAMM convention."

Bissonette connection aside, Musselman wound up in the DLR camp via another Roth backing musician, Brett Tuggle. "So Brett sends me an email and says, 'Learn these songs.' It's "Hot for Teacher," it's "Runnin' with the Devil." . . . I get this list of songs to learn. Brett has worked with everybody and Fleetwood Mac was going through some changes because they were kicking out Lindsey Buckingham and they were getting Mike Campbell in there. Brett and Lindsey are closer than Brett is with anybody else . . . I thought Brett was gonna say, 'Hey, Lindsey's going on tour,' and that would have my mind just as well. But he sends me 'Hot for Teacher' and I immediately know, 'Holy shit, Dave is going out. It's happening.'"

Musselman did not have the gig necessarily, just more of a friendly recommendation. "I meet with Greatti and Ryan Wheeler in a rehearsal, a pay-by-the-hour rehearsal space in Echo Park. As I'm setting up, I set up a China cymbal and for some weird reason it triggers Ryan Wheeler to play King Crimson from the album *Red*." Musselman paused. "I grew up listening to that shit, I hit my China on accident while I'm setting it up and he goes right into the riff and I just go in with him and I play until I can't remember what the hell happens next. Ryan looked up at Greatti and just went, 'He's got the gig.'"

I asked Musselman about that original lineup and how long he remembered rehearsals going on for. "Greatti was the original. It started there and then: Greatti got his buddy and bandmate Ryan Wheeler and then Gerri [Leonard] the manager called Brett. She said, 'Come be the boss of these youngins.' Greatti had worked with this guy named Tom Syrowski and they just remembered him from some random session and said, 'He's the guy, Greatti's the guy.'" After Kane's scheduling did not work out, it boiled down to a family connection for Musselman. "Brett's son, Matt Tuggle, he's an audio engineer, he used to work at Henson [Studios]. . . . He was having an engagement party and I saw Brett there, and Brett said, 'Mikey, what's going on with you?' I said, 'I have a show in Austin, Texas, and then I'm completely free.' I think that was like 2018 or something. Then Brett goes, 'Alright, well, look in your email. I'm going to email you some stuff.'"

Turns out that Kane and Musselman did know one another. "Brett Tuggle's son and I were in a band and we would always play shows with Kane's bands. . . . So I was always playing with Kane and his friends were like dating some of my friends. I was always seeing him and when I found out that he was the first drummer for this, those Vegas shows, I was so stoked. I was like, 'He's going to nail it.' I love watching him, he's so amazing, he studied under Gregg Bissonette as well." Further onto the small world tip, Brett Tuggle's son Matt took guitar lessons from former Roth guitarist Brian Young as a teenager, and both Bissonette and Musselman have played with Ryan Cabrera.

While Brett Tuggle is primarily thought of as a keyboardist, turns out he had plenty more to do as part of this guy. "I think what happened was that

Dave wanted, instead of just one guitar player, he wanted two, rhythm and lead. So Brett started playing guitar on most of the songs and then playing a Rhodes or B3 organ . . . Brett was switching between rhythm guitar and then keyboards."

Musselman agreed with Ritchotte that rehearsals under DLR were not lax for musicians. "It demands a lot from your body. We would rehearse four times a week, five times a week, four or five hours, just hitting it over and over and over. I think we wanted to keep Brett fresh, so it's like, 'Let's give rhythm guitar to Brett.'" Enter Danny Wagner. "Danny was supposed to be the drum tech."

Continued Musselman about Wagner: "Danny was doing keyboards, but when he wasn't doing keyboards, he was playing a lot of synthesized bass, doing the low end with his left hand. If you see some of the shows he's just pressing with one finger, he's going from note to note. Something like 'Just Like Paradise,' which I believe is keyboard bass on the recording, he would play keys on that with some dialed-in patch. Where Brett was able to get the actual sound from some old weird floppy disc that's been converted and now it's in his keyboard."

Rocket Ritchotte echoed what Musselman had said at the end of that last one. "Tug's been in and out. Dave used to always call Tug when he went on the road, even if Tug wasn't on the road with him, 'cause he needed to get the keyboards for 'Jump.'" Kane Ritchotte agreed. "Brett has the stuff off the record. I was talking to him in rehearsal. . . . Back in the day when you guys were all playing together, he got the tapes from Warner, transferred them. So he could get the 'Jump' keyboard patch, then sample that off the record, he got some background vocals. . . . He has this keyboard just full of these awesome Van Halen stems."

However, when playing Kane Ritchotte was rehearsing with the band—before Danny Wagner joined—he did not remember keyboard samples being used: "The part that I liked most, conceptually about the way the rehearsals were being run and the show was going to happen when I was playing, it was no tracks. It was no click. It was completely wide open and free."

I asked Warrant guitarist Joey Allen about former Warrant drummer and keyboardist Danny Wagner, who declined to be interviewed for the book. Allen never met Wagner, as it turns out. "When I was out [of Warrant], there were a bunch of different drummers in Warrant, I think it kind of got Spinal

Tap-y, to be honest with you. After Steven [Sweet] and I left after the first three records, there were many lineup changes in Warrant and there were some guys I knew and some guys I didn't know. I never met Danny but I heard good things about him from the other guys, that he was a nice guy. I heard that when Dave was on that tour with Danny playing keyboards that he said some nice things about Warrant, even though he slags 'hair bands' and a lot of bands that had some Van Halen in their blood."

Musselman also recalled not seeing Diamond Dave much during rehearsals, like Kane. "We rehearsed with Brett, Greatti, and Ryan for, like, three weeks. We did not see Dave at all. Dave just wanted us to just grind it out and get together as a unit, his thought process behind the *Eat 'Em and Smile* crew. . . . Just make them sound like they've been together for ten years when it's really been six months. So that's how it started and it shape shifted and evolved in many ways." He further noted: "There were three guitar players onstage at one point."

Any idea why the lineup changed so many times? "If I had to guess what my old boss Dave was thinking, it's probably he's just looking for perfection. He's like, 'What is gonna be the right combo?'" Who was that third guitarist? "We had a guitar player, who's more of like a Keith Richards kind of guy. He's so fucking cool, his name is Andrew Martin and he's an amazing guitar player. He worked with Greatti on a lot of stuff."

"Turns out that Brett Tuggle, Chris Greatti, and Andrew Martin did perform in a public setting once with Roth," as Musselman recalled. "There was one 'friends and family' show where it was Brett doing keys and guitar, Andrew doing guitar, Chris Greatti doing guitar, and then Ryan and I doing our thing. It was a wild show." Footage from this show was initially used in promotional materials published to YouTube, and Greatti and Tuggle can be seen in it.

Lineup aside, did Musselman remember the band's setlist changing much over time? "It was going to be a revolving setlist. . . . We might have got up to twenty-one songs. . . . When it came to the shows, we would write the setlist." Surprising, because many recall Roth calling the shots, creatively speaking. "He would sit us all together and Dave would eat some tacos and say, 'What do you guys want to play?' We're all fans of this legend that we're with and he's just asking us, 'What do you guys want to do?' So we're like, 'Tobacco Road.' We're shouting out some deep cuts from the solo stuff or from Van

Halen and he would be like, 'Alright.' . . . Obviously we did 'Big Train' and that was something he really wanted to play. He made sure we knew 'Big Train.'"

Shows from this era were missing one of Roth's biggest solo hits, "Yankee Rose." Any idea why, Mike? "What he said about 'Yankee Rose,' he said he thought it was too much of a novelty song. He thought you could only play that song on the Fourth of July." Any other solo songs he remembers rehearsing? "We learned 'She's My Machine' from *Your Filthy Little Mouth* . . . I feel like that song took a little bit more energy or brain power for me to remember everything that's happening. . . . Those are the only two from that album that we did."

A surprising addition to the setlist was a cover of "Fresh Out" by Christone "Kingfish" Ingram. When interviewing Kingfish in 2022, I threw in a question as to whether he was familiar with Roth's cover of his song. "Actually the morning after it happened, when he did that show in Vegas, someone sent it to me and we all listened to it. I pretty much enjoy his version of it. It's very slow, raw, and gritty, for sure." Is he otherwise a fan of Roth and Van Halen? "Oh most definitely, most definitely."

With Tuggle gone from the band, Musselman recalls control shifting over to Ryan Wheeler. "Dave just pointed to him and said, 'You're in charge.' What that meant was, 'Make sure the guitars are in tune, they're loud enough, my vocals sound a specific way,' because we would show up two or three hours before a rehearsal and make sure that everything is perfect before Dave gets in there. That was Ryan's job and then he kind of took on some more responsibilities behind the scenes, working with Dave's engineer [Tom Syrowski]. . . . All of that shit was up to Ryan."

Ryan Wheeler, who remains in Roth's band as of this book's writing and had moved to Los Angeles from New Jersey only a few months before getting the gig, also came into the DLR picture via an previously mentioned guitarist. "I got the gig through my dear friend Chris Greatti, whom I've known since 2007." Frankie Lindia, who would find his way into the Roth band as a guitarist, described Greatti as a "great player, great guy."

While speaking with Frankie Lindia in 2021, I asked how he wound up in the Roth band. "My buddy Brent [Woods]—who plays for Sebastian Bach—a family friend of mine, he was like, 'Roth needs a guitar player. Would you want to try out? I can throw your name around.' That was when Al [Estrada] was playing and I came in." Al Estrada would ultimately replace Chris Greatti. "It was right after the three [guitar lineup]."

How much of the DLR and Van Halen catalogs did Frankie Lindia know before getting the gig? "I started playing because of Van Halen back when I was in sixth grade. My dad showed me Van Halen, Eddie was #1 from the start . . . I knew the entire catalog." He admitted needing to learn how to play "Big Train," but showing knowledge of Roth deep cuts he told me he wished the band had played "Damn Good."

Ryan Wheeler also reinforced that the "eighty rehearsals" line may be inaccurate in our 2022 Q&A over email. "Looking back at the Roth band inception, it's kind of wild how long it's actually been. People probably don't realize, since we've only played around thirty shows, but since 2019 I have spent an entire *year* rehearing for this project. Six months before the KISS World Tour and six months leading up to this canceled Vegas residency. That's . . . a lot."

I asked Wheeler how much prep he did beyond the in-room rehearsals. Did he watch a lot of live videos? "Honestly, I didn't look at a ton of live stuff at all. I just hunkered down and learned a fuck ton of Van Halen and DLR songs." He continued: "It's really kind of impossible to anticipate what an artist wants in a band and even recent history is still history. Being able to adapt on the spot and *fast* is always what matters in those situations. And showing up on time . . . Van Halen's success as a band wasn't 'lucky.' Those dudes were *highly* intelligent and super-hard workers. I think that gets lost in the era and the stereotypes they came up in." Added Wheeler: "If you're a musician reading this, *show up on time*. On time is fifteen minutes early by the way."

Frankie Lindia agreed with the assessment of a DLR rehearsal being close to as intense as a live performance in front of a crowd: "You're 100 percent on. You're dressed up. . . . Just follow the protocol and do what you gotta do. . . . Be on your A-game, but it's cool, it's a great way of being."

Lindia, like Kane Ritchotte, accepted the Roth gig with the understanding that it was going to be just a few shows in Las Vegas. He had other scheduled obligations after January 2020 he had to step away for. On the small world end, he wound up joining the Stephen Pearcy–fronted Ratt in 2021, and 2022 would find him joining the Dave-approved Van Halen tribute band known as The Atomic Punks.

Speaking of DLR-related musical chairs, former Roth guitarist Brian Young almost wound up performing with the band as part of the Vegas residency. He recalled receiving a mid-2019 call from Brett Tuggle: "He just said that they were going to be doing this residency with Dave in Vegas and they were working with guys, still kind of checking out guys, and was I interested in doing it?" He continued: "It wasn't like an offer, but it was more like a 'just checking to see.' We talked a little bit and the truth was that my 2020 calendar was booked solid and I was happy with what I was doing."

When I spoke with guitarist Andy Timmons, he told me a story about a late 1980s interaction he had related to Roth guitarist Steve Vai. He had also mentioned in passing that his producer Josh Smith nearly joined Roth's band. I reached out to Smith's rep and was declined an interview, but he noted the following: "He was only asked if he was interested and he had conflicts because I remember us talking about it. . . . He has never even met him. It can stay in 'rumor' land because he is not going to officially talk about it."

Following the January 2020 shows performed at Las Vegas' House of Blues inside the Mandalay Bay Hotel & Casino, Roth and band hit the road as openers for KISS on its *End of the Road* farewell tour. Jake Faun joined on guitar in place of Frankie Lindia. An LA resident by way of England, Faun came into the fold via Ryan Wheeler, as he told me in 2022. "I jumped in a few weeks before we went on the road and the rest is history. We did a great six weeks on the road. Amazing playing with a wall of Marshall stacks."

One of the highlights for Faun was the Los Angeles show of the tour. "Steve Vai, because when we did the Staples Center show, which is like the LA hometown show. . . . When we finished playing, we're walking around backstage, and David's business manager was like running up to us. . . . She was like, 'Where's Ryan? . . . Steve is here. He wants to come and say hi to the band.' Cool. Let's go say hi." Continued Faun: "Steve's very nice, very humble and 'nice to meet you all' kind of thing. He said to the band, 'It's funny hearing my own songs being played back to me.' Then he says to us, 'The only thing is you're not supposed to pay them better than me.' Then we all laugh. He was very nice and obviously no one's gonna play any better than him, but at the same time, it's just fun to hear him say that. That was a cool moment."

Another 2020 lineup change for David Lee Roth's band was Michael Musselman being replaced mid–KISS tour by Francis Valentino, another New

Jersey native. "I got the call from our MD/bassist Ryan Wheeler," he explained via email. "I was very familiar with the material before getting the gig."

Ryan Wheeler clarified: "Me and Francis have been friends and playing music together since 2009. There is so much trust, nuance, and syncopation with long-term musical relationships that simply cannot be faked when playing with new people. I've done most of my '10,000 hours' with him and when I was looking for new drummers for the Roth band it was a no-brainer."

In turn, not a lot of drama among the musicians backing Diamond Dave in this era. "Ten percent of your workday is performing, the rest of it . . . you have to be friends with everyone, you have to get along, and so we're all good friends," Faun told me. He recapped a telling interaction he had with Wheeler after auditioning: "A week later he phones me up. . . . 'So do you want to come be in the band?' I was like, 'Sounds good.' After that he was like, 'You know, I just want to say thank you for being a normal person.' Because he had so many people audition who were just weird or didn't learn the material." As further telling of how "normal" Faun and band were: "I remember we went bowling once or twice when we were on the road."

A unique thing about Faun was that he, unlike some of his bandmates, did not come into the DLR fold just thinking that they were playing Vegas shows and moving on. "We were supposed to do from the end of January, when we flew out to the first show, which was on the East Coast in Allentown, Pennsylvania. . . . Then we were gonna do six weeks on the road with KISS kind of going around, which we just about did. Then we were supposed to do a two-week Vegas residency straight after that. And then we're gonna have a break from the tour. And then it was going to be more like David was going to do some of his own stuff without KISS. There's a whole bunch of festivals lined up, we were supposed to play at this one that Metallica put on. . . . There was another one that was more of like a pop one, big pop artists are gonna play like Billie Eilish. . . . Then the tour is gonna resume again in the summer, which is going to be from, like, August until October, another two months on the road. And then at that point, who knows? That was the year's schedule."

But a little pandemic happened to get in the way. "We started, obviously, and we did six weeks, right before we were supposed to go to Vegas, and then COVID happened. At that point, we were like, 'Okay, well, we have to stop the tour, fine, whatever. But we'll be two weeks and we're back on the road again.' . . . Then like a week would go by and like, 'Yeah, Vegas is still going, it's still on the website online as you can buy tickets.' Another week went by and, 'Okay, well, we're gonna postpone that for another couple of weeks.' As things went on, it was like, 'Yeah, we're still gonna go back out. . . . Maybe it's three months later.'"

Faun looks back at his time with DLR very fondly: "I had such a blast playing on those shows. What guitarist wouldn't want to play Van Halen with David himself, playing arenas in America?" He later added: "One thing I think COVID taught us is that the live-playing industry, at any moment can be taken away from us, just because if something comes up and stopped us from playing, it shuts us down. You have to have something else to do."

In turn, Faun changed up his strategy related to his musical endeavors: "If you're a writer and a composer, then at least you can fall back on that and turn that into more of a way of making money . . . I also notice that the older you get, you don't want to be playing necessarily 'til two in the morning when you're like sixty years old, because you might be wanting to settle down and relax." Since his time with Roth, Faun has also worked as fill-in guitarist on the road for Winger.

But as you will soon read, this was not to be the "end of the road" for David Lee Roth, even though he at some points hinted that it would be.

COVID-19

(and Vegas: Part IV)

In March 2020, like most things in the world that involved crowds of people, touring abruptly stopped for David Lee Roth. The coming months led many creative types to take up new home-based hobbies while waiting on next steps.

"It was so cool to open the *New York Times* today and see almost a full page in the Arts & Leisure section about the quarantine art that he is producing during this upside-down moment in history, so he still carries a huge cachet," former Roth publicist Mitch Schneider said to me and *DLR Cast* cohost Steve Roth in 2020.

Continued Schneider: "It has to be larger than life, just like the *New York Times* today, that photo of him. It's almost like painting overalls if you look closely at what he's wearing, it's like, 'Oh my god this is so well thought out.' I looked at it and it just made me smile, saying he still gets it right. . . . What you see is what you get."

Author and photographer Lisa S. Johnson also had appreciation for what Roth was doing on the canvas: "They give us light on the interior of his mind and soul. He has a lot to say in a visual way that is thought provoking and lends a different side most have likely not seen." Continued Johnson: "The work personifies the truth of who he is, which reveals to me he is an artist in every sense of his being. I like that I can see what's in his mind versus hearing him talk about what's in it."

In the midst of the COVID-19 pandemic, Roth also unveiled *The Roth Project*. A seventeen-chapter graphic novel that featured his narration and a soundtrack of his music, it can aptly be described as a cross between *Tokyo Story*, *No Holds Bar-B-Que*, and *Dave TV*. Some of its background music was, interestingly, songs recorded during the previously discussed recording sessions with John 5.

One of the songs featured in *The Roth Project* was "Somewhere Over the Rainbow Bar & Grill." Shortly after the passing of Eddie Van Halen in October 2020, Roth stated that the song was related to Eddie: "I don't usually write autobiographically, but this was a specific effort to replicate a time and a place." But the jury is out on that one because Roth's 2013 interview with *USA Today* noted that song to have been intended for a "jukebox musical," and those songs had been offered to the Van Halens and subsequently declined.

Aside from an appearance on Joe Rogan's podcast, Roth's only documented public appearance in 2021 was at MTV's Video Music Awards. Roth appeared as a surprise on air to announce a performance by rapper Lil Nas X and briefly worked the red carpet before the event.

Shortly after that VMA appearance, DLR announced a new residency in Las Vegas, kicking off on New Year's Eve 2021. A few weeks later, Roth declared these five House of Blues performances to be his "final" shows as he was "throwing in the shoes." The reason why, he told a Las Vegas newspaper, was locked away in a metaphorical "safe." And that he would not be commenting further. And a few weeks after that, he opted to add additional shows.

Simply put, everyone was confused. Including this writer, who booked a trip out to Las Vegas to see some of the "final" shows. And then extended his Vegas trip with his wife to see some of the add-on shows. Only for the first show to be canceled about twenty-four hours before showtime—a story that was broken by the *Metal Sludge* website, whose CEO Stevie Rachelle you heard from earlier in *DLR Book*—and all following shows canceled shortly after. COVID-19 was to blame, but per inside sources wishing to remain anonymous, David Lee Roth did not have the virus. The retirement shows were not rescheduled, although Roth issued a comment to *Fox News Digital* in early January 2022 that implied he was not retired: "It's not about me anymore. When the benefits for Kentucky, Colorado, and Farm Aid kick in; call me."

Per Ryan Wheeler, the lineup of Roth's backing band for the 2021/2022 shows was to be a power trio: "It's how the music was written, recorded and performed and that's how it should be. I love the other guys who were playing in the ensemble dearly, but as a lineup, it was overkill." He added: "I'm sad the Vegas shows got canceled because the band and song list was sounding *hot*. No tracks, just the four of us giving it our all."

Vocal prep was a key part of rehearsals, according to Wheeler: "Before this last Vegas run got canceled, I was singing more of Ed's parts and Al Estrada was handling the Michael parts. That man can get up there!"

Rumor was that Van Halen bassist Michael Anthony himself was going to appear at one or more of the "final" shows for Roth, as he was doing the 2020 run of Vegas shows. He confirmed this to me during our 2022 interview: "The original one that he did there, I was actually going to show up. But then, unfortunately, some Circle shows came up and I couldn't make it out there. And then again, I was also contemplating going out there this last time when he was supposed to do it over New Year's."

Ratt's Stephen Pearcy was also hoping to join in on the "final" shows, per our 2021 interview: "We'll see what happens, maybe you'll see me out here [in Vegas] following Sam and Dave. Everybody else is coming through here, you got Bruce Dickinson, you got Scorpions . . , You name it, I'm in the right place at the right time."

In May 2022, a reporter with a camera spotted David Lee Roth leaving Los Angeles International Airport, after performing at what this author confirmed to be a private gig at the Montage Resort in Cabo San Lucas, Mexico. Pressed for comment, after referencing *Rocky* and *Rambo* sequels, Roth stated the following: "I'm only in the middle of my first retirement." Further research efforts conducted by this author confirmed that Cardi B and Coolio were also on the billing for that evening in Cabo, a fiftieth birthday celebration for PayPal cofounder David O. Sacks, who made guests sign a nondisclosure agreement to attend; "Poker Brat" Phil Hellmuth is among the event's rumored attendees. And just a few months later, Roth relaunched his *Roth Show* podcast, beyond releasing songs said to be recorded at Henson Studios in May 2022. And less than a year later, Roth would make a Vegas return of sorts, playing a corporate gig for Home Depot at the Mandalay Bay Arena alongside the previously mentioned Steve Stevens, who nearly became his lead guitarist almost forty years prior.

Yet apparently all of this turns out to be nothing new, as Roth declared twenty-five years earlier in a 1997 interview published via *Slawterhouse*: "I threaten retirement four times a day and I threaten never to retire five times." And just six years prior to that in 1991's "A Lil' Ain't Enough" music video, his "final tour" had been declared to take place in 2020 . . .

Dave's Legacy

While the true history of David Lee Roth is filled with countless unanswered and/or unanswerable questions, one thing that cannot be denied is that David Lee Roth changed the world in a variety of ways.

"People ask me about him and I always say he was very meticulous, very detailed, very exacting about what he wanted. It's never necessarily 'easy' to work with artists like that, but it really asks you to step up your game as a publicist, so I definitely thrived on the challenge," declared former publicist Mitch Schneider. "I considered it a privilege and I would work with him in a heartbeat again."

Former cohort of Schneider—and an A-list publicist in her own right—Amanda Cagan told me that working with Roth taught her a lot: "How to be patient and take lots of deep breaths when things get hectic!" After a laugh, she added: "He was such a 'larger than life' kind of person, so working with him taught me how to absorb all of the moments and really take pride in the final results of any press we put together, because there was always a lot of time and energy placed into whatever it was that we were arranging for him."

Cagan, who is specifically thanked in Roth's *Crazy from the Heat* memoir, had more to say: "On a personal level, I also just loved how open he always was whenever he met fans or met anyone in general. I only had one-on-one time with him after a show a couple of times, and he always took the time to say hello and 'thank you' for my work, even if it was only for a few minutes before he was pulled in another direction by someone else who wanted to talk to him."

Henry Rollins, a friend who had also worked professionally with Roth, called Roth "one of the greats, absolutely. Along with Iggy Pop, Mick Jagger, Lux Interior, David Bowie, Perry Farrell, etc." Aldo Nova dubbed Roth "probably one of the greatest frontmen that ever existed." Former Roth musician Melissa Elena Reiner added: "I feel like he's the kind of guy that does things really well when he puts his mind to it." Ted Nugent told me: "Thank you, David, for enriching our lives with your incredible music. God bless you."

Per Fozzy's Rich Ward in 2022: "I think David Lee Roth is the best frontman that rock and roll has ever seen." Former Guns N' Roses guitarist DJ Ashba told me in 2021: "Van Halen was the reason I got into music." Helmet's Page Hamilton told me that same year that "Hot for Teacher" is "maybe the greatest MTV music video ever made." Linkin Park's Dave Farrell is yet another influential musician who spoke highly of Van Halen, and when asked who his favorite Van Halen frontman was, in 2020 he said: "It's gotta be David Lee Roth, come on."

John Blenn agrees with Rollins, Reiner, Nugent, Nova, Ward, Ashba, Hamilton, and Farrell: "He's right at the head of the class. . . . As a personality, he's second to none, your personal feelings on what comes out of his mouth aside. He's one of the brightest people I've ever met. He fully understood what this job was from the get-go. I think he did some of his finest work after Van Halen—*A Little Ain't Enough* and *Your Filthy Little Mouth* are remarkable lyrical albums. . . . Dave made some great music when he didn't have to compromise his muse. He made some mediocre stuff too, by no means do I think everything he did was flawless. But he really has a legacy to be proud of."

Continued Blenn: "I think, unlike most of his peers, Dave understands the legend he's created and that you can tarnish it by hanging around and becoming a faltering caricature of yourself. I don't think he needs the money, but it always comes down to missing the attention. If he's comfortable in his own skin these days and embraces a quieter life, I think he'll walk away. If not, what's Ozzy's record for unretirements . . . ?"

Roth's influence not only lives on in the rock world but in plenty of other genres as well. For example, Tone Loc's hit "Wild Thing" sampled Van Halen favorite "Jamie's Cryin'." I asked "Wild Thing" cowriter Marvin "Young MC" Young about this in 2021: "Most of the stuff was produced by Mike Ross and

Matt Dike and The Dust Brothers, all samples were other people's stuff. They had to deal with it." In other words, Young MC was not one of the people responsible for the song's unauthorized Van Halen sample, for which a six-figure settlement had been paid out.

Armin Van Buuren—one of the world's top DJs for decades—released a remix of "Jump" in 2019. Roth was invited to join Van Buuren onstage at 2019's Ultra Music Festival, which he accepted. Elsewhere in the EDM space, decades prior, A440 scored a hit with a Van Halen–sampling track called "Ain't Talkin' 'Bout Dub."

The Bird & The Bee—the duo of vocalist Inara George and Grammy-winning songwriter and producer Greg Kurstin—released an album of mostly Van Halen covers in 2019 titled *Interpreting the Masters, Vol. 2: A Tribute to Van Halen*. The full-length album features a piano-based take on a lone original titled "Diamond Dave" about you-know-who, as originally heard on 2008's *Ray Guns Are Not Just the Future*. The song was reportedly inspired by George seeing Van Halen live for the first time in 2007.

Weezer's studio album released in 2021—as recorded between 2018 and 2020—was titled *Van Weezer*. The album has a dedication to Eddie Van Halen. And of course Van Halen's long-time logo, often dubbed "the Flying W," does resemble both the *Wonder Woman* logo and the classic winged Van Halen logo.

When Dave Grohl decided to host a birthday show for himself at The Forum in Los Angeles in January 2015, he brought out some of his favorite artists to collaborate onstage with the Foo Fighters. This included David Lee Roth, who performed "Panama" and "Ain't Talkin' 'Bout Love" with the Foos. A few years later at 2019's Beach Life Festival, Foo Fighters drummer Taylor Hawkins would front Chevy Metal for an all-Roth-era Van Halen covers set, including a cameo from Weezer's Pat Wilson. Bringing things full circle, a pair of posthumous tribute concerts to Hawkins in 2022 would feature The Darkness' Justin Hawkins—no relation to Taylor—and Wolfgang Van Halen performing two early Roth-era Van Halen tracks with Grohl on bass at each show. Also in late 2022, the original Van Halen recording of "Unchained" would air as part of an episode of the Netflix series *Cobra Kai*.

Early into the COVID-19 pandemic, when it was in vogue for bands to be recording songs remotely and performing live sets in rehearsal spaces, there were plenty of Van Halen covers from high-profile artists. This included

Mr. Bungle—featuring Faith No More's Mike Patton and Anthrax's Scott Ian—performing "Loss of Control," members of High on Fire and Fall Out Boy handling "Unchained," and a makeshift Van Halen tribute band called PanaMama playing a four-song "Slay at Home Festival" set to benefit Black Lives Matter.

As of this book's writing, we remain unsure about the status of discussions between Roth and Alex Van Halen about a "tribute tour" to Van Halen; in a September 2022 interview done for *Rolling Stone*, Sammy Hagar claimed he was asked to partake in such a tour. Neither Van Halen nor Roth would be present for the public dedication of a Van Halen Stage by the city of Pasadena. We also do not know what remains unreleased for Van Halen and whether "the vaults" will ever open up, nor the status of Roth's personal collection of unreleased recordings; Roth's latest official releases were live-in-the-studio performances of some of Van Halen's earliest hits, as recorded in May 2022 with Ryan Wheeler, Francis Valentino, and Al Estrada backing him. We also have no idea if or when Roth will ever tour again. But at the very least, DLR diehards can smile, knowing that they have close to five decades' worth of recordings, videos, and interviews to continually enjoy.

"One of the great things that David Lee Roth would say, and I use it to this day and I always quote him. It's such a great David Lee Rothism—because it doesn't really make sense, but it does make sense—is when he didn't like something, he would just say '1-800-SEE-YA,'" Mitch Schneider told me toward the end of our conversation. "It's confusing but it's such a great line because you get it, it's stamped with his vision, so indelibly '1-800-SEE-YA.'"

Acknowledgments

DLR Book would not exist without the help of my wife, Melissa Paltrowitz. Melissa has been the backbone of all of my creative projects and brainstorms for the past decade. She got me back into writing articles in the early 2010s, pushed me to launch the Paltrocast.com website, and—perhaps most importantly—she agreed to take time off from work to go see David Lee Roth in Las Vegas on more than one occasion, none of that is intended to be a Jay Mohr reference, Melissa. However, I cannot confirm nor deny whether she does a fantastic Roth-style "yow!" on a daily basis.

My parents, Stuart and Donna Paltrowitz, have written dozens of books, absolutely fostering my appreciation both for reading and writing at an early age. While my mother did some early proofreading of this book, I'm still not sure whether she appreciates "Yankee Rose" more in English or Spanish. My brother Adam, who is mentioned throughout the book, taught me how to play "Jump" on the piano; hopefully you and Blair will eventually teach "Jump" to Lyla and Nolan. My sister Shari went to college on a full ride for the bassoon, so she probably can play "Jump" on bassoon better than I can on piano; Mike, please explain the cultural significance of "Jump" to Shari when you have the chance.

Lee Sobel, it still blows my mind that you were able to find a publisher for *DLR Book* less than seventy-two hours after I gave you my pitch packet. Everything you said would happen ultimately did happen, and how many authors can say that about their literary agent? Thanks to you for connecting me with the wonderful John Cerullo and team at Backbeat/Rowman & Littlefield.

Immediate family pleasantries and industry brownnosing aside, the following people were ultrasupportive throughout the making of this book, provided inspiration, and/or are owed a beer: Steve Roth (always great to dig into the "DLR Cast" rabbit holes with you); Steve Herold (sorry you got turned down for the DLR fan club); Kevin Baldes (beyond your excellent photos and the great quotes you provided, I remain a huge fan of Lit); Payge and Diamond Dallas Page (still the most famous person saved in my cell phone); Matthew Speddings (he knows which Hard Rock Cafes to find Van Halen memorabilia in); Velo Andreev (The Great Khan); Laurie Andreev (please watch my Brandon Boyd interview); Barry Andreev (next time I control the jukie); Sharon, Adam, Sadie, and Sydney Bergstein Family (best of luck with your pizza problems); Mary, Nick, and Chris Crispino (am I still invited to the next Melendez Family Christmas?); Anthony, Jacqui, Aaliyah, and Caleb Trichter (the only people I'll do karaoke with); Marina Maher (Carlow's Finest); Tony Lo (Top Ten); Anthony, Kerry, Olive, and Alex Dalto ("Who's High Pitch?"); Erin and Grog Zeichner ("Goo fa you"); Jac, Nico, Oliver, and Steve Schiltz ("Go with Gene, get the green"); Joe and Jessica Hasan (Brucie's Angels); James Lance (Trunkshot); Chris and Allison Balas (does Ben know who DLR is yet?); Elaine and Efrain Calderon Jr. (Jake Hager's best friends); John and Lauren Weishahn ("I don't feel tardy"); Jesus and Becca Garcia (New York misses you); Cari, Gary, and Parker Deduke (Hoppycats); Cousin Gwyneth; Dante, Garrett, Janan, Chris, Jeff, and the JAG International family; Thea and Atif, Bryant and Heather; JT Turret; Suzanne and Mark Piro; Jillian and Tom; Kate and Andy Levine; Dan, Kelly, and Abby Platt; Jon Adler; Pat, Tracy, and Clyde Parrino; TJ Penzone and These People; Eric Senich and Van Halen News Desk; Richard Lee and Sidewalks Entertainment; Aaron, Paula, and Carolina March; Donald and Liz Mones; Jeff Tobias; Lucy Woodward; Stuttering John Melendez; Yoshi Kato; Rachael Yamagata; Dan Pasternack; Steph and Chance Dennis; the other Milmans (Chad, I know you owned "Skyscraper" in the late 1980s); the other Kalmyks; the other "DLR Cast" listeners; Maxwell Jacob Friedman; Erin Brady and Joel Miller; Chuck Shute; Rina and Andy Collins; and Shine's Bar of Long Beach, New York (still hosting a *DLR Book* event party, Megan?).

Thanks for the interviews and/or clarifications (in alphabetical order): Jason Aldean; Joey Allen; Michael Anthony; DJ Ashba; Kevin Baldes; Rob Baker; Ronnie Barnett; Justin Beck; Robert "Kool" Bell; Jason Biggs; Gregg Bissonette; Matt Bissonette; John Blenn; Bobby Boling; Albert Bouchard; Adam Busch; Johnny Brennan; Lenny Bronstein; Steve Brown; Amanda Cagan; Jeff Cardoni; Desmond Child; Jason Consoli; Stewart Copeland; Billy Corgan; Jersey Dagger; Katie Daryl; Chris Demakes; Eric Dover; Marc Elmer; Scotty Emerick; Dave Farrell; Jake Faun; Sammy Figueroa; Dana Gould; Adam Green; Tracii Guns; Page Hamilton; Albert Hammond Jr.; Jesse Harms; Richard Hilton; Ross Hogarth; Will Hunt; John "Hutch" Hutchinson; Sam Ingraffia; Christone "Kingfish" Ingram; Jack Irons; Takurô Ishizaka; Whynot Jansveld; David Jellison; John 5; Lisa S. Johnson; Stacy Jones; Chris Kattan; Frankie Kazarian; Kennedy; Kerri Kenney-Silver; David Krebs; Marc LaFrance; Rob Lane; Ronni Le Tekro; Tom Lennon; Tom Lilly; Frankie Lindia; Linus of Hollywood; Kenny Loggins; LP; Steve Lukather; Ray Luzier; Gary Marino; Bob Marlette; Durga McBroom; Andrew McMahon; Frank Meyer; Ginger Minj; Billy Mira; Isaiah Mitchell; Aki Mizutani; Michael Musselman; Dave Mustaine; Margo Z. Nahas; Paul Natkin; Robbie Nevil; Ted Nugent; Aldo Nova; John Oates; Ian Paice; Diamond Dallas Page; Adam Paltrowitz; Kyary Pamyu Pamyu; Stephen Pearcy; Todd Perlmutter; Slim Jim Phantom; Jeremy Popoff; Stevie Rachelle; Jaret Reddick; Melissa Elena Reiner; Linda Reissman; Greg Renoff; Adam Richman; Andy Ridings; Garry Rindfuss; Kane Ritchotte; Rocket Ritchotte; Krista Rodriguez; Kira Roessler; Henry Rollins; David Lee Roth; Dr. Jack Roth; Lisa Roth; Jordan Rudess; Angela Sampras-Stabile; Ralph Saenz; Rudy Sarzo; Mitch Schneider; Billy Sheehan; Kazuhiro Shinagawa; Jonathan Shlafer; Gene Simmons; Doug Short; Bobby Slayton; Aron Stevens; Hannah Storm; Ruyter Suys; Jon Taffer; ET Tecosky; Andy Timmons; Brad Tolinski; Travis Tritt; Robin Trower; Francis Valentino; Brian Vanderark; Steve Vai; Butch Vig; Mike Viola; Rich Ward; Mark Weiss; Brian Weinstein; Ryan Wheeler; Joe Whiting; Edgar Winter; Konishiki Yasokichi; Brian Young; and Danny Zelisko.

Diamond Dave, as this book's title points out, you changed the world. You continue to have millions of fans all over the world. We'd like to hear more from you soon, whatever the medium.

Otherwise, thanks and sorry!

—Darren Paltrowitz, March 2023

Index

Note: Album and song titles are shown in *italics* and "quotations" respectively.